UNDERSTANDING
AMERICAN HISTORY
THROUGH FICTION

UNDERSTANDING AMERICAN HISTORY THROUGH FICTION
Volume II

Warren A. Beck

California State University-Fullerton

Myles L. Clowers

San Diego City College

McGraw-Hill Book Company

New York   St. Louis   San Francisco   Düsseldorf
Johannesburg   Kuala Lumpur   London   Mexico   Montreal   New Delhi   Panama
Paris   São Paulo   Singapore   Sydney   Tokyo   Toronto

Library of Congress Cataloging in Publication Data

Beck, Warren A   comp.
  Understanding American history through fiction.

  1. American literature. 2. United States—
History—Literary collections. I. Clowers, Myles L.,
joint comp. II. Title.
PS509.U52B4   813'.03   74-11266
ISBN 0-07-004217-9 (v. 1)
ISBN 0-07-004218-7 (v. 2)

UNDERSTANDING
AMERICAN HISTORY
THROUGH FICTION
Volume II

1234567890DODO7987654

This book was set in Times Roman by Compucomp Corporation.
The editors were Robert P. Rainier and Michael Weber;
the cover was designed by Anne Canevari Green;
the production supervisor was Leroy A. Young.
R. R. Donnelley & Sons Company Press, Inc., was printer and binder.

Contents

3   THE GROWTH OF AMERICAN CAPITALISM   41

4   EMPIRE AND WAR   75

8   COLD WAR, KOREA, AND VIETNAM   189

Preface

In their constant effort to interpret the past, historians have used every possible tool from documents to computers to carbon dating. Among the oldest tools they have used are works of creative literature. From the time man first spun tales of valor around the campfire in his cave, creative stories have been indispensable in capturing the spirit of an age. Whether such writing was a Homeric saga glorifying the deeds of heroic Greeks, a song of the troubadors of the Middle Ages, a Shakespearean historical drama, or a novel of the American Revolution, creative literature has aided historians in their efforts to recapture the mood and spirit of times far removed from their own.

America's heritage has been especially enriched by numerous outstanding works of historical fiction. No historian has aroused the popular imagination or excited the public's interest in the Revolutionary era as has Kenneth Roberts. Abraham Lincoln acknowledged the importance of *Uncle Tom's Cabin* when he greeted its author, Harriet Beecher Stowe, with the comment, "So this is the little lady that caused the war." More Americans have learned the story of the South during the years of the Civil War and Reconstruction from Margaret Mitchell's *Gone with the Wind* than from all of the learned volumes on this period. Upton Sinclair's *The Jungle,* by triggering the passage of the Meat Inspection Act of 1906, played a key role in the movement for federal regulation of many facets of American life. For better or worse, Americans have learned of their past and have been influenced in their understanding of that past by historical fiction.

Historians have, of course, not entirely overlooked the value of fiction in classroom reading. With the availability of paperbooks a novel or two is often assigned as required reading in the hope that it will stimulate the interest of students in the subject matter as a whole. But in teaching the basic American history course it is obviously impossible to find one or even several novels which will adequately introduce beginning students to the extensive treasure of fiction available.

In the present work the authors attempt to meet this problem by providing students with a sampling of the way fiction writers have treated important epochs in American history. The selections are intended to supplement basic text materials and to arouse the students' interest so that they will do further reading. Of course, America's past is so varied and complex that not all subjects can be treated fully. Size limitations have also dictated the brevity of the selections. But the most important periods are thoroughly treated. Special attention has been paid to often neglected areas, such as the parts played by women and ethnic minorities in American history. Above all, social history is stressed in an effort to introduce students to the way people of yesteryear lived. From the hundreds of novels, poems, and short stories consulted in the preparation of this anthology, the authors have selected works of such famous writers as Lewis, Fitzgerald, Steinbeck, and Michener, as well as those of many obscure authors.

To the members of the historical profession who may feel that supplemental books of readings like this one are "sugarcoating" the pill of learning, the authors would like to stress that accuracy in his subject matter is as important to the writer of historical fiction as it is to the author of a scholarly monograph. And if students can be encouraged to read because the selections are entertaining instead of dull and prosaic, the learning process is advanced. In an age in which students are often motivated mainly by visual material, an introduction to the wonders of the historical past by a sampling of fiction may be a worthwhile innovation.

The authors have had a great deal of help and advice in this project. They would like to thank Donald Estes, Cathy Jones, Celia Violet, and Rex Painter of San Diego City College; Professors B. Carmon Hardy, Arthur Hansen, Jackson Putnam, and Edward H. Parker of California State University-Fullerton; and Kent M. Beck of the University of California-Irvine.

Warren A. Beck
Myles L. Clowers

UNDERSTANDING AMERICAN HISTORY THROUGH FICTION

Chapter 1

Reunion

Reading 1

Good Old Rebel

Innes Randolph

The bitterness that had developed between the North and South in the decade before the Civil War fanned to a white heat during the conflict, and this hatred could not be turned off simply because the fighting stopped. Both sides continued to express their attitudes in many ways. Northern hatred was an integral part of the harsh radical reconstruction plan. Southern hatred was nurtured inwardly for many generations and was expressed through many outlets, including this song.

Oh, I'm a good old Rebel,
Now that's just what I am;
For this fair land of Freedom
I do not care a dam.
I'm glad I fit against it
I only wish we'd won,
And I don't want no pardon
For anything I've done.

I hates the Constitution
This great Republic, too;
I hates the Freedmen's Buro,
In uniforms of blue.
I hates the nasty eagle,
With all his brag and fuss;
The lyin', thievin' Yankees,
I hates 'em wuss and wuss.

I hates the Yankee Nation
And everything they do;
I hates the Declaration
Of Independence, too.
I hates the glorious Union,
'Tis dripping with our blood;
I hates the striped banner—
I fit it all I could.

I followed old Marse Robert

For four years, near about,
Got wounded in three places,
And starved at Pint Lookout.
I cotch the roomatism
A-campin' in the snow.
But I killed a chance of Yankees—
I'd like to kill some mo'.

Three hundred thousand Yankees
Is stiff in Southern dust;
We got three hundred thousand
Before they conquered us.
They died of Southern fever
And Southern steel and shot;
I wish it was three millions
Instead of what we got.

I can't take up my musket
And fight 'em now no more,
But I ain't goin' to love 'em
Now that is sartin sure.
And I don't want no pardon
For what I was and am;
I won't be reconstructed,
And I don't care a dam.

Reading 2

Main Travelled Roads

Hamlin Garland

The following selection tells something of the struggle of the farm wives left behind in the North. As usual, it was the woman who had to do the day-by-day chores, care for the children, and, most difficult of all, wait for her husband to come home. The return of the private in the North was a sober affair as the weary and often battle-scarred veteran made his way home. Unlike after recent wars, the government did not provide transportation home for the soldier; in fact, he was lucky even to get his fare home.

From *Main Travelled Roads* by Hamlin Garland. Published in 1890.

Furthermore, the soldier could not look forward to the generous GI benefits that the government now extends to its veterans.

The nearer the train drew toward La Crosse, the soberer the little group of "vets" became. On the long way from New Orleans they had beguiled tedium with jokes and friendly chaff; or with planning with elaborate detail what they were going to do now, after the war. A long journey, slowly, irregularly, yet persistently pushing northward. When they entered on Wisconsin territory they gave a cheer, and another when they reached Madison, but after that they sank into a dumb expectancy. Comrades dropped off at one or two points beyond, until there were only four or five left who were bound for La Crosse County.

Three of them were gaunt and brown, the fourth was gaunt and pale, with signs of fever and ague upon him. One had a great scar down his temple, one limped, and they all had unnaturally large, bright eyes, showing emaciation. There were no hands greeting them at the station, no banks of gayly dressed ladies waving handkerchiefs and shouting "Bravo!" as they came in on the caboose of a freight train into the towns that had cheered and blared at them on their way to war. As they looked out or stepped upon the platform for a moment, while the train stood at the station, the loafers looked at them indifferently. Their blue coats, dusty and grimy, were too familiar now to excite notice, much less a friendly word. They were the last of the army to return, and the loafers were surfeited with such sights.

The train jogged forward so slowly that it seemed likely to be midnight before they should reach La Crosse. The little squad grumbled and swore, but it was no use; the train would not hurry, and, as a matter of fact, it was nearly two o'clock when the engine whistled "down brakes."

All of the group were farmers, living in districts several miles out of the town, and all were poor.

"Now, boys," said Private Smith, he of the fever and ague, "we are landed in La Crosse in the night. We've got to stay somewhere till mornin'. Now I ain't got no two dollars to waste on a hotel. I've got a wife and children, so I'm goin' to roost on a bench and take the cost of a bed out of my hide."

"Same here," put in one of the other men. "Hide'll grow on again, dollars'll come hard. It's going to be mighty hot skirmishin' to find a dollar these days."

"Don't think they'll be a deptuation of citizens waitin' to 'scort us to a hotel, eh?" said another. His sarcasm was too obvious to require an answer.

Smith went on, "Then at daybreak we'll start for home—at least, I will."

"Well, I'll be dummed if I'll take two dollars out o' *my* hide," one of the younger men said. "I'm goin' to a hotel, ef I don't never lay up a cent."

"That'll do f'r you," said Smith; "but if you had a wife an' three young uns dependin' on yeh—"

"Which I ain't, thank the Lord! and don't intend havin' while the court knows itself."

The station was deserted, chill, and dark, as they came into it at exactly a quarter to two in the morning. Lit by the oil lamps that flared a dull red light over the dingy benches, the waiting room was not an inviting place. The younger man went off to look up a hotel, while the rest remained and prepared to camp down on the floor and benches. Smith was attended to tenderly by the other men, who spread their blankets on the bench for him, and, by robbing themselves, made quite a comfortable bed, though the narrowness of the bench made his sleeping precarious.

It was chill, though August, and the two men, sitting with bowed heads, grew stiff with cold and weariness, and were forced to rise now and again and walk about to warm their stiffened limbs. It did not occur to them, probably, to contrast their coming home with their going forth, or with the coming home of the generals, colonels, or even captains——but to Private Smith, at any rate, there came a sickness at heart almost deadly as he lay there on his hard bed and went over his situation.

In the deep of the night, lying on a board in the town where he had enlisted three years ago, all elation and enthusiasm gone out of him, he faced the fact that with the joy of home-coming was already mingled the bitter juice of care. He saw himself sick, worn out, taking up the work on his half-cleared farm, the inevitable mortgage standing ready with open jaw to swallow half his earnings. He had given three years of his life for a mere pittance of pay, and now!—

Morning dawned at last, slowly, with a pale yellow dome of light rising silently above the bluffs, which stand like some huge storm-devastated castle, just east of the city. Out to the left the great river swept on its massive yet silent way to the south. Bluejays called across the water from hillside to hillside through the clear, beautiful air, and hawks began to skim the tops of the hills. The older men were astir early, but Private Smith had fallen at last into a sleep, and they went out without waking him. He lay on his knapsack, his gaunt face turned toward the ceiling, his hands clasped on his breast, with a curious pathetic effect of weakness and appeal.

An engine switching near woke him at last, and he slowly sat up and stared about. He looked out of the window and saw that the sun was lightening the hills across the river. He rose and brushed his hair as well as he could, folded his blankets up, and went out to find his companions. They stood gazing silently at the river and at the hills.

"Looks natcher'l, don't it?" they said, as he came out.

"That's what it does," he replied. "An' it looks good. D' yeh see that peak?" He pointed at a beautiful symmetrical peak, rising like a slightly truncated cone, so high that it seemed the very highest of them all. It was touched by the morning sun and it glowed like a beacon, and a light scarf of gray morning fog was rolling up its shadowed side.

"My farm's just beyond that. Now, if I can only ketch a ride, we'll be home by dinner-time."

"I'm talkin' about breakfast," said one of the others.

"I guess it's one more meal o' hardtack f'r me," said Smith.

They foraged around, and finally found a restaurant with a sleepy old German behind the counter, and procured some coffee, which they drank to wash down their hardtack.

"Time'll come," said Smith, holding up a piece by the corner, "when this'll be a curiosity."

"I hope to God it will! I bet I've chawed hardtack enough to shingle every house in the coolly. I've chawed it when my lampers was down, and when they wasn't. I've took it dry, soaked, and mashed. I've had it wormy, musty, sour, and blue-mouldy. I've had it in little bits and big bits; 'fore coffee an' after coffee. I'm ready f'r a change. I'd like t' git holt jest about now o' some of the hot biscuits my wife c'n make when she lays herself out f'r company."

"Well, if you set there gabblin', you'll never *see* yer wife."

"Come on," said Private Smith. "Wait a moment, boys; less take suthin'. It's on me." He led them to the rusty tin dipper which hung on a nail beside the wooden water-pail, and they grinned and drank. Then shouldering their blankets and muskets, which they were "takin' home to the boys," they struck out on their last march.

"They called that coffee Jayvy," grumbled one of them, "but it never went by the road where government Jayvy resides. I reckon I know coffee from peas."

They kept together on the road along the turnpike, and up the winding road by the river, which they followed for some miles. The river was very lovely, curving down along its sandy beds, pausing now and then under broad basswood trees, or running in dark, swift, silent currents under tangles of wild grapevines, and drooping alders, and haw trees. At one of these lovely spots the three vets sat down on the thick green sward to rest, "on Smith's account." The leaves of the trees were as fresh and green as in June, the jays called cheery greetings to them, and kingfishers darted to and fro with swooping, noiseless flight.

"I tell yeh, boys, this knocks the swamps of Loueesiana into kingdom come."

"You bet. All they c'n raise down there is snakes, niggers, and p'rticler hell."

"An' fighting men," put in the older man.

"An' fightin' men. If I had a good hook an' line I'd sneak a pick'rel out o' that pond. Say, remember that time I shot that alligator——"

"I guess we'd better be crawlin' along," interrupted Smith, rising and shouldering his knapsack, with considerable effort, which he tried to hide.

"Say, Smith, lemme give you a lift on that."

"I guess I c'n manage," said Smith, grimly.

"Course. But, yo' see, I may not have a chance right off to pay yeh back for the times you've carried my gun and hull caboodle. Say, now, gimme that gun, anyway."

"All right, if yeh feel like it, Jim," Smith replied, and they trudged along doggedly in the sun, which was getting higher and hotter each half-mile.

"Ain't it queer there ain't no teams comin' along," said Smith, after a long silence.

"Well, no, seein's it's Sunday."

"By jinks, that's a fact. It *is* Sunday. I'll git home in time f'r dinner, sure!" he exulted. "She don't hev dinner usually till about *one* on Sundays." And he fell into a muse, in which he smiled.

"Well, I'll git home jest about six o'clock, jest about when the boys are milkin' the cows," said old Jim Cranby. "I'll step into the barn, an' then I'll say: *'Heah!* why ain't this milkin' done before this time o' day?' An' then won't they yell!" he added, slapping his thigh in great glee.

Smith went on. "I'll jest go up the path. Old Rover'll come down the road to meet me. He won't bark; he'll know me, an' he'll come down waggin' his tail an' showin' his teeth. That's his way of laughin'. An' so I'll walk up the kitchen door, an' I'll say, *'Dinner* f'r a hungry man!' An' then she'll jump up, an'——"

He couldn't go on. His voice choked at the thought of it. Saunders, the third man, hardly uttered a word, but walked silently behind the others. He had lost his wife the first year he was in the army. She died of pneumonia, caught in the autumn rains while working in the fields in his place.

They plodded along till at last they came to a parting of the ways. To the right the road continued up the main valley; to the left it went over the big ridge.

"Well boys," began Smith, as they grounded their muskets and looked away up the valley, "here's where we shake hands. We've marched together a good many miles, an' now I s'pose we're done."

"Yes, I don't think we'll do any more of it f'r a while. I don't want to, I know."

"I hope I'll see yeh once in a while, boys, to talk over old times."

"Of course," said Saunders, whose voice trembled a little, too. "It ain't *exactly* like dyin'." They all found it hard to look at each other.

"But we'd ought'r go home with you," said Cranby. "You'll never climb that ridge with all them things on yer back."

"Oh, I'm all right! Don't worry about me. Every step takes me nearer home, yeh see. Well, good-by, boys."

They shook hands. "Good-by. Good luck!"

"Same to you. Lemme know how you find things at home."

"Good-by."

"Good-by."

He turned once before they passed out of sight, and waved his cap, and they did the same, and all yelled. Then all marched away with their long, steady, loping, veteran step. The solitary climber in blue walked on for a time with his mind filled with the kindness of his comrades, and musing upon the many wonderful days they had had together in camp and field.

He though of his chum, Billy Tripp. Poor Billy! A "minie" ball fell into his breast one day, fell wailing like a cat, and tore a great ragged hole in his heart. He looked forward to a sad scene with Billy's mother and sweetheart. They would want to know all about it. He tried to recall all that Billy had said, and the particulars of it, but there was little to remember, just that wild wailing sound high in the air, a dull slap, a short, quick, expulsive groan, and the boy lay with his face in the dirt in the ploughed field they were marching across.

That was all. But all the scenes he had since been through had not dimmed the horror, the terror of that moment, when his boy comrade fell, with only a breath between a laugh and a deathgroan. Poor handsome Billy! Worth millions of dollars was his young life.

These sombre recollections gave way at length to more cheerful feelings as he began to approach his home coolly. The fields and houses grew familiar, and in one or two he was greeted by people seated in the doorways. But he was in no mood to talk, and pushed on steadily, though he stopped and accepted a drink of milk once at the well-side of a neighbor.

The sun was burning hot on that slope, and his step grew slower, in spite of his iron resolution. He sat down several times to rest. Slowly he crawled up the rough, reddish-brown road, which wound along the hillside, under great trees, through dense groves of jack oaks, with tree-tops far below him on his left hand, and the hills far above him on his right. He crawled along like some minute, wingless variety of fly.

He ate some hardtack, sauced with wild berries, when he reached the summit of the ridge, and sat there for some time, looking down into his home coolly.

Sombre, pathetic figure! His wide, round, gray eyes gazing down into the beautiful valley, seeing and not seeing, the splendid cloudshadows sweeping over the western hills and across the green and yellow wheat far below. His head drooped forward on his palm, his shoulders took on a tired stoop, his cheek-bones showed painfully. An observer might have said, "He is looking down upon his own grave."

A man in a blue coat, with a musket on his back, was toiling slowly up the hill on the sun-bright, dusty road, toiling slowly, with bent head half hidden by a heavy knapsack. So tired it seemed that walking was indeed a process of falling. So eager to get home he would not stop, would not look aside, but plodded on, amid the cries of the locusts, the welcome of the crickets, and the rustle of the yellow wheat. Getting back to God's country, and his wife and babies!

Laughing, crying, trying to call him and the children at the same time, the little wife, almost hysterical, snatched her hat and ran out into the yard. But the soldier had disappeared over the hill into the hollow beyond, and, by the time she had found the children, he was too far away for her voice to reach him. And, besides, she was not sure it was her husband, for he had not turned his head at their shouts. This seemed so strange. Why didn't he stop to rest at his old neighbor's house? Tortured by hope and doubt, she hurried up the coolly as fast as she could push the baby wagon, the blue-coated figure just ahead pushing steadily, silently forward up the coolly.

When the excited, panting little group came in sight of the gate they saw the blue-coated figure standing, leaning upon the rough rail fence, his chin on his palms, gazing at the empty house. His knapsack, canteen, blankets, and musket lay upon the dusty grass at his feet.

He was like a man lost in a dream. His wide, hungry eyes devoured the scene. The rough lawn, the little unpainted house, the field of clear yellow wheat behind it, down across which streamed the sun, now almost ready to touch the high hill to the west, the crickets crying merrily, a cat on the fence near by, dreaming, unmindful of the stranger in blue——

How peaceful it all was. O God! How far removed from all camps, hospitals, battle lines. A little cabin in a Wisconsin coolly, but it was majestic in its peace. How did he ever leave it for those years of tramping, thirsting, killing?

Trembling, weak with emotion, her eyes on the silent figure, Mrs. Smith hurried up to the fence. Her feet made no noise in the dust and grass, and they were close upon him before he knew of them. The oldest boy ran a little ahead. He will never forget that figure, that face. It will always remain as something epic, that return of the private. He fixed his eyes on the pale face covered with a ragged beard.

"Who *are* you, sir?" asked the wife, or, rather, started to ask, for he turned, stood a moment, and then cried:

"Emma!"

"Edward!"

The children stood in a curious row to see their mother kiss this bearded, strange man, the elder girl sobbing sympathetically with her mother. Illness had left the soldier partly deaf, and this added to the strangeness of his manner.

But the youngest child stood away, even after the girl had recognized her father and kissed him. The man turned then to the baby, and said in a curiously unpaternal tone:

"Come here, my little man; don't you know me?" But the baby backed away under the fence and stood peering at him critically.

"My little man!" What meaning in those words! This baby seemed like some other woman's child, and not the infant he had left in his wife's arms. The war had come between him and his baby—he was only a strange man to him, with big eyes; a soldier, with mother hanging to his arm, and talking in a loud voice.

"And this is Tom," the private said, drawing the oldest boy to him. "*He'll* come and see me. *He* knows his poor old pap when he comes home from the war."

The mother heard the pain and reproach in his voice and hastened to apologize.

"You've changed so, Ed. He can't know yeh. This is papa, Teddy; come and kiss him—Tom and Mary do. Come, won't you?" But Teddy still peered through the fence with solemn eyes, well out of reach. He resembled a half-wild kitten that hesitates, studying the tones of one's voice.

"I'll fix him," said the soldier, and sat down to undo his knapsack, out of which he drew three enormous and very red apples. After giving one to each of the older children, he said:

Now I guess he'll come. Eh, my little man? Now come see your pap."

Teddy crept slowly under the fence, assisted by the overzealous Tommy, and a moment later was kicking and squalling in his father's arms. Then they entered the house, into the sitting room, poor, bare, art-forsaken little room, too, with its rag carpet, its square clock, and its two or three chromos and pictures from *Harper's Weekly* pinned about.

"Emma, I'm all tired out," said Private Smith, as he flung himself down on the carpet as he used to do, while his wife brought a pillow to put under his head, and the children stood about munching their apples.

"Tommy, you run and get me a pan of chips, and Mary, you get the tea-kettle on, and I'll go and make some biscuit."

And the soldier talked. Question after question he poured forth about the crops, the cattle, the renter, the neighbors. He slipped his heavy government brogan shoes off his poor, tired blistered feet, and lay out with utter, sweet relaxation. He was a free man again, no longer a soldier under a command. At supper he stopped once, listened and smiled. "That's old Spot. I know her voice. I s'pose that's her calf out there in the pen. I can't milk her to-night, though. I'm too tired. But I tell you, I'd like a drink of her milk. What's become of old Rove?"

"He died last winter. Poisoned, I guess." There was a moment of sadness for them all. It was some time before the husband spoke again, in a voice that trembled a little.

"Poor old feller! He'd a' known me half a mile away. I expected him to come down the hill to meet me. It 'ud 'a' been more like comin' home if I could 'a' seen him comin' down the road an' waggin' his tail, an' laughin' that way he has. I tell yeh, it kind o' took hold o' me to see the blinds down an' the house shut up."

"But, yeh see, we—we expected you'd write again 'fore you started. And then we thought we'd see you if you did come," she hastened to explain.

"Well, I ain't worth a cent on writin'. Besides, it's just as well yeh didn't know when I was comin'. I tell you, it sounds good to hear them chickens out there, an' turkeys, an' the crickets. Do you know they don't have just the same kind o' crickets down South? Who's Sam hired t' help cut yer grain?"

"The Ramsey boys."

"Looks like a good crop; but I'm afraid I won't do much gettin' it cut. This cussed fever an' ague has got me down pretty low. I don't know when I'll get rid of it. I'll bet I've took twenty-five pounds of quinine if I've taken a bit. Gimme another biscuit. I tell yeh, they taste good, Emma. I ain't had anything like it——Say, if you'd 'a' hear'd me braggin' to th' boys about your butter 'n' biscuits I'll bet your ears 'ud 'a' burnt.'

The private's wife colored with pleasure. "Oh, you're always a-braggin' about your things. Everybody makes good butter."

"Yes; old lady Snyder, for instance."

"Oh, well, she ain't to be mentioned. She's Dutch."

"Or old Mis' Snively. One more cup o' tea, Mary. That's my girl! I'm feeling better already. I just b'lieve the matter with me is, I'm starved."

This was a delicious hour, one long to be remembered. They were like lovers again. But their tenderness, like that of a typical American family, found utterance in tones, rather than in words. He was praising her when praising her biscuit, and she knew it. They grew soberer when he showed where he had been struck, one ball burning the back of his hand, one cutting away a lock of hair from his temple, and one passing through the calf of his leg. The wife shuddered to think how near she had come to being a soldier's widow. Her waiting no longer seemed hard. This sweet, glorious hour effaced it all.

Then they rose, and all went out into the garden and down to the barn. He stood beside her while she milked old Spot. They began to plan fields and crops for next year.

His farm was weedy and encumbered, a rascally renter had run away with his machinery (departing between two days), his children needed clothing, the years were coming upon him, he was sick and emaciated, but his heroic soul did not quail. With the same courage with which he had faced his Southern march he entered upon a still more hazardous future.

Oh, that mystic hour! The pale man with big eyes standing there by the well, with his young wife by his side. The vast moon swinging above the eastern peaks, the cattle winding down the pasture slopes with jangling bells, the crickets singing, the stars blooming out sweet and far and serene; the katydids rhythmically calling, the little turkeys crying querulously, as they settled to roost in the poplar tree near the open gate. The voices at the well drop lower, the little ones nestle in their father's arms at last, and Teddy falls asleep there.

The common soldier of the American volunteer army had returned. His war with the South was over, and his fight, his daily running fight with nature and against the injustice of his fellowmen, was begun again.

Reading 3

Gone with the Wind

Margaret Mitchell

No matter how difficult it was for the Union soldier to reach home, he was far more fortunate than his Southern counterpart, for at least the Northerner was returning home victorious. The Confederate veteran had to make his trek home defeated and frequently without boots. Usually, he walked because many of the Southern railroads had been destroyed during the war. And, when he reached his destination, he often found his home town destroyed by the ravages of war, his farm buildings in a state of collapse or near-collapse, his fields in weeds, his livestock gone or dead, and perhaps even his loved ones missing. This tragedy is seen in the following selection.

In that warm summer after peace came, Tara suddenly lost its isolation. And for months thereafter a stream of scarecrows, bearded, ragged, footsore and always hungry, toiled up the red hill to Tara and came to rest on the shady front steps, wanting food and a night's lodging. They were Confederate soldiers walking home. The railroad had carried the remains of Johnston's army from North Carolina to Atlanta and dumped them there, and from Atlanta they began their pilgrimages afoot. When the wave of Johnston's men had passed, the weary veterans from the Army of Virginia arrived and then men from the Western troops beating their way south toward homes which might not exist and families which might be scattered or dead. Most of them were walking, a few fortunate ones rode bony horses and mules which the terms of the surrender had permitted them to keep, gaunt animals which even an untrained eye could tell would never reach far-away Florida and south Georgia.

Going home! Going home! That was the only thought in the soldiers' minds. Some were sad and silent, others gay and contemptuous of hardships, but the thought that it was all over and they were going home was the one thing that sustained them. Few of them were bitter. They left bitterness to their women and their old people. They had fought a good fight, had been licked and were willing to settle down peaceably to plowing beneath the flag they had fought.m

Going home! Going home! They could talk of nothing else, neither battles nor wounds, nor imprisonment nor the future. Later, they would refight battles and tell children and grandchildren of pranks and forays and charges, of hunger, forced marches and wounds, but not now. Some of them lacked an arm or a leg or an eye, many had scars which would ache in rainy weather if they lived for seventy years but these seemed small matters now. Later it would be different.

Old and young, talkative and taciturn, rich planter and sallow Cracker, they all had two things in common, lice and dysentery. The Confederate soldier was so accustomed to his verminous state he did not give it a thought and scratched unconcernedly even in the presence of ladies. As for dysentery —the "bloody flux" as the ladies delicately called it—it seemed to have spared no one from private to general. Four years of half-starvation, four years of rations which were coarse or green or half-putrefied, had done its work with them and every soldier who stopped at Tara was either just recovering or was actively suffering from it.

"Dey ain' a soun' set of bowels in de whole Confedrut ahmy," observed Mammy darkly as she sweated over the fire, brewing a bitter concoction of blackberry roots which had been Ellen's sovereign remedy for such afflictions. "It's mah notion dat 'twarn't de Yankees whut beat our gempmum. Twuz dey own innards. Kain no gempmum fight wid his bowels tuhnin' ter water."

One and all, Mammy dosed them, never waiting to ask foolish questions about the state of their organs and, one and all, they drank her doses meekly and with wry faces, remembering, perhaps, other stern black faces in far-off places and other inexorable black hands holding medicine spoons.

In the matter of "comp'ny" Mammy was equally adamant. No lice-ridden soldier should come into Tara. She marched them behind a clump of thick bushes, relieved them of their uniforms, gave them a basin of water and strong lye soap to wash with and provided them with quilts and blankets to cover their nakedness, while she boiled their clothing in her huge wash pot. It was useless for the girls to argue hotly that such conduct humiliated the soldiers. Mammy replied that the girls would be a sight more humiliated if they found lice upon themselves.

When the soldiers began arriving almost daily, Mammy protested against their being allowed to use the bedrooms. Always she feared lest some louse had escaped her. Rather than argue the matter, Scarlett turned the parlor with its deep velvet rug into a dormitory. Mammy cried out equally loudly at the sacrilege of soldiers being permitted to sleep on Miss Ellen's rug but Scarlett was firm. They had to sleep somewhere. And, in the months after the surrender, the deep soft nap began to show signs of wear and finally the heavy warp and woof showed through in spots where heels had worn it and spurs dug carelessly.

Reading 4

Bricks without Straws

Albion Tourgee

With Reconstruction came the desire to assist the newly freed blacks in the South. One of the progressive proposals was free public education for all. In many cases blacks and poor whites went to school for the first time. Despite these accomplishments, however, the tasks facing blacks were often beyond their talents because they did not receive the education and other assistance they needed from the federal government to aid their transition from slavery to freedom. Instead, they were expected to "make bricks without straws." Tourgee, an Ohio-born carpetbagger active in North Carolina politics, wrote several novels based upon his experiences in the South.

From *Bricks without Straws* by Albion Tourgee. Published in 1880.

Two days afterward, Mollie Ainslie took the train for the North, accompanied by Lugena and her children. At the same time went Captain Pardee, under instructions from Hesden Le Moyne to verify the will, discover who the testator really was, and then ascertain whether he had any living heirs.

To Mollie Ainslie the departure was a sad farewell to a life which she had entered upon so full of abounding hope and charity, so full of love for God and man, that she could not believe that all her bright hopes had withered and only ashes remained. The way was dark. The path was hedged up. The South was "redeemed."

The poor, ignorant white man had been unable to perceive that liberty for the slave meant elevation to him also. The poor, ignorant colored man had shown himself, as might well have been anticipated, unable to cope with intelligence, wealth, and the subtle power of the best trained political intellects of the nation; and it was not strange. They were all alone, and their allies were either as poor and weak as themselves, or were handicapped with the brand of Northern birth. These were their allies—not from choice, but from necessity. Few, indeed, were there of the highest and the best of those who had fought the nation in war as they had fought against the tide of liberty before the war began—who would accept the terms on which the nation gave re-established and greatly-increased power to the States of the South.

So there were ignorance and poverty and a hated race upon one side, and, upon the other, intelligence, wealth, and pride. The former *outnumbered* the latter; but the latter, as compared with the former, were a Grecian phalanx matched against a scattered horde of Scythian bowmen. The Nation gave the jewel of liberty into the hands of the former, armed them with the weapons of self-government, and said: "Ye are many; protect what ye have received." Then it took away its hand, turned away its eyes, closed its ears to every cry of protest or of agony, and said: "We will not aid you nor protect you. Though you are ignorant, from you will we demand the works of wisdom. Though you are weak, great things shall be required at your hands." Like the ancient taskmaster, the Nation said; *"There shall no straw be given you, yet shall ye deliver the tale of bricks."*

But, alas! they were weak and inept. The weapon they had received was two-edged. Sometimes they cut themselves; again they caught it by the blade, and those with whom they fought seized the hilt and made terrible slaughter. Then, too, they were not always wise—which was a sore fault, but not their own. Nor were they always brave, or true—which was another grievous fault: but was it to be believed that one hour of liberty would efface the scars of generations of slavery? Ah! well might they cry unto the Nation, as did Israel unto Pharaoh: "There is no straw given unto thy servants, and they say to us, 'Make brick': and behold thy servants are beaten; but the fault is in thine own people." They had simply demonstrated that in the years of Grace of the nineteenth century liberty could not be maintained nor prosperity achieved by ignorance and poverty, any more than in the days of Moses adobe bricks could be made without straw. The Nation gave the power of the South into the hands of ignorance and poverty and inexperience, and then demanded of them the fruit of intelligence, the strength of riches, and the skill of experience. It put before a keen-eyed and unscrupulous minority—a minority proud, aggressive, turbulent, arrogant, and scornful of all things save their own will and pleasure —the temptation to enhance their power by seizing that held by the trembling hands of simple-minded and unskilled guardians. What wonder that it was ravished from their care?

Mollie Ainslie thought of these things with some bitterness. She did not doubt the outcome. Her faith in truth and liberty, and her proud confidence in the ultimate destiny of the grand Nation whose past she had worshiped from childhood, were too strong to permit that. She believed that some time in the future light would come out of the darkness; but between then and the present was a great gulf, whose depth of horror no man knew, in which the people to serve whom she had given herself must sink and suffer—she could not tell how long. For them there was no hope.

She did not, indeed, look for a continuance of the horrors which then prevailed. She knew that when the incentive was removed the acts would cease. There would be peace, because there would no longer be any need for violence. But she was sure there would be no real freedom, no equality of right, no certainty of justice. She did not care who ruled, but she knew that this people —she felt almost like calling them *her* people—needed the incentive of liberty, the inspiriting rivalry of open and fair competition, to enable them to rise. Ay, to prevent them from sinking lower and lower. She greatly feared that the words of a journal which gloried in all that had been done toward abbreviating and annulling the power, rights, and opportunities of the recent slaves might yet become verities if these people were deprived of such incentives. She remembered how deeply-rooted in the Southern mind was the idea that slavery was a social necessity. She did not believe, as so many had insisted, that it was founded merely in greed. She believed that it was with sincere conviction that a leading journal had declared: "The evils of free society are insufferable. Free society must fail and give way to a *class society*—a social system old as the world, universal as man."

She knew that the leader of a would-be nation had declared: "A thousand must die as slaves or paupers in order that one gentleman may live. Yet they are cheap to any nation, even at that price."

So she feared that the victors in the *post-bellum* strife which was raging around her would succeed, for a time at least, in establishing this ideal "class society." While the Nation slumbered in indifference, she feared that these men, still full of the spirit of slavery, in the very name of law and order, under the pretense of decency and justice, would re-bind those whose feet had just begun to tread the path of liberty with shackles only less onerous than those which had been dashed from their limbs by red-handed war. As she thought of these things she read the following words from the pen of one who had carefully watched the process of "redemption," and had noted its results and tendency—not bitterly and angrily, as she had done, but coolly and approvingly:

"We would like to engrave a prophecy on stone, to be read of generations in the future. The Negro, in these [the Southern] States, will be slave again or cease to be. His sole refuge from extinction will be in slavery to the white man."

She remembered to have heard a great man say, on a memorable occasion, that "the forms of law have always been the graves of buried liberties." She feared that, under the "forms" of *subverted* laws, the liberties of a helpless people would indeed be buried. She had little care for the Nation. It was of those she had served and whose future she regarded with such engrossing interest that she thought. She did not dream of remedying the evil. That was beyond her power. She only thought she might save some from its scath. To that she devoted herself.

The day before, she had visited the cemetery where her brother's ashes reposed. She had long ago put a neat monument over his grave, and had herself supplemented the national appropriation for its care. It was a beautiful inclosure, walled with stone, verdant with soft turf, and ornamented with rare shrubbery. Across it ran a little stream, with green banks sloping either way. A single great elm drooped over its bubbling waters. A pleasant drive ran with easy grade and graceful curves down one low hill and up another. The iron gate opened upon a dusty highway. Beside it stood the keeper's neat brick lodge. In front, and a little to the right, lay a sleepy Southern town half hidden in embowering trees. Across the little ravine within the cemetery, upon the level plateau, were the graves, marked, in some cases, by little square white monuments of polished marble, on which was but the single word, "Unknown." A few bore the names of those who slept below. But on one side there were five long mounds, stretching away, side by side, as wide as the graves were long, and as long as four score graves. Smoothly rounded from end to end, without a break or a sign, they seemed a fit emblem of silence. Where they began, a granite pillar rose high, decked with symbols of glory interspersed with emblems of mourning. Cannon, battered and grim, the worn-out dogs of war, gaped with silent jaws up at the silent sky. No name was carved on base or capital, nor on the marble shield upon the shaft. Only, "Sacred to the memory of the unknown heroes who died——."

How quick the memory fills out the rest! There had been a military prison of the Confederacy just over the hill yonder, where the corn now grew so rank and thick. Twelve thousand men died there and were thrown into those long trenches where are now heaped-up mounds that look like giants' graves—not buried one by one, with coffin, shroud, and funeral rite, but one upon another heaped and piled, until the yawning pit would hold no more. No name was kept, no grave was marked, but in each trench was heaped one undistinguishable mass of dead humanity!

Reading 5

A Fool's Errand

Albion Tourgee

Tourgee was very pessimistic about the results of Reconstruction and described the efforts of the North to superimpose its values upon the South as "a fool's errand." Tourgee also stressed the fact that the two sections of the country represented two separate and distinctive societies and suggested that they were going to remain that way indefinitely.

It was shortly after the rupture of his home-life and his departure from Warrington, that Sérvosse visited, by special invitation, Doctor Enos Martin, the ancient friend who had been at first his instructor, and afterward his revered and trusted counselor. In the years which had elapsed since the Fool had seen him, he had passed from a ripe manhood of surpassing vigor into that riper age which comes without weakness, but which, nevertheless, brings not a little of philosophic calm,—that true "sunset of life which gives mystical lore." It is in those calm years which come before the end, when ambition is dead and aspiration ceases; when the restless clamor of busy life sweeps by unheeded as the turmoil of the crowded thoroughfare by the busy worker; when the judgment acts calmly, unbiased by hope or fear,—it is in these declining years that the best work of the best lives is usually done. The self which makes the balance waver is dead; but the heart, the intellect, the keen sympathy with that world which is fast slipping away, remain, and the ripened energies act without the wastefulness of passion. It was in this calm brightness which precedes the twilight, that Enos Martin sat down to converse with the

From *A Fool's Errand* by Albion Tourgee. Published in 1879.

man, now rugged and mature, whom he had watched while he grew from youth into manhood, and from early manhood to its maturity. A score of years had passed since they had met. To the one, these years had been full of action. He had been in the current, had breasted its bufferings, and been carried away out of the course which he had marked out for himself on life's great chart, by its cross-currents and counter-eddies. He had a scar to show for every struggle. His heart had throbbed in harmony with the great world-pulse in every one of the grand purposes with which it had swelled during those years. The other had watched with keenest apprehension those movements which had veered and whirled about in their turbid currents the life of the other, himself but little moved, but ever seeking to draw what lessons of value he might from such observation, for the instruction and guidance of other young souls who were yet but skirting the shore of the great sea of life.

This constant and observant interest in the great social movements of the world which he overlooked from so serene a height had led him to note with peculiar care the relations of the nation to the recently subjugated portion of the South, and more especially the conditions of the blacks. In so doing, he had been led to consider especially that transition period which comes between Chattelism, or some form of individual subordination and dependence, and absolute individual autonomy. This is known by different names in different lands and ages,—villenage in England, serfdom in Russia. In regard to this, his inquiries had been most profound, and his interest in all those national questions had accordingly been of the liveliest character: hence his keen desire to see his old pupil, and to talk with one in whom he had confidence as an observer, in regard to the phenomena he had witnessed and the conclusions at which he had arrived, and to compare the same, not only with his own more remote observations, but also with the facts of history. They sat together for a long time in the library where the elder had gathered the intellectual wealth of the world and the ages, and renewed the personal knowledge of each other which a score of years had interrupted. The happenings of the tumultuous life, the growth of the quiet one, were both recounted; and then their conversation drifted to that topic which had engrossed so much of the thought of both,— that great world-current of which both lives were but unimportant incidents.

"And so," said the elder gravely, "you think, Colonel Servosse, that what has been termed Reconstruction is a magnificent failure?"

"Undoubtedly," was the reply, "so far as concerns the attainment of the result intended by its projectors, expected by the world, and to be looked for as a logical sequence of the war."

"I do not know that I fully understand your limitation," said Martin doubtfully.

"I mean," said the younger man, "that Reconstruction was a failure so far as it attempted to unify the nation, to make one people in fact of what had been one only in name before the convulsion of civil war. It was a failure, too, so far as it attempted to fix and secure the position and rights of the colored race. They were fixed, it is true, on paper, and security of a certain sort taken to prevent the abrogation of that formal declaration. No guaranty whatever was provided against their practical subversion, which was accomplished with an ease and impunity that amazed those who instituted the movement."

"You must at least admit that the dogma of 'State Rights' was settled by the war and by that system of summary and complete national control over the erring commonwealths which we call Reconstruction," said Martin.

"On the contrary," answered Servosse, "the doctrine of 'State Rights' is altogether unimpaired and untouched by what has occurred, except in one particular; to wit, *the right of peaceable secession.* The war settled that. The Nation asserted its right to defend itself against disruption."

"Did it not also assert its right to re-create, to make over, to reconstruct?" asked the elder man.

"Not at all," was the reply. "Reconstruction was never asserted *as a right,* at least not formally and authoritatively. Some did so affirm; but they were accounted visionaries. The act of reconstruction was *excused* as a necessary sequence of the failure of attempted secession: it was never defended or promulgated as a *right of the nation,* even to *secure its own safety.*"

"Why, then, do you qualify the declaration of failure?" asked Martin. "It seems to me to have been absolute and complete."

"Not at all," answered Servosse with some vehemence. "A great deal was gained by it. Suppose a child does wrong a hundred times, is reproved for it each time, and only at the last reproof expresses sorrow, and professes a desire to do better, and the very next day repeats the offense. The parent does not despair, nor count the repentance as nothing gained. On the contrary, a great step has been made: the wrong has been admitted, and is thereafter without excuse. Thenceforward, Nathan-like, the parent can point the offender to his own judgment on his own act. So Reconstruction was a great step in advance, in that it formulated a confession of error. It gave us a construction of 'we the people' in the preamble of our Federal Constitution which gave the lie to that which had formerly prevailed. It recognized and formulated the universality of manhood in governmental power, and, in one phase or another of its development, compelled the formal assent of all sections and parties."

"And is this all that has been gained by all these years of toil and struggle and blood?" asked the old man with a sigh.

"Is it not enough, my friend?" replied the Fool, with a reproachful tone. "Is not almost a century of falsehood and hypocrisy cheaply atoned by a decade of chastisement? The confession of error is the hardest part of repentance, whether in a man or in a nation. It is there the Devil always makes his strongest fight. After that, he has to come down out of the mountain, and fight in the valley. He is wounded, crippled, and easily put to rout."

"You do not regard the struggle between the North and the South as ended, then," said Martin.

"Ended?" ejaculated the Fool sharply. "It is just begun! I do not mean the physical tug of war between definitely defined sections. That is a mere incident of a great underlying struggle,—a conflict which is ever going on between two antagonistic ideas. It was like a stream with here and there an angry rapid, before the war; then, for a time, it was like a foaming cascade; and since then it has been the sullen, dark, but deep and quiet whirlpool, which lies below the fall, full of driftwood and shadows, and angry mutterings, and unseen currents, and hidden forces, whose farther course no one can foretell, only that it must go on.

> The deepest ice that ever froze
> Can only o'er the river close:
> The living stream lies quick below,
> And flows—and can not cease to flow"

"Do you mean to say that the old battle between freedom and slavery was not ended by the extinction of slavery?" asked the doctor in surprise.

"I suppose it would be," answered the Fool, with a hint of laughter in his tones, "if slavery *were* extinct. I do not mean to combat the old adage that 'it takes two to make a quarrel;' but that is just where our mistake—the mistake of the North, for the South has not made one in this matter—has been. We have *assumed* that slavery was dead, because we had a Proclamation of Emancipation, a Constitutional Amendment, and 'laws passed in pursuance thereof,' all reciting the fact that involuntary servitude, except for crime, should no more exist. Thereupon, we have thrown up our hats, and crowed lustily for what we had achieved, as we had a good right to do. The Antislavery Society met, and congratulated itself on the accomplishment of its mission, on having no more worlds to conquer, no more oppression to resist, and no more victims to succor. And thereupon, in the odor of its self-laudation, it dissolved its own existence, dying full of good works, and simply for the want of more good works to be done. It was an end that smacks of the millennium; but, unfortunately, it was farcical in the extreme. I don't blame Garrison and Phillips and yourself, and all the others of the old guard of abolitionists. It was natural that you should at least wish to try on your laurels while alive."

"Really, Colonel," said the old doctor laughingly, "you must not think that was our motive."

"Not confessedly, nor consciously of course," said the Fool. "Real motives are rarely formulated. I don't wonder, though, that men who had been in what our modern slang denominates the 'racket' of the antislavery reform should be tired. I fully realize that a life-time of struggle takes away a man's relish for a fight. Old men never become missionaries. Being in a conflict of ideas, they may keep up the fight till the last minute and the last breath. Old men have made good martyrs ever since Polycarp's day, but they don't long for martyrdom, nor advertise for it. If it is just as convenient to avoid it, they prefer to do so; and in this case they certainly deserved a rest, and more honor and glory than they will ever get, alive or dead.

"It was our fault,—the then youngsters who had just come out of the furnace-fire in which the shackles were fused and melted away from the cramped and shriveled limbs. We ought to have seen and known that only the shell was gone. Slavery as a formal state of society was at an end: as a force, a power, a moral element, it was just as active as before. Its conscious evils were obliterated: its unconscious ones existed in the dwarfed and twisted natures which had been subjected for generations to its influences,—master and slave alike. As a form of society, it could be abolished by proclamation and enactment: as a moral entity, it is as indestructible as the souls on which it has left its mark."

"You think the 'irrepressible conflict' is yet confronting us, then?" said Martin.

"Undoubtedly. The North and the South are simply convenient names for two distinct, hostile, and irreconcilable ideas,—two civilizations they are sometimes called, especially at the South. At the North there is somewhat more of intellectual arrogance; and we are apt to speak of the one as civilization, and of the other as a species of barbarism. These two must always be in conflict until the one prevails, and the other falls. To uproot the one, and plant the other in its stead, is not the work of a moment or a day. That was our mistake. We tried to superimpose the civilization, the idea of the North, upon the South at a moment's warning. We presumed, that, by the suppression of rebellion, the Southern white man had become identical with the Caucasian of the North in thought and sentiment; and that the slave, by emancipation, had become a saint and a Solomon at once. So we tried to build up communities there which should be identical in thought, sentiment, growth, and development, with those of the North. It was A FOOL'S ERRAND."

Chapter 2

The Last Frontier

Reading 6
Starving to Death on a Government Claim

During the period of the last frontier (1865–1890), the vast area from the 100th meridian to the Rocky Mountains was settled by the white man. The Indian was again pushed aside to make way for the miner, the cattleman, and the farmer, in that order. But the grasslands of the Great Plains were a different kind of frontier for the American pioneer. The following poem is the lament of an Oklahoma farmer, but it is also representative of Lane County, Kansas settlers who were disillusioned with their lot. The same lament could have come from settlers in most counties from Montana south to Texas.

My name is Tom Hight, and old bach'lor I am,
You'll find me out west in the country of fame,
You'll find me out west on elegant plan,
A starving to death on my government claim.

Chorus (to be sung between each of the stanzas):
Hurrah for Greer County, the land of the free,
The land of the bedbug, grasshopper and flea;
I'll sing of its praises, I'll tell of its fame,
While starving to death on my government claim.

My house, it is built out of national soil,
Its walls are erected according to Hoyle,
Its roof has no pitch, but is level and plain,
I always get wet if it happens to rain.

My clothes are all ragged, as my language is rough;
My bread is corndodgers, both solid and tough;
But yet I am happy and live at my ease
On sorghum molasses, bacon and cheese.

Now happy am I when I crawl into bed,
A rattlesnake hisses a tune at my head,
A gay little centipede, all without fear,

Starving to Death on a Government Claim, as published in Tremaine McDowell, ed., *America in Literature.*

Crawls over my pillow and into my ear.

Now all you claim holders, I hope you will stay
And chew your hardtack till you're toothless and gray,
But for myself I'll no longer remain
To starve like a dog on my government claim.

Good-by to Greer County where blizzards arise,
Where the sun never sinks and the flea never dies,
And the wind never ceases but always remains
Till it starves us all out on our government claims.

Farewell to Greer County, farewell to the West,
I'll travel back East to the girl I love best,
I'll travel to Texas and marry me a wife,
And quit corndodger the rest of my life.

Reading 7

The Shadow Catcher

James Horan

During the first phase of the last frontier, the Indians, the first Americans, contested the white man for almost every piece of territory. From 1868 to about 1890 there was almost incessant warfare between the whites and the natives, who usually had fine horses and occasionally had better weapons than the settlers or even the soldiers. The result, however, was foreordained. The railroad not only brought settlers rapidly, it also destroyed the buffalo, the Indian food staple, forcing the first Americans onto reservations. Fortunately, during the earlier years the government sent out exploring parties that were usually accompanied by a painter, who recorded the life of the tribes. The "shadow catchers," as the Indians called such men, painted many valuable scenes before they were gone forever.

"How many times have you been out, Jim?" I asked, when we had finished.
    He looked into space a moment. "Four treaties and three field trips—

about ten paintings. Well, the colonel wants me to give you all the help I can."

While the servant was clearing the table, we strolled over to the easel under the elm. I saw the portrait of a young Indian with a crown of brilliantly colored feathers and a broad slash of red paint across the center of his face. He stared out with a curious mixture of fierce pride and animal shyness.

"He's the Chippewa chief I met when the Fond du Lac treaty was signed," Lewis said. "Note the importance of ornaments and decorations. Also the coloring of the feathers on his headpiece; they were all carefully selected from a drake's breast by his squaw. That wide neckband is horsehair dyed with vermilion. The feathers on the pipe are from the drake's wings. That decoration on the bowl is the carefully dyed head of a woodpecker." He leaned closer to the painting. "See this line above his eyebrows? It's a sacred tatoo; you'll find a lot of tattoo work out there among the Crows. They use porcupine quills dipped in a mixture of charcoal and pine. They take hours to make their designs. I would advise you to study them carefully."

"But how do you get them to stand still?"

"The farther west you go the more difficult it will be. You might get them to pose by either appealing to their pride or giving them presents. However, keep a careful guard over your finished work. Indians are frightened to death of even seeing their reflection in a calm pond. They're afraid of losing their shadows, as they say. But don't worry. Most men—red, white, yellow, or black —can scarcely resist the lure of immortality. By the way, how much experience have you had in oils?"

In the next hour I absorbed enough information about paints, texture, the care and treatment of equipment in the wilderness (chipmunks and Indian dogs will chew the brushes, while young bucks will steal strips of canvas to sew on their buffalo shields as good medicine) to set my head whirling.

"The main thing is to observe. Before you paint a buffalo pony, study it, watch the play of sinews and muscles. The same with the Indians. Remember they are all human; you'll find them suspicious, afraid, happy. Study them— then put into your painting what you see. Always remember this, Matt. You are not painting for your time, you are painting for your children's children. You are painting because you want them to know exactly what these redmen looked like—you will be a painter of a lost people."

"A lost people? They occupy half the continent!"

He shrugged. "We whites are peculiarly ruthless. Once we start moving west—and that will be within our generation—we will exterminate more and more of these people with lies, threats, disease, and whiskey. We will repeat what happened when the Mayflower landed, only on a larger scale." He glanced at a battered old silver watch. "Dammit, where has the afternoon gone? I think you and Charles had better be getting back." He hesitated. Then: "Would it be prying to ask what made you decide to go?"

The question was unexpected and I hesitated. "Well, let's say personal reasons. . . ."

Apparently believing I meant affairs of the heart, he whispered in a conspiratorial fashion, "I can assure you, you'll find the Crow women very attractive."

"I'm sure Montero will take care of the ladies," I said.

"Yes, I suppose so. God, the stories I heard about that man!"

"Rather strange man, isn't he?"

Lewis thought for a moment. "Strange? Perhaps. But unlike most of us, Dana has been lucky enough to be born in the right century. He belongs to the Nations, the buffalo, the mountains. Many of us can walk out there, but we need someone to lead us, a man who can be as hard and ruthless as the country. Once the wagons come, men like that will be gone." He held out his hand. "Well, Matt, good-by and good luck."

I looked at the man and a question that had been plaguing me all afternoon came to my lips.

"From what I heard, the government only allows you thirty-three dollars a portrait?"

"Thirty-three dollars is the *maximum*. Most of the time we get twenty."

"And, this is for work done under the greatest hardships."

"You can lose your hair too," King said. "Once a drunken Chippewa tried to brain Jim."

"In addition to such miserable payment you have to put up with the insults of politicians."

King said, "Sam Houston's mad because the colonel made the Cherokee agent stop peddling whiskey."

I turned to Lewis. "Knowing all this, why do you continue to paint these pictures?"

There was a long silence. They looked at each other for a moment, then Lewis said in a thoughtful, measured voice, "Why, Matt? Well, I guess I'm one of God's hungry people, who want to possess—no, imprison is a better word—a part of life that will be soon gone. In fact, it will pass so quickly most men will think it vanished overnight." He stopped and seemed to be staring at something I wasn't privileged to see.

"It's like a fever. You want to get everything on canvas—the Dog Soldiers, hunters, medicine men, women, and the great vastness of their country. God, it *is* big; wait until you get there, Matt. You'll get the itch for the brush, you won't even stop to eat. It's something you just can't help, you must do it." He held out his hands, palms up as though he was begging me to understand. "So I guess if you feel that way about something, thirty-three dollars and all the yelping of that Missouri titmouse doesn't mean anything, now does it?"

After a last handshake Charles and I drove off in his carriage. Just before we turned into Pennsylvania Avenue I looked back. The street was empty. Jim Lewis was already back at his easel under the big elm.

Reading 8

The Big Rock Candy Mountain

Wallace Stegner

The frontier bestowed a legacy of restlessness upon America. Since colonial days men "have been born with the itch in (their) bones." To many it has provided an excuse to pull up roots wherever they were bored and move on to greener pastures. This brief selection, describing the constant movement in search of opportunity in the early twentieth century, is in essence descriptive of all American frontiersmen. Bo, the hero of the novel, is engaged in a lifetime quest for the "Big Rock Candy Mountain."

Pinky Jordan never returned for the poker game, though Bo tried all the next day to locate him around town. But he had done his work. He left behind him a few dollars' worth of gold dust in a shot glass behind Bo Mason's bar. He also left behind him a vision of clean wilderness, white rivers and noble mountains, forests full of game and fabulously valuable fur, sand full of glittering grains. And he left in Bo, fretted by hard times and the burden of an unpaid mortgage and the worry and wear of keeping his nose too long to an unprofitable grindstone, a heightened case of that same old wandering itch that had driven him from town to town and job to job since he was fourteen.

He was born with the itch in his bones, Elsa knew. He was always telling stories of men who had gone over the hills to some new place and found a land of Canaan, made their pile, got to be big men in the communities they fathered. But the Canaans toward which Bo's feet had turned had not lived up to their promise. People had been before him. The cream, he said, was gone. He should have lived a hundred years earlier.

Yet he would never quite grant that all the good places were filled up. There was somewhere, if you knew where to find it, some place where money could be made like drawing water from a well, some Big Rock Candy Mountain where life was effortless and rich and unrestricted and full of adventure and action, where something could be had for nothing. He hadn't found it in Chicago or Milwaukee or Terre Haute or the Wisconsin woods or Dakota; there was no place and no business where you took chances and the chances paid off, where you played, and the play was profitable. Ball playing might have been it, if he had hit the big time, but bad luck had spoiled that chance. But in the Klondike . . . the Klondike, Elsa knew as soon as he opened his mouth to say something when Pinky Jordan was gone, was the real thing, the thing he had been looking for for a lifetime.

"Let me show you," he said, and brought the shot glass containing Pinky Jordan's immortal dust. His mind was whitehot with visions, and he vibrated like a harp to his own versions of Pinky's yarns. There was a place without the scorching summers that fried the meat on your bones; there was a place where banks didn't close and panics didn't reach, where they had no rules and regulations a man had to live by. You stood on your own two feet and to hell with the rest of the world. In the Klondike the rivers ran gold and silver fox skins fetched four hundred dollars apiece and the woods were full of them.

She was not surprised when he proposed selling the hotel and lighting out. It took him only three or four days to arrive at that plan, but she was ready for it.

Reading 9

Coarse Gold

Edwin Corle

Mining acted as a catalytic agent in the settling of the last frontier. Ever since gold had first been discovered in California in 1848, settlers had swarmed westward in search of precious metals. Once the rich placer deposits in the Golden State declined, men sought gold and silver in the rugged mountains, deep canyons, and high plateaus that dominate the Far West. A pattern in mining discoveries evolved: there was a flurry of excitement at the discovery of a new find, followed by a mad stampede to the new site, the hasty building of a tent city, the erection of more durable buildings, and the influx of a large number of prospectors. In most cases these high hopes were soon dashed, and people left for greener pastures. There was usually a new discovery just

From *Coarse Gold* by Edwin Corle. Published in 1942. Reprinted with permission of Mrs. Jean A. Corle.

when a strike was playing out. From Montana to Arizona large numbers of
ghost towns, in various stages of disintegration, remain as mute testimony
of this process. A very few miners succeeded abundantly, but most received
only a modest return on their investment of time and money. Still, many who
sought precious metals in the West remained and provided the nuclei of
future settlements. This selection tells of one prospector's discovery.

Out from the open door of the town's only bank a rabbit hopped. He was a
large dun-colored jack rabbit and he squatted on the sand in the light of a
setting sun, his long ears pointing skyward and his nose twitching and his eyes
staring blankly at the sagebrush across the street. For a long time he did
nothing but continue to sit in the twilight and blend with the landscape and
wrinkle his nose.

The sun touched the rim of the Funeral Mountains to the west and
apparently went down into Death Valley. Its final minutes bathed the two-
story bank and the street and the rabbit in a copper light. Four blocks down
Main Street the sagging, leaning, eroding buildings ended abruptly. Four
blocks in any direction from the bank grew the sagebrush surrounding the
town on all sides, stretching on far across the floor of the desert, an impersonal
sea flecked with patches of greasewood washing up to the distant purple
mountains on the horizon. And into the town itself advance guards of greasewood and sage sprang up incongrously in streets, in the middle of houses
whose floors had long since rotted away, and whose walls crumbling and
wearing down from years of desert sun and wind, were slowly being reduced
to oblivion.

To the north, beyond the shambles of a stamp mill, was the Hill—a rise
of ground five hundred feet above the streets of the town, a mountain in
miniature, honeycombed and pockmarked with shafts and tunnels. Smaller
hills of slag and waste and ore dumpings and tailings were pimples on the hill
itself, and from the timbered opening of the largest tunnel a narrow-gauge
railway led out to a dump-rack. On the rack were three heavy and cumbersome
iron dump-cars once used for carrying ore from the internal depths of the hill
to the world outside. The cars had not been moved in years. They were rusted
and oxidized until they seemed fastened to the spot, and the tiny rails over
which their heavy wheels had once rolled were sprung and useless. The view
from the hill gave a comprehensive picture of the town; four streets east and
west, four streets north and south had formed the heart of it. The outlying
houses and streets had been taken over entirely by the steadily encroaching
desert growth, but the bank building and several dozen others remained in
various stages of preservation but badly marked by the scars of the battle: no

glass, empty windows, sagging doors, rotting floors and collapsed roofs. The business district was making the last stand, fighting the tightening grip of the sagebrush and the greasewood house by house, falling back foot by foot as the desert horde advanced, and then finding itself suddenly caught from the rear —for in the heart of the bank itself, up through the rotting planks of the floor where once had been the cashier's window, a small greasewood bush was pushing its way. The desert had advanced on the town from four directions, and from within the fifth column was at work. Only the formality of surrender remained.

The desert was not overstepping its bounds; it was merely reclaiming its own and returning this area to the condition it had enjoyed fifty years earlier. For then there had been no town and the greasewood and the sagebrush had stretched from the horizon to the hill, and had even crept up on the hill until the scrub growth had taken root around and among the rocks in which Lucky Sam Branahan had wandered one day and finally had sat down on gold.

Sam had been prospecting all his life and was sixty-five years old when he made the strike that created a town. He had been looking for gold for so long that the search had become reflexive, like breathing. It was said he would rather look for gold than eat. In truth, Sam was more consistently a searcher than an eater. There had been times in his life when he was down to bacon and beans, and there had been times when there wasn't even bacon and beans, but at no time had he ever stopped searching for gold. Sam never saw a rock; he saw instead the possibilities and potentialities within the rock. He knew that the day must come when he would "strike it rich" and he pursued that day through the sequence of conscious time. At twenty-five he had a burro and a blanket and a pick and a canteen and some camping equipment and for the next forty years he had little else. He swore that he would turn over every rock in Nevada if need be, for the gold was there and that gold he was going to find.

He did.

I went up to the ledge and took a look at the quartz outcropping. I picked up a rock and I took a look and I guess the old heart skipped a beat. Maybe she skipped two beats—or three or four. Because there it was. I held it in my two hands and I just stood there lookin' at it. Maybe I stood there a long time. I don't know. It was as pretty a piece of rock full of free gold as any man could ask God to let him see. It set me to thinkin' fast—not about the claim, but about a lot of things. Almost everything. Here it was the year of our lord 1891 —January 10—and I'm standin' with my own two feet on a quartz blowout that means this here hill under me is rich enough to buy and sell maybe the whole blasted state of Nevada. And there ain't nobody but me and God and the burro that knows it right at that minute. "Gold," I says to the jackass, and he don't even bat an eye. From the hill I look across the desert. There ain't a livin' soul around me. Far off to the west is the Funeral Range, but no matter where I look there ain't nobody. "Jesus," I said, and I wasn't swearin'. "Jesus, this is it. I thank ya." And then I sat down before I fell down. I sat down on that quartz blowout and I'm a little dizzy. "I'm sittin' on a million dollars," I think. Maybe two million. Maybe twenty million—or forty, or fifty. This whole damned hill is a quartz blowout and only God knows how much gold is hid away here. "I'm rich," I says, and I can hardly believe that it is my own voice tellin' me that. I sit there thinkin' that I've got to file on this pronto and I'm so punch drunk from the shock that I begin figurin' on foolish things like what'll I call this mine and how I'll spend all the money. And pretty soon, just for the hell of it, I take my pick and I begin to break into that hill and no matter in what direction I swing it, there she is, good gold, pure gold, virgin gold, fine gold, coarse gold—just gold, gold, gold, and I go on swingin' the pick just for the sheer pleasure of it. And the damn fool jackass ain't even got brains enough to give a hee-haw. . . .

When the sun disappeared behind the Funeral Mountains the rabbit came to life and took three hops down the main street and then sat still again. There was no other movement in the town, but with the cooling evening air a slight breeze began to whisper through the greasewood, carrying the pungent creosote odor of the bush over the town and through the glassless windows of the bank. The bank building was merely a shell; the fixtures had long since been removed. Only the safe remained: but its heavy iron door had been pried off and lay on the dirt floor. BANK OF COARSE GOLD was spelled out in letters on the safe, and just beyond was the space formerly occupied by Mr. Roland Fredericks, one-time president. Mr. Fredericks had never been a banker until he came to the town in 1893. The mushrooming tent and shack city had no bank in 1893 and when Mr. Fredericks arrived he had no business. He had been Mr. Fred E. Ricks, mining promoter, real-estate promoter and general opportunist in New Mexico and in Arizona (in earlier days he would have had a carpetbag). And as his last promotion had run afoul of Arizona's territorial law, Mr. Ricks suddenly decided to change states and even names. Fred E. Ricks disappeared from Arizona and entrepreneur Roland Fredericks arrived in Nevada. The town of Coarse Gold (first known as Branahan's Strike) was then only two years old, and Mr. Fredericks arrived by Wells Fargo stagecoach with five dollars in his pocket and an eye to business. The new town, to his practiced eye, looked promising. Quickly he noted that it had no bank. Thus Mr. Fredericks became a banker.

Reading 10

Main Travelled Roads

Hamlin Garland

Some farmers always believed, much to the dismay of their long-suffering
wives, that greater prosperity lay just a little farther westward. The family of
Hamlin Garland, whose fiction usually reflected his own experiences, is a
good example of this type of thinking. His family first moved from Wisconsin
to Iowa and then, after several years, pulled up stakes from South Dakota.
The following selection, especially the song, reflects the hostility of women
toward the pioneer life.

Sometime in the spring of 1868, a merchant from LaCrosse, a plump man who
brought us candy and was very cordial and condescending, began negotiations
for our farm, and in the discussion of plans which followed, my conception
of the universe expanded. I began to understand that "Minnesota" was not a
bluff but a wide land of romance, a prairie, peopled with red men, which lay
far beyond the big river. And then, one day, I heard my father read to my
mother a paragraph from the county paper which ran like this, "It is reported
that Richard Garland has sold his farm in Green's Coulee to our popular
grocer, Mr. Speer. Mr. Speer intends to make of it a model dairy farm."

This intention seemed somehow to reflect a ray of glory upon us, though
I fear it did not solace my mother, as she contemplated the loss of home and
kindred. She was not by nature an emigrant,—few women are. She was content
with the pleasant slopes, the kindly neighbors of Green's Coulee. Furthermore,
most of her brothers and sisters still lived just across the ridge in the valley
of the Neshonoc, and the thought of leaving them for a wild and unknown
region was not pleasant.

To my father, on the contrary, change was alluring. Iowa was now the
place of the rainbow, and the pot of gold. He was eager to push on toward it,
confident of the outcome. His spirit was reflected in one of the songs which
we children particularly enjoyed hearing our mother sing, a ballad which
consisted of a dialogue between a husband and wife on this very subject of
emigration. The words as well as its wailing melody still stir me deeply, for
they lay hold of my sub-conscious memory—embodying admirably the debate
which went on in our home as well as in the homes of other farmers in the
valley,—only, alas! our mothers did not prevail.

From *Main Travelled Roads* by Hamlin Garland. Published in 1890.

It begins with a statement of unrest on the part of the husband who confesses that he is about to give up his plow and his cart—

> Away to Colorado a journey I'll go,
> For to double my fortune as other men do,
> *While here I must labor each day in the field*
> *And the winter consumes all the summer doth yield.*

To this the wife replies:

> Dear husband, I've noticed with a sorrowful heart
> That you long have neglected your plow and your cart
> Your horses, sheep, cattle at random do run,
> And your new Sunday jacket goes every day on.
> *Oh, stay on your farm and you'll suffer no loss,*
> *For the stone that keeps rolling will gather no moss.*

But the husband insists:

> Oh, wife, let us go; Oh, don't let us wait;
> I long to be there, and I long to be great,
> While you some fair lady and who knows but I
> May be some rich governor long 'fore I die,
> *Whilst here I must labor each day in the field,*
> *And the winter consumes all the summer doth yield.m*

But wife shrewdly retorts:

> Dear husband, remember those lands are so dear
> They will cost you the labor of many a year.
> Your horses, sheep, cattle will all be to buy,
> You will hardly get settled before you must die.
> Oh, stay on the farm,—etc.

The husband then argues that as in that country the lands are all cleared to the plow, and horses and cattle not very dear, they would soon be rich. Indeed, "we will feast on fat venison one-half of the year." Thereupon the wife brings in her final argument:

> Oh, husband, remember those lands of delight
> Are surrounded by Indians who murder by night.
> Your house will be plundered and burnt to the ground
> While your wife and your children lie mangled around.

This fetches the husband up with a round turn:

> Oh, wife, you've convinced me, I'll argue no more,
> I never once thought of your dying before.
> I love my dear children although they are small
> And you, my dear wife, I love greatest of all.

Refrain (both together)

> We'll stay on the farm and we'll suffer no loss
> For the stone that keeps rolling will gather no moss.

This song was not an especial favorite of my father. Its minor strains and its expressions of womanly doubts and fears were antipathetic to his sanguine, buoyant, self-confident nature. He was inclined to ridicule the conclusions of its last verse and to say that the man was a molly-coddle—or whatever the word of contempt was in those days. As an antidote he usually called for "O'er the hills in legions, boys," which exactly expressed his love of exploration and adventure.

This ballad which dates back to the conquest of the Allegheny mountains opens with a fine uplifting note.

> Cheer up, brothers, as we go
> O'er the mountains, westward ho,
> Where herds of deer and buffalo
> Furnish the fare.

and the refrain is at once a bugle call and a vision:

> Then o'er the hills in legions, boys,
> Fair freedom's star
> Points to the sunset regions, boys,
> Ha, ha, ha-ha!

and when my mother's clear voice rose on the notes of that exultant chorus, our hearts responded with a surge of emotion akin to that which sent the followers of Daniel Boone across the Blue Ridge, and lined the trails of Kentucky and Ohio with the canvas-covered wagons of the pioneers.

A little farther on in the song came these words,

> When we've wood and prairie land,
> Won by our toil,
> We'll reign like kings in fairy land,
> Lords of the soil!

which always produced in my mind the picture of a noble farm-house in a park-like valley, just as the line, "We'll have our rifles ready, boys," expressed the boldness and self-reliance of an armed horseman.

The significance of this song in the lives of the McClintocks and the Garlands cannot be measured. It was the marching song of my Grandfather's generation and undoubtedly profoundly influenced my father and my uncles in all that they did. It suggested shining mountains, and grassy vales, swarming with bear and elk. It called to green savannahs and endless flowery glades. It voiced as no other song did, the pioneer impulse throbbing deep in my father's blood. That its words will not bear close inspection today takes little from its power. Unquestionably it was a directing force in the lives of at least three generations of my pioneering race. Its strains will be found running through this book from first to last, for its pictures continued to allure my father on and on toward "the sunset regions," and its splendid faith carried him through many a dark vale of discontent.

. . .

There, on a low mound in the midst of the prairie, in the shadow of the house we had built, beneath the slender trees we had planted, we were bidding farewell to one cycle of emigration and entering upon another. The border line had moved on, and my indomitable Dad was moving with it. I shivered with dread of the irrevocable decision thus forced upon me. I heard a clanging as of great gates behind me and the field of the future was wide and wan.

From this spot we had seen the wild prairies disappear. On every hand wheat and corn and clover had taken the place of the wild oat, the hazelbush and the rose. Our house, a commonplace frame cabin, took on grace. Here Hattie had died. Our yard was ugly, but there Jessie's small feet had worn a slender path. Each of our lives was knit into these hedges and rooted in these fields and yet, notwithstanding all this, in response to some powerful yearning call, my father was about to set out for the fifth time into the still more remote and untrodden west. Small wonder that my mother sat with bowed head and tear-blinded eyes, while these good and faithful friends crowded around her to say goodbye.

She had no enemies and no hatreds. Her rich singing voice, her smiling face, her ready sympathy with those who suffered, had endeared her to every home into which she had gone, even as a momentary visitor. No woman in childbirth, no afflicted family within a radius of five miles had ever called for her in vain. Death knew her well, for she had closed the eyes of youth and age, and yet she remained the same laughing, bounteous, wholesouled mother of men that she had been in the valley of the Neshonoc. Nothing could permanently cloud her face or embitter the sunny sweetness of her creed.

One by one the women put their worn, ungraceful arms about her, kissed her with trembling lips, and went away in silent grief. The scene became too painful for me at last, and I fled away from it—out into the fields, bitterly asking, "Why should this suffering be? Why should mother be wrenched from all her dearest friends and forced to move away to a strange land?"

Reading 11

East of Eden

John Steinbeck

John Steinbeck, who wrote so movingly of frontier life, especially in California, portrays an often neglected aspect of it in the following selection. In the West, the center of social life was generally either the church or the whorehouse. The role of the church is frequently treated, but the part played by the whorehouse is usually neglected for obvious reasons. Whether they were essential parts of the cultural expression of the frontier is left for the reader to decide.

A new country seems to follow a pattern. First come the openers, strong and brave and rather childlike. They can take care of themselves in a wilderness, but they are naïve and helpless against men, and perhaps that is why they went out in the first place. When the rough edges are worn off the new land, businessmen and lawyers come in to help with the development—to solve problems of ownership, usually by removing the temptations to themselves. And finally comes culture, which is entertainment, relaxation, transport out of the pain of living. And culture can be on any level, and is.

The church and the whorehouse arrived in the Far West simultaneously. And each would have been horrified to think it was a different facet of the same thing. But surely they were both intended to accomplish the same thing: the singing, the devotion, the poetry of the churches took a man out of his bleakness for a time, and so did the brothels. The sectarian churches came in swinging, cocky and loud and confident. Ignoring the laws of debt and repayment, they built churches which couldn't be paid for in a hundred years. The sects fought evil, true enough, but they also fought each other with a fine lustiness. They fought at the turn of a doctrine. Each happily believed all the others were bound for hell in a basket. And each for all its bumptiousness brought with it the same thing: the Scripture on which our ethics, our art and poetry, and our relationships are built. It took a smart man to know where the difference lay between the sects, but anyone could see what they had in common. And they brought music—maybe not the best, but the form and sense of it. And they brought conscience, or, rather, nudged the dozing conscience. They were not pure, but they had a potential of purity, like a soiled white shirt. And any man could make something pretty fine of it within himself. True enough, the Reverend Billing, when they caught up with him, turned out to be a thief, an adulterer, a libertine, and a zoophilist, but that didn't change the fact that he had communicated some good things to a great number of receptive people. Billing went to jail, but no one ever arrested the good things he had released. And it doesn't matter much that his motive was impure. He used good material and some of it stuck. I use Billing only as an outrageous example. The honest preachers had energy and go. They fought the devil, no holds barred, boots and eye-gouging permitted. You might get the idea that they howled truth and beauty the way a seal bites out the National Anthem on a row of circus horns. But some of the truth and beauty remained, and the anthem was recognizable. The sects did more than this, though. They built the structure of social life in the Salinas Valley. The church supper is the grandfather of the country club, just as the Thursday poetry reading in the basement under the vestry sired the little theater.

While the churches, bringing the sweet smell of piety for the soul, came in prancing and farting like brewery horses in bock-beer time, the sister evangelism, with release and joy for the body, crept in silently and grayly, with its head bowed and its face covered.

You may have seen the spangled palaces of sin and fancy dancing in the false West of the movies, and maybe some of them existed—but not in the Salinas Valley. The brothels were quiet, orderly, and circumspect. Indeed, if after hearing the ecstatic shrieks of climactic conversion against the thumping beat of the melodeon you had stood under the window of a whorehouse and listened to the low decorous voices, you would have been likely to confuse the identities of the two ministries. The brothel was accepted while it was not admitted.

I will tell you about the solemn courts of love in Salinas. They were about the same in other towns, but the Salinas Row has a pertinence to this telling.

You walked west on Main Street until it bent. That's where Castroville Street crossed Main. Castroville Street is now called Market Street, God knows why. Streets used to be named for the place they aimed at. Thus Castroville Street, if you followed it nine miles, brought you to Castroville. Alisal Street to Alisal, and so forth.

Anyway, when you came to Castroville Street you turned right. Two blocks down, the Southern Pacific tracks cut diagonally across the street on their way south, and a street crossed Castroville Street from east to west. And for the life of me I cannot remember the name of that street. If you turned left on that street and crossed the tracks you were in Chinatown. If you turned right you were on the Row.

It was a black 'dobe street, deep shining mud in winter and hard as rutted iron in summer. In the spring the tall grass grew along its sides—wild oats and mallow weeds and yellow mustard mixed in. In the early morning the sparrows shrieked over the horse manure in the street.

Do you remember hearing that, old men? And do you remember how an easterly breeze brought odors in from Chinatown, roasting pork and punk and black tobacco and yen shi? And do you remember the deep blatting stroke of the great gong on the Joss House, and how its tone hung in the air so long?

Remember, too, the little houses, unpainted, unrepaired? They seemed very small, and they tried to efface themselves in outside neglect, and the wild overgrown front yards tried to hide them from the street. Remember how the shades were always drawn with little lines of yellow light around their edges? You could hear only a murmur from within. Then the front door would open to admit a country boy, and you'd hear laughter and perhaps the soft sentimental tone of an open-face piano with a piece of toilet chain across the strings, and then the door would close it off again.

Then you might hear horses' hoofs on the dirt street, and Pet Bulene would drive his hack up in front, and maybe four or five portly men would get out—great men, rich or official, bankers maybe, or the courthouse gang. And Pet would drive around the corner and settle down in his hack to wait for them. Big cats would ripple across the street to disappear in the tall grass.

And then—remember?—the train whistle and the boring light and a freight from King City would go stomping across Castroville Street and into Salinas and you could hear it sighing at the station. Remember?

Every town has its celebrated madams, eternal women to be sentimentalized down the years. There is something very attractive to men about a madam. She combines the brains of a businessman, the toughness of a prize fighter, the warmth of a companion, the humor of a tragedian. Myths collect around her, and, oddly enough, not voluptuous myths. The stories remembered and repeated about a madam cover every field but the bedroom. Remembering, her old customers picture her as philanthropist, medical authority, bouncer, and poetess of the bodily emotions without being involved with them.

For a number of years Salinas had sheltered two of these treasures; Jenny, sometimes called Fartin' Jenny, and the Nigger, who owned, and operated the Long Green. Jenny was a good companion, a keeper of secrets, a giver of secret loans. There is a whole literature of stories about Jenny in Salinas.

The Nigger was a handsome, austere woman with snow-white hair and a dark and awful dignity. Her brown eyes, brooding deep in her skull, looked out on an ugly world with philosophic sorrow. She conducted her house like a cathedral dedicated to a sad but erect Priapus. If you wanted a good laugh and a poke in the ribs, you went to Jenny's and got your money's worth; but if the sweet world-sadness close to tears crept out of your immutable loneliness, the Long Green was your place. When you came out of there you felt that something pretty stern and important had happened. It was no jump in the hay. The dark beautiful eyes of the Nigger stayed with you for days.

When Faye came down from Sacramento and opened her house there was a flurry of animosity from the two incumbents. They got together to drive Faye out, but they discovered she was not in competition.

Faye was the motherly type, big-breasted, big-hipped, and warm. She was a bosom to cry on, a soother and a stroker. The iron sex of the Nigger and the tavern bacchanalianism of Jenny had their devotees, and they were not lost to Faye. Her house became the refuge of young men puling in puberty, mourning over lost virtue, and aching to lose some more. Faye was the reassurer of misbegotten husbands. Her house took up the slack for frigid wives. It was the cinnamon-scented kitchen of one's grandmother. If any sexual thing happened to you at Faye's you felt it was an accident but forgivable. Her house led the youths of Salinas into the thorny path of sex in the pinkest, smoothest way. Faye was a nice woman, not very bright, highly moral, and easily shocked. People trusted her and she trusted everyone. No one could want to hurt Faye once he knew her. She was no competition to the others. She was a third phase.

Just as in a store or on a ranch the employees are images of the boss, so in a whorehouse the girls are very like the madam, partly because she hires that kind and partly because a good madam imprints her personality on the business. You could stay a very long time at Faye's before you would hear an ugly or suggestive word spoken. The wanderings to the bedrooms, the payments, were so soft and casual they seemed incidental. All in all, she ran a hell of a fine house, as the constable and the sheriff knew. Faye contributed heavily to every charity. Having a revulsion against disease, she paid for regular inspection of her girls. You had less chance of contracting a difficulty at Faye's than with your Sunday School teacher. Faye soon became a solid and desirable citizen of the growing town of Salinas.

Chapter 3

The Growth of
American Capitalism

Reading 12

Ladies Day

Chard Smith

After the Civil War Jay Cooke commented, "Through all the grades I see the all-pervading, all-engrossing anxiety to grow rich. That is the only thing for which men live." To some the dollar sign had replaced the cross as the national symbol. This emphasis on the attainment of material wealth at the expense of moral values is stressed in this selection. The oilman referred to by Cleveland is, of course, John D. Rockefeller, and the young "Scotchman" in the steel business is Andrew Carnegie. These two men were among the most notable practitioners of this "gospel of wealth." Note especially that it is the women who defend the higher values.

"You mentioned religion, Miss Sally," he began. "Well, I'll tell you what strikes me as the only religion these days for anybody who isn't shy of his shadow. It's the religion of this whoppin' big country, Miss Sally, and it's such a big religion there just ain't any room in it for your respectable, old-fashioned, ladies' God with all his pretty-prettiness and his decency. What's goin' on right now here in this nation is about the biggest thing ever happened on this earth since God Almighty set it to spinnin' to no special purpose among the stars.

"Take the thirty years I've been alive, Miss Sally." Race fished with his fingers in his waistcoat pockets and drew out a slip of paper. "During that time we've built a whole new world, accomplished most as much as everybody before us in all of history put together. In that time we've settled about a quarter of a billion acres of land. Built a hundred and sixteen thousand miles of railroad, crossin' the second highest mountains in the world four times. Strung four hundred and fifty thousand miles of telegraph. Dug up almost a billion and a half dollars' worth of gold. Over half a billion dollars' worth of silver. A hundred and twenty million tons of iron. Over a billion tons of coal. Ten billion gallons of oil. Made over ten million tons of steel. Grown over eight billion bushels of wheat. Over thirty billion of corn. A hundred and twenty-five million bales of cotton. I could go on readin' you about some of our increase in manufactures that have made us the biggest manufacturin' country in the world, though I haven't set down a thousandth part of the figures. Let alone the inventions that have changed our whole way of livin'.'"

Race paused, stuck the paper back in his pocket, remembered to take off his hat, and leaned across the tea tray, as he continued with mounting zest. The cynicism in his smile, the smile itself, left his face, and his cheeks were flushed. Sally's anger had evaporated while he was speaking, and though the figures he had been quoting meant nothing to her, his enthusiasm stirred her, and she had lowered her eyes in conscious terror lest her own color rise in response to it.

"All this, Miss Sally," Race went on, "has happened in thirty years. And it's hardly a beginnin'. While your decent friends have been in college learnin' what people were up to two thousand years ago, I've crossed the continent twice, the first time mostly by stagecoach. There's power still to be won that'll make Napoleon and Grant look like tin soldiers, and Vanderbilt and Astor and Stewart and the rest seem like Jole Haddock's poor folks. The new trick, Miss Sally, is goin' to be to get all of a business under one head and kill competition. There's a young fella I know in Cleveland has already made the oil business into somethin' about as big as the Roman Empire—and he let me buy a little of his stock! Young Scotchman in Pittsburgh is aimin' to do the same thing with steel—and he's goin' to let me have some of his stock too! These'll be the biggest businesses the world has ever seen, Miss Sally, and there can be thousands of them. From now on the old fellas like your pa who aim just to hang on to their little concerns are goin' to slip back pretty fast. But for us youngsters that are thinkin' of the future, it's like lookin' up in the sky on a starry night and knowin' we can fly. There are millions up there glitterin' for anybody who'll take the gamble of leavin' the comfortable earth. There's plenty of stars for everybody, but at the same time it might be—it just might be—that the smartest of us can get 'em all for himself. When you think of these things, Miss Sally, it's so big that a fella can't grasp it all, let alone havin' any room left for your God and your decency, and all that."

Race paused, smiling boyishly at Sally, but she kept her eyes down. Involuntarily her hand went out and touched the *Democratic Union,* though she dared not speak. But Race understood what she meant. "Jole Haddock's poor folks?" he said, his mouth again taking its cynical twist as he descended from the higher to the lower plane. "The folks that can't get work and haven't enough to eat? The Knights of Labor, the Anarchists and Communists, and all that? The poor critters your pa is worried about?" Sally glanced up and down quickly, but she said nothing.

"Well, Miss Sally," Race went on, "they just make the game more dangerous, sometimes more fun. They're the boys we all have to fight together, at the same time we're knifin' each other. We're the boys have got it now, and they're the boys are goin' to take it away from us if they can, same as we'd try to take it away from them if things were the other way round. Don't blame 'em a bit.

They've plenty of nerve, no doubt of that—at least some of 'em have, marchin' out with bricks and clubs to face bullets and soldiers. You had to admire 'em in the telegraph strike last year, stoppin' most o' the important business o' the country."

Race smiled to himself a moment, then continued: "O, I respect 'em plenty, Miss Sally! But they've got to be kept down, same as the South had to be licked if Northern business was to prosper. Fact is, the smartest of 'em are slippin' out all the time and beginnin' to take a hand in the big game with the rest of us. Outside of the foreigners, they mostly see the same vision we do, and they're for us even when they're fightin' us. That's what your Democrats don't understand. The Republicans with their big war, their big ideas, their big talk, and their big money, are what the folks really like, what they'll really holler for, even if they're starvin', because they hope to be there themselves some day. It's the new religion, Miss Sally, the biggest show in human history. Got P. T. Barnum backed off the map, let alone the churches. Make way for the big peerade, Miss Sally! Make way for the Republicans and the millions! Make way for America! Or if you don't make way, Miss Sally, don't blame us if you get run over!"

Race chuckled at his mock oratory. Sally now had herself in hand, and looked up with a cool, social smile. "And so," she said with light sarcasm, "old-fashioned religion doesn't matter any more?"

"Not to anybody who has his eyes open," said Race.

"Or any of the things," Sally continued, "that we've always been told were important? Decency? Politeness? Kindness? Sweet thoughts? Beautiful things? Poetry? Pictures? Music? Do I understand you correctly, Mr. Kirkwood, that none of these things are of any importance any more?" Sally's voice trembled ever so little. She swallowed involuntarily and glanced down.

"No, Miss Sally," said Race, at first speaking in a candid tone and also looking at the ground. "When our pas were youngsters, maybe those things had somethin' to do with a man's life, a real man's life. But nowadays a man with brains and a little gumption just hasn't time for them. We'll leave all that to the ladies—includin' "—his voice turned sweet with contempt—"all the nice, decent ladies in trousers who have gone to college. We can have a game with Jole Haddock's poor people. We fellas who are tryin' to build up the country will starve 'em as fast as we can, and you ladies feed 'em as fast as you can. We can see who's winnin' by countin' corpses."

Race chuckled a little coarsely. When he glanced up he met an expression of Sally's face as overwhelming as the smile had been earlier. Now it was an utterly blank expression, an absence of expression, perfect beauty motionless and looking at him with large, fearless eyes whose usual clear blue was darkened to the color of steel.

Startled, Race dropped his eyes, whereat his mouth curled slightly in contempt at himself for a nincompoop. Wearing this trivial expression, he looked up at Sally slantwise, studying her. Her defiant look did not change, except that her white forehead lifted a little so that it was delicately lined, and her nostrils were slightly dilated so he could see the light of the low sun through one of them.

Abruptly his own mood changed. Something in him deeper than consciousness began to feel a complete and absorbing challenge in that beautiful marble gaze. He raised his head and let his own large, dark brown eyes look directly into hers. His recent, quizzical look gave way to a candid expressionlessness as simple and elemental as Sally's. They sat looking at each other, without self-consciousness, without any trace of insinuation, invitation or embarrassment, two natural forces facing one another in a state of challenge inevitably given and accepted.

For perhaps half a minute their eyes held in that gaze that was less man and woman than the man's world and the woman's world as Race had just described them, power against charity. Then there was a distant, rhythmed scraping of the pebbles in the driveway. Sally knew both steps without looking, and suddenly was fighting back an impulse to cry. But she neither flickered an eyelash nor changed color. Race did not know the footsteps, and turned his head quickly to see.

Reading 13

Julius

Horatio Alger

Perhaps the most popular writer in America during the last thirty years of the nineteenth century was Horatio Alger. In some 130 novels which sold over 20 million copies, Alger stressed the fact that anyone could become rich if he were honest, worked hard, persevered, and refrained from the vices of tobacco and alcohol (Alger was an ordained cleric). This "rags-to-riches" myth became a stereotype in American literature. In *Julius* the general theme of Alger's stories is revealed. In the Lodging House of the poor newsboy Corny and Mr. O'Connor espouse this idea that a pot of gold is just over the rainbow and that if the boys only follow their advice, they, like everyone else, can achieve their dream.

From *Julius* by Horatio Alger. Published in 1870.

Julius and his companions were readily excused by the superintendent, on explaining the cause of their delay.

After supper was over, Mr. O'Connor said, "Boys, this is the last time you will be all together. Tomorrow probably many of you will set out for new homes. Now, how shall we pass the time?"

"A speech from Corny Donovan!" cried one boy.

"Speech from Corny!" was heard from all parts of the hall.

"Corny, have you anything to say to the boys?" asked the superintendent, smiling.

Corny was a short, wiry little fellow, apparently twelve, but in reality two years older. He was noted among the boys for his drollery, and frequently amused them with his oratory. He came forward with a twinkle of merriment in his eye.

"The Honorable Corny Donovan will speak to the meetin'," said Julius, acting as temporary chairman.

Corny took his place on the platform, and with perfect gravity took out a small, red handkerchief, and blew his nose explosively, in imitation of a gentleman who once addressed the boys at the Lodging House. The boys greeted this commencement with vociferous applause.

"Go in, Corny!" "Spit it out!" were heard from different parts of the hall.

"Boys," said Corny, extending his right arm horizontally, "I've come here from my manshun in Fifth Avenoo to give you some good advice. You're poor, miserable bummers, ivery mother's son of you. You don't know much anyhow. Once't I was as poor as you." ("Hi! hi!" shouted his auditors.) "You wouldn't think to look at my good clo'es that I was once a poor bummer like the rest of yez." ("Yes we would. Where's your gold watch?") "Where's my gold watch? I left it at home on the pianner. Maybe you'd like to grow up gentlemen like me. But you can't do it. It aint in you." ("Oh, dry up!") "Boys, where's your manners? Don't you know no more'n to interrupt me in my speech? Me and Mr. O'Connor have brought you out here to make men of you. We want you to grow up 'spectable. Blackin' boots won't make men of you." ("You're only a bootblack yourself!") "I only blacked boots for amoosement, boys. I'd have you know I used to leave my Fifth Avenoo manshun in disguise, and pass the day round Printin' House Square, blackin' boots, 'cause my doctor told me I must have exercise, or I'd die of eatin' too much rich food." ("Rich hash, you mean!") "No, I don't. I never allow my cook to put hash on the table, 'cause you can't tell what it's made of, no more'n sassidges. There's lots of dogs and cats disappear in New York, and it's pop'larly supposed that they commits suicide; but the eatin'-house keepers know what 'comes of 'em." ("You bet! That's so, Corny!")

"Now I want you, boys, to leave off bummin', and try to be 'spectable members of s'ciety. I don't want yer to spend yer money for cigars, an' chew cheap tobaccer, just as ef you was men. Once't I saw a four-year-old bummer sittin' on a doorstep, smokin 'a cigar that was half as big as he was. All at once't his rags took fire, and he went up in a balloon." ("Hi! Hi!")

"I tell you, boys, the West is the place for you. Who knows but what you'll git to be Congressmen, or even President?" ("Hear the boy talk!") "I didn't mean you, Jim Malone, so you needn't say nothin'. They don't make Congressmen out'n sich crooked sticks as you be. Maybe you'll keep a corner grocery some time, or a whiskey-shop, an' lay on the floor drunk half the time." ("Pitch into him, Corny!") "But that aint what I was a goin' to say. You'll be great men, ef you don't miss of it; and if you're good and honest and industrious like I am," ("Dry up! Simmer down!"), "you'll come to live in fine houses, and have lots of servants to wait on you, and black yer boots, instead of blackin' 'em yourself." ("I'll take you for my bootblack, Corny," interrupted Julius.) "No, you won't. I expect to be governor before that time, and maybe you'll be swallered by the bear that scared you so this afternoon." (Laughter from the boys.) "But I've most got through." ("Oh, drive ahead, Corny!") "If you want to be great men, all you've got to do is to imertate me. Me and Mr. Connor are goin' to watch you, to see that you behave the way you ought to. When you're rich you can come back to New York, and go to the Lodgin' House, and make a speech to the boys, and tell 'em you was once a poor bummer like they be, and advise 'em to go West, if they want to be somebody.

"Now, boys, I won't say no more. I'm afeared you won't remember what I've said already. I won't charge you nothin' for my advice."

Corny descended from the platform amid the laughter and applause of his comrades.

Mr. O'Connor said, "Boys, Corny's advice is very good, and I advise you to follow it, especially as to avoiding cigars and tobacco, which can only do boys harm. I am not sure that any of you stand a chance of becoming a Congressman or President, as he suggests, but there is one thing pretty certain —you can, if you are honest, industrious, and improve your opportunities at the schools which you will have a chance to attend, obtain a respectable position in society. Some of the boys who in former years have gone to the West have become prosperous, having farms or shops of their own. I don't see why you can't be just as successful as they. I hope you will be, and if, some years hence, you come to New York, I hope you will visit the Lodging House. If I am still there, I shall be glad to see you, and have you speak to the boys, and encourage them, by the sight of your prosperity, to work as you have done. Now I would suggest that you sing one or two of the songs we used to sing on Sunday evenings at the Lodging House. After that you may go out for an hour, but you must keep near this hall, as the evening is coming on."

Reading 14

The Fable of the Honest Money-Maker and the Partner of His Joys, Such as They Were

George Ade

George Ade wrote hundreds of fables satirizing virtually every aspect of American life. The following selection is concerned with the distortions of values in a society based solely on profit-making. It depicts avarice not confined to the moneychangers in the temple but present in some of its worst aspects in everyday life as well. The fate suffered by the wife of the prosperous farmer was a common one on the farms of the nation where men were so concerned with wealth that they ignored human values. In many states prosperous farmers kept records of their sons' school attendance; once their sons satisfied minimum requirements, they were kept home to work. Note too the community's stress upon success.

The Prosperous Farmer lived in an Agricultural Section of the Middle West. He commanded the Respect of all his Neighbors. He owned a Section, and had a Raft of big Horses and white-faced Cows and Farm Machinery, and Money in the Bank besides. He still had the first Dollar he ever made, and it could not have been taken away from him with Pincers.

Henry was a ponderous, Clydesdale kind of Man, with Warts on his Hands. He did not have to travel on Appearances, because the whole County knew what he was Worth. Of course he was Married. Years before he had selected a willing Country Girl with Pink Cheeks, and put her into his Kitchen to serve the Remainder of her Natural Life. He let her have as high as Two Dollars a Year to spend for herself. Her Hours were from 6 a.m. to 6 a.m., and if she got any Sleep she had to take it out of her Time. The Eight-Hour Day was not recognized on Henry's Place. After Ten Years of raising Children, Steaming over the Washtub, Milking the Cows, Carrying in Wood, Cooking for the Hands, and other Delsarte such as the Respected Farmer usually Frames Up for his Wife, she was as thin as a Rail and humped over in the Shoulders. She was Thirty, and looked Sixty. Her Complexion was like Parchment and her Voice had been worn to a Cackle. She was losing her Teeth, too, but Henry could not afford to pay Dentist Bills because he needed all his

From *More Fables* by George Ade. Published in 1900.

Money to buy more Poland Chinas and build other Cribs. If she wanted a Summer Kitchen or a new Wringer or a Sewing Machine, or Anything Else that would lighten her Labors, Henry would Moan and Grumble and say she was trying to land him in the Poorhouse.

They had a dandy big Barn, painted Red with White Trimmings, and a Patent Fork to lift the Hay into the Mow, and the Family lived in a Pine Box that had not been Painted in Years and had Dog-Fennel all around the Front of it.

The Wife of the Respected Farmer was the only Work Animal around the Place that was not kept Fat and Sleek. But, of course, Henry did not count on Selling her. Henry often would fix up his Blooded Stock for the County Fair and tie Blue Ribbons on the Percherons and Herefords, but it was never noticed that he tied any Blue Ribbons on the Wife.

And yet Henry was a Man to be Proud of. He never Drank and he was a Good Hand with Horses, and he used to go to Church on Sunday Morning and hold a Cud of Tobacco in his Face during Services and sing Hymns with Extreme Unction. He would sing that he was a Lamb and had put on the Snow-White Robes and that Peace attended him. People would see him there in his Store Suit, with the Emaciated Wife and the Scared Children sitting in the Shadow of his Greatness, and they said that she was Lucky to have a Man who was so Well Off and lived in the Fear of the Lord.

Henry was Patriotic as well as Pious. He had a Picture of Abraham Lincoln in the Front Room, which no one was permitted to Enter, and he was glad that Slavery had been abolished.

Henry robbed the Cradle in order to get Farm-Hands. As soon as the Children were able to Walk without holding on, he started them for the Corn-Field, and told them to Pay for the Board that they had been Sponging off of him up to that Time. He did not want them to get too much Schooling for fear that they would want to sit up at Night and Read instead of Turning In so as to get an Early Start along before Daylight next Morning. So they did not get any too much, rest easy. And he never Foundered them on Stick Candy or Raisins or any such Delicatessen for sale at a General Store. Henry was undoubtedly the Tightest Wad in the Township. Some of the Folks who had got into a Box through Poor Management, and had been Foreclosed out of House and Home by Henry and his Lawyer, used to say that Henry was a Skin, and was too Stingy to give his Family enough to Eat, but most People looked up to Henry, for there was no getting around it that he was Successful.

When the Respected Farmer had been Married for Twenty Years and the Children had developed into long Gawks who did not know Anything except to get out and Toil all Day for Pa and not be paid anything for it, and after Henry had scraped together more Money than you could load on a Hay-Rack, an Unfortunate Thing happened. His Wife began to Fail. She was now Forty, but the Fair and Fat did not go with it. At that Age some Women are Buxom and just blossoming into the Full Charm of Matronly Womanhood. But Henry's Wife was Gaunt and Homely and all Run Down. She had been Poorly for Years, but she had to keep up and do the Chores as well as the House-Work, because Henry could not afford to hire a Girl. At last her Back gave out, so that she had to sit down and Rest every Once in a While. Henry would come in for his Meals and let her know how Hearty all the Calves seemed to be, and he began to Notice that she was not very Chipper. It Worried him more than a little, because he did not care to pay any Doctor Bills. He told her she had better go and get some Patent Medicine that he had seen advertised on the Fence coming out from Town. It was only Twenty-Five cents a Bottle, and was warranted to Cure Anything. So she tried it, but it did not seem to restore her Youth and she got Weaker, and at last Henry just had to have the Doctor, Expense or No Expense. The Doctor said that as nearly as he could Diagnose her Case, she seemed to be Worn Out. Henry was Surprised, and said she had not been Complaining any more than Usual.

Next Afternoon he was out Dickering for a Bull, and his Woman, lying on the cheap Bedstead, up under the hot Roof, folded her lean Hands and slipped away to the only Rest she had known since she tied up with a Prosperous and Respected Farmer.

Henry was all Broken Up. He Wailed and Sobbed and made an Awful Fuss at the Church. The Preacher tried to Comfort him by saying that the Ways of Providence were beyond all Finding Out. He said that probably there was some Reason why the Sister had been taken right in the Prime of her Usefulness, but it was not for Henry to know it. He said the only Consolation he could offer was the Hope that possibly she was Better Off. There did not seem to be much Doubt about that.

In about a Month the Respected Farmer was riding around the Country in his Buck-Board looking for Number Two. He had a business Head and he knew it was Cheaper to Marry than to Hire one. His Daughter was only Eleven and not quite Big Enough as yet to do all the Work for five Men.

Finally he found one who had the Reputation of being a Good Worker. When he took her over to his House to Break Her In, the Paper at the County Seat referred to them as the Happy Couple.

MORAL: *Be Honest and Respected and it Goes.*

Reading 15

The Fable of the Corporation Director and the Mislaid Ambition

George Ade

In the following selection Ade treats the dream of every American schoolboy to rescue civilization by his own good works. Once the former schoolboy joins the business world, however, he becomes a prisoner of it and quickly forgets his earlier high aspirations. For his own health he has to be sheltered from reminders of them.

One of the Most Promising Boys in a Graded School had a Burning Ambition to be a Congressman. He loved Politics and Oratory. When there was a Rally in Town he would carry a Torch and listen to the Spellbinder with his Mouth open.

The Boy wanted to grow up and wear a Black String Tie and a Bill Cody Hat and walk stiff-legged, with his Vest unbuttoned at the Top, and be Distinguished.

On Friday Afternoons he would go to School with his Face scrubbed to a shiny pink and his Hair roached up on one side, and he would Recite the Speeches of Patrick Henry and Daniel Webster and make Gestures.

When he Graduated from the High School he delivered an Oration on "The Duty of the Hour," calling on all young Patriots to leap into the Arena and with the Shield of Virtue quench the rising Flood of Corruption. He said that the Curse of Our Times was the Greed for Wealth, and he pleaded for Unselfish Patriotism among those in High Places.

He boarded at Home for a while without seeing a chance to jump into the Arena, and finally his Father worked a Pull and got him a Job with a Steel Company. He proved to be a Handy Young Man, and the Manager sent Him out to make Contracts. He stopped roaching his Hair, and he didn't give the Arena of Politics any serious Consideration except when the Tariff on Steel was in Danger.

In a little while he owned a few Shares, and after that he became a Director. He joined several Clubs and began to enjoy his Food. He drank a Small Bottle with his Luncheon each Day, and he couldn't talk Business unless he held a Scotch High Ball in his Right Hand.

From *More Fables* by George Ade. Published in 1900.

With the return of Prosperity and the Formation of the Trust and the Whoop in all Stocks he made so much Money that he was afraid to tell the Amount.

His Girth increased—he became puffy under the Eyes—you could see the little blue Veins on his Nose.

He kept his Name out of the Papers as much as possible, and he never gave Congress a Thought except when he talked to his Lawyer of the Probable Manner in which they would Evade any Legislation against Trusts. He took two Turkish Baths every week and wore Silk Underwear. When an Eminent Politician would come to his Office to shake him down he would send out Word by the Boy in Buttons that he had gone to Europe. That's what he thought of Politics.

One day while rummaging in a lower Drawer in his Library, looking for a Box of Poker Chips, he came upon a Roll of Manuscript and wondered what it was. He opened it and read how it was the Duty of all True Americans to hop into the Arena and struggle unselfishly for the General Good. It came to him in a Flash—this was his High School Oration!

Then suddenly he remembered that for several Years of his Life his consuming Ambition had been—to go to Congress!

With a demoniacal Shriek he threw himself at full length on a Leather Couch and began to Laugh.

He rolled off the Sofa and tossed about on a $1,200 Rug in a Paroxysm of Merriment.

His Man came running into the Library and saw the Master in Convulsions. The poor Trust Magnate was purple in the Face.

They sent for a Great Specialist, who said that his Dear Friend had ruptured one of the smaller Arteries, and also narrowly escaped Death by Apoplexy.

He advised Rest and Quiet and the avoidance of any Great Shock.

So they took the High School Oration and put it on the Ice, and the Magnate slowly recovered and returned to his nine-course Dinners.

MORAL: *Of all Sad Words of Tongue or Pen, the Saddest are these, "It Might Have Been."*

Reading 16

Success

Samuel Hopkins Adams

The Sears, Roebuck catalog was one of the most popular books in America in the late nineteenth century. In some isolated areas it even surpassed the Good Book. Citizens of all ages consulted its pages to fulfill their needs, both real or fancied. The North Dakota farm girl could order a dress in the latest Chicago fashion from its treasure-laden pages, and the Oklahoma ranch-hand could while away hours in his bunkhouse poring over them. Even when it was outdated, the catalog performed a common service a more sophisticated age could not appreciate.

The lonely station of Manzanita stood out, sharp and unsightly, in the keen February sunlight. A mile away in a dip of the desert, lay the town, a sorry sprawl of frame buildings, patternless save for the one main street, which promptly lost itself at either end of a maze of cholla, prickly pear, and the lovely, golden-glowing roseo. Far as the eye could see, the waste was spangled with vivid hues, for the rare rains had come, and all the cacti were in joyous bloom, from the scarlet stain of the ocatilla to the pale, dream-flower of the yucca. Overhead the sky shone with a hard serenity, a blue, enameled dome through which the imperishable fires seemed magnified as they limned sharp shadows on the earth; but in the southwest clouds massed and lurked darkly for a sign that the storm had but called a truce.

East to west, along a ridge bounding the lower desert, ran the railroad, a line as harshly uncompromising as the cold mathematics of the engineers who had mapped it. To the north spread unfathomably a forest of scrub pine and piñon, rising, here and there, into loftier growth. It was as if man, with his imperious interventions, had set those thin steel parallels as an irrefragable boundary to the mutual encroachments of forest and desert, tree and cactus. A single, straggling trail squirmed its way into the woodland. One might have surmised that it was winding hopefully if blindly toward the noble mountain peak shimmering in white splendor, mystic and wonderful, sixty miles away, but seeming in that lucent air to be brooding closely over all the varied loveliness below.

Though nine o'clock had struck on the brisk little stationclock, there was still a tang of night chill left. The station-agent came out, carrying a chair

From *Success* by Samuel Hopkins Adams. Published in 1921.

which he set down in the sunniest corner of the platform. He looked to be hardly more than a boy, but firm-knit and self-confident. His features were regular, his fairish hair slightly wavy, and in his expression there was a curious and incongruous suggestion of settledness, of acceptance, of satisfaction with life as he met it, which an observer of men would have found difficult to reconcile with his youth and the obvious intelligence of the face. His eyes were masked by deeply browned glasses, for he was bent upon literary pursuits, witness the corpulent, paper-covered volume under his arm. Adjusting his chair to the angle of ease, he tipped back against the wall and made tentative entry into his book.

What a monumental work was that in the treasure-filled recesses of which the young explorer was straightway lost to the outer world! No human need but might find its contentment therein. Spread forth in its alluringly illustrated pages was the whole universe reduced to the purchasable. It was a perfect and detailed microcosm of the world of trade, the cosmogony of commerce *in petto*. The style was brief, pithy, pregnant; the illustrations—oh, wonder of wonders! —unfailingly apt to the text. He who sat by the Damascus Road of old marveling as the caravans rolled dustily past bearing "emeralds and wheat, honey and oil and balm, fine linen and embroidered goods, iron, cassia and calamus, white wool, ivory and ebony," beheld or conjectured no such wondrous offerings as were here gathered, collected, and presented for the patronage of this heir of all the ages, between the gay-hued covers of the great Sears-Roebuck Semiannual Mail Order Catalogue. Its happy possessor need but cross the talisman with the ready magic of a postal money order and the swift genii of transportation would attend, servile to his call, to deliver the commanded treasures at his very door.

But the young reader was not purposefully shopping in this vast marketplace of print. Rather he was adventuring idly, indulging the amateur spirit, playing a game of hit-or-miss, seeking oracles in those teeming pages. Therefore he did not turn to the pink insert, embodying the alphabetical catalogue (Abdominal Bands to Zither Strings), but opened at random.

"Supertoned Banjos," he read, beginning at the heading; and, running his eye down the different varieties, paused at "Pride of the Plantation, a full-sized, well-made, snappy-toned instrument at a very moderate price. 12 T 4031/4."

The explorer shook his head. Abovestairs rested a guitar (the Pearletta, 12 S 206, price $7.95) which he had purchased at the instance of Messrs. Sears-Roebuck's insinuating representation as set forth in catalogue item 12 S 01942, "Self-mastery of the Guitar in One Book, with All Chords, Also Popular Solos That Can Be Played Almost at Sight." The nineteen-cent instruction-book had gone into the fire after three days of unequal combat between it and its owner, and the latter had subsequently learned something of the guitar (and more of life) from a Mexican-American girl with lazy eyes and the soul of a capricious and self-indulged kitten, who had come uninvited to Manzanita to visit an aunt, deceased six months previously. With a mild pang of memory for those dreamy, music-filled nights on the desert, the youth decided against further experiments in stringed orchestration.

Telescopes turned up next. He lingered a moment over 20 T 3513, a nickel-plated cap pocket-glass, reflecting that with it he could discern any signal on the distant wooded butte occupied by Miss Camilla Van Arsdale, back on the forest trail, in the event that she might wish a wire sent or any other service performed. Miss Camilla had been very kind and understanding at the time of the parting with Carlotta, albeit with a grimly humorous disapproval of the whole inflammatory affair; as well as at other times; and there was nothing that he would not do for her. He made a neat entry in a pocket ledger (3 T 9901) against the time when he should have spare cash, and essayed another plunge.

Arctics and Lumberman's Overs he passed by with a grin as inappropriate to the climate. Cod Liver Oil failed to interest him, as did the Provident Cast Iron Range and the Clean-Press Cider Mill. But he paused speculatively before Punching Bags, for he had the clean pride of body, typical of lusty Western youth, and loved all forms of exercise. Could he find space, he wondered, to install 6 T 1441 with its Scientific Noiseless Platform & Wall Attachment (6 T 1476) in the portable house (55 S 17) which, purchased a year before, now stood in the clearing behind the station crammed with purchases from the Sears-Roebuck wonderbook. Anyway, he would make another note of it. What would it be like, he wondered, to have a million dollars to spend, and unlimited access to the Sears-Roebuck treasures. Picturing himself as such a Croesus, he innocently thought that his first act would be to take train for Chicago and inspect the warehoused accumulations of those princes of trade with his own eager eyes!

He mused humorously for a moment over a book on "Ease in Conversation." ("No trouble about conversation," he reflected; "the difficulty is to find anybody to converse with," and he thought first of Carlotta, and then of Miss Camilla Van Arsdale, but chiefly of the latter, for conversation had not been the strong point of the passionate, light-hearted Spanish girl.) Upon a volume kindly offering to teach astronomy to the lay mind without effort or trouble (43 T 790) and manifestly cheap at $1.10, he bestowed a more respectful attention, for the desert nights were long and lonely.

Eventually he arrived at the department appropriate to his age and the almost universal ambition of the civilized male, to wit, clothing. Deeply, judiciously, did he meditate and weigh the advantages as between 745 J 460 ("Something new—different—economical—efficient. An all-wool suit embodying all the features that make for clothes satisfaction. This announcement is of tremendous importance"—as one might well have inferred from the student's rapt expression) and 776 J 017 ("A double-breasted, snappy, yet semi-conservative effect in dark-green worsted, a special social value"), leaning to the latter because of a purely literary response to that subtle and deft appeal of the attributive "social." The devotee of Messrs. Sears-Roebuck was an innately social person, though as yet his gregarious proclivities lay undeveloped and unsuspected by himself. Also he was of a literary tendency; but of this he was already self-conscious. He passed on to ulsters and raincoats, divagated into the colorful realm of neckwear, debated scarfpins and cuff-links, visualized patterned shirtings, and emerged to dream of composite sartorial grandeurs which, duly synthesized into a long list of hopeful entries, were duly filed away within the pages of 3 T 9901, the pocket ledger.

Reading 17

The Jungle

Upton Sinclair

The most influential of all muckraking novels was *The Jungle*. It told of the poor sanitary conditions in the Chicago stockyards in such a graphic manner that many people became vegetarians, at least temporarily. The following passage was quoted in Congress and was the direct cause of the passage of the Federal Meat Inspection Act of 1906. As this law was among the first of scores of regulatory measures passed by Congress, *The Jungle* might even be described as one of the most important books in American history.

It was a long, narrow room, with a gallery along it for visitors. At the head there was a great iron wheel, about twenty feet in circumference, with rings here and there along its edge. Upon both sides of this wheel there was a narrow space, into which came the hogs at the end of their journey; in the midst of them stood a great burly Negro, bare-armed and bare-chested. He was resting for the moment, for the wheel had stopped while men were cleaning up. In a minute or two, however, it began slowly to revolve, and then the men upon each side of it sprang to work. They had chains which they fastened about the leg of the nearest hog, and the other end of the chain they hooked into one

From *The Jungle* by Upton Sinclair. Published in 1906.

of the rings upon the wheel. So, as the wheel turned, a hog was suddenly jerked off his feet and borne aloft.

At the same instant the ear was assailed by a most terrifying shriek; the visitors started in alarm, the women turned pale and shrank back. The shriek was followed by another, louder and yet more agonizing—for once started upon that journey, the hog never came back; at the top of the wheel he was shunted off upon a trolley, and went sailing down the room. And meantime another was swung up, and then another, and another, until there was a double line of them, each dangling by a foot and kicking in frenzy—and squealing. The uproar was appalling, perilous to the eardrums; one feared there was too much sound for the room to hold—that the walls must give way or the ceiling crack. There were high squeals and low squeals, grunts, and wails of agony; there would come a momentary lull, and then a fresh outburst, louder then ever, surging up to a deafening climax. It was too much for some of the visitors —the men would look at each other, laughing nervously, and the women would stand with hands clenched, and the blood rushing to their faces, and the tears starting in their eyes.

Meantime, heedless of all these things, the men upon the floor were going about their work. Neither squeals of hogs nor tears of visitors made any difference to them; one by one they hooked up the hogs, and one by one with a swift stroke they slit their throats. There was a long line of hogs, with squeals and lifeblood ebbing away together; until at last each started again, and vanished with a splash into a huge vat of boiling water.

It was all so very businesslike that one watched it fascinated. It was porkmaking by machinery, porkmaking by applied mathematics. And yet somehow the most matter-of-fact person could not help thinking of the hogs; they were so innocent, they came so very trustingly; and they were so very human in their protests—and so perfectly within their rights! They had done nothing to deserve it; and it was adding insult to injury, as the thing was done here, swinging them up in this cold-blooded, impersonal way, without a pretense at apology, without the homage of a tear. Now and then a visitor wept, to be sure; but this slaughtering machine ran on, visitors or no visitors. It was like some horrible crime committed in a dungeon, all unseen and unheeded, buried out of sight and of memory.

One could not stand and watch very long without becoming philosophical, without beginning to deal in symbols and similes, and to hear the hog squeal of the universe. Was it permitted to believe that there was nowhere upon the earth, or above the earth, a heaven for hogs, where they were requited for all this suffering? Each one of these hogs was a separate creature. Some were white hogs, some were black; some were brown, some were spotted; some were old, some young; some were long and lean, some were monstrous. And each of them had an individuality of his own, a will of his own, a hope and a heart's desire; each was full of self-confidence, of self-importance, and a sense of dignity. And trusting and strong in faith he had gone about his business, the while a black shadow hung over him and a horrid Fate waited in his pathway. Now suddenly it had swooped upon him, and had seized him by the leg. Relentless, remorseless, it was; all his protests, his screams, were nothing to it—it did its cruel will with him, as if his wishes, his feelings, had simply no existence at all; it cut his throat and watched him gasp out his life. And now was one to believe that there was nowhere a god of hogs, to whom this hog personality was precious, to whom these hog squeals and agonies had a meaning? Who would take this hog into his arms and comfort him, reward him for his work well done, and show him the meaning of his sacrifice? Perhaps some glimpse of all this was in the thoughts of our humble-minded Jurgis, as he turned to go with the rest of the party, and muttered: *"Dieve*—but I'm glad I'm not a hog!"

Reading 18

The Jungle
Upton Sinclair

Basically reformers, the Progressives directed their attention toward politics. Much of their concern was with correcting political abuses on the local level, where political bosses often held sway. Such local leaders were frequently corrupt, but they did perform many useful social functions, a fact which many of the reformers overlooked. The political boss often provided the newly arrived immigrant, like Jurgis in this selection, his only contact with the American political system.

In the place where he had come from there had not been any politics—in Russia one thought of the government as an affliction like the lightning and the hail. "Duck, little brother, duck," the wise old peasants would whisper; "everything passes away." And when Jurgis had first come to America he had supposed that it was the same. He had heard people say that it was a free country—but what did that mean? He found that here, precisely as in Russia, there were rich men who owned everything; and if one could not find any work, was not the hunger he began to feel the same sort of hunger?

From *The Jungle* by Upton Sinclair. Published in 1906.

When Jurgis had been working about three weeks at Brown's, there had come to him one noontime a man who was employed as a night watchman, and who asked him if he would not like to take out naturalization papers and become a citizen. Jurgis did not know what that meant, but the man explained the advantages. In the first place, it would not cost him anything, and it would get him half a day off, with his pay just the same; and then when election time came he would be able to vote—and there was something in that. Jurgis was naturally glad to accept, and so the night watchman said a few words to the boss, and he was excused for the rest of the day. When, later on, he wanted a holiday to get married he could not get it; and as for a holiday with pay just the same—what power had wrought that miracle heaven only knew! However, he went with the man, who picked up several other newly landed immigrants, Poles, Lithuanians, and Slovaks and took them all outside, where stood a great four-horse tallyho coach, with fifteen or twenty men already in it. It was a fine chance to see the sights of the city, and the party had a merry time, with plenty of beer handed up from inside. So they drove downtown and stopped before an imposing granite building, in which they interviewed an official, who had the papers all ready, with only the names to be filled in. So each man in turn took an oath of which he did not understand a word, and then was presented with a handsome ornamented document with a big red seal and the shield of the United States upon it, and was told that he had become a citizen of the Republic and the equal of the President himself.

A month or two later Jurgis had another interview with this same man, who told him where to go to "register." And then finally, when election day came, the packing houses posted a notice that men who desired to vote might remain away until nine that morning, and the same night watchman took Jurgis and the rest of his flock into the back room of a saloon, and showed each of them where and how to mark a ballot, and then gave each two dollars, and took them to the polling place, where there was a policeman on duty especially to see that they got through all right. Jurgis felt quite proud of his good luck till he got home and met Jonas, who had taken the leader aside and whispered to him, offering to vote three times for four dollars, which offer had been accepted.

And now in the union Jurgis met men who explained all this mystery to him; and he learned that America differed from Russia in that its government existed under the form of a democracy. The officials who ruled it, and got all the graft, had to be elected first; and so there were two rival sets of grafters, known as political parties, and the one got the office which bought the most votes. Now and then the election was very close, and that was the time the poor man came in. In the stockyards this was only in national and state elections, for in local elections the Democratic Party always carried everything. The ruler of the district was therefore the Democratic boss, a little Irishman named Mike Scully. Scully held an important party office in the state, and bossed even the mayor of the city, it was said; it was his boast that he carried the stockyards in his pocket. He was an enormously rich man—he had a hand in all the big graft in the neighborhood. It was Scully, for instance, who owned that dump which Jurgis and Ona had seen the first day of their arrival. Not only did he own the dump, but he owned the brick factory as well; and first he took out the clay and made it into bricks, and then he had the city bring garbage to fill up the hole, so that he could build houses to sell to the people. Then, too, he sold the bricks to the city, at his own price, and the city came and got them in its own wagons. And also he owned the other hole near by, where the stagnant water was; and it was he who cut the ice and sold it; and what was more, if the men told truth, he had not had to pay any taxes for the water, and he had built an icehouse out of city lumber, and had not had to pay anything for that. The newspapers had got hold of that story, and there had been a scandal; but Scully had hired somebody to confess and take all the blame, and then skip the country. It was said, too, that he had built his brick-kiln in the same way, and that the workmen were on the city payroll while they did it; however, one had to press closely to get these things out of the men, for it was not their business, and Mike Scully was a good man to stand in with. A note signed by him was equal to a job any time at the packing houses; and also he employed a good many men himself, and worked them only eight hour a day, and paid them the highest wages. This gave him many friends.

Reading 19

A Far Country

Winston Churchill

The Progressive movement raised fundamental questions about the basic values of American industrial society. Many wondered if a commitment to the profit motive, to the exclusion of everything else, was really the proper course of action. In the following selection two former Harvard classmates meet after a bitter mayoralty campaign in which they were on opposite sides; one is a reformer and the other a representative of traditional business values. In this exchange the reformer wins his former friend to his point of view.

From *A Far Country* by Winston Churchill. Published in 1915.

My eye fell upon the long line of sectional book-cases that lined one side of the room. "Why, you've got quite a library here," I observed.

"Yes. I've managed to get together some good books. But there is so much to read nowadays, so much that is really good and new, a man has the hopeless feeling he can never catch up with it all. A thousand writers and students are making contributions to-day where fifty years ago there was one."

"I've been following your speeches, after a fashion.—I wish I might have been able to read more of them. Your argument interested me. It's new, unlike the ordinary propaganda of—"

"Of agitators," he supplied, with a smile.

"Of agitators," I agreed, and tried to return his smile. "An agitator who appears to suggest the foundations of a constructive programme and who isn't afraid to criticise the man with a vote as well as the capitalist is an unusual phenomenon."

"Oh, when we realize that we've only got a little time left in which to tell what we think to be the truth, it doesn't require a great deal of courage, Paret. I didn't begin to see this thing until a little while ago. I was only a crude, hot-headed revolutionist. God knows I'm crude enough still. But I began to have a glimmering of what all these new fellows in the universities are driving at." He waved his hand towards the book-cases. "Driving at collectively, I mean. And there are attempts, worthy attempts, to coordinate and synthesize the sciences. What I have been saying is not strictly original. I took it on the stump, that's all. I didn't expect it to have much effect in this campaign, but it was an opportunity to sow a few seeds, to start a sense of personal dissatisfaction in the minds of a few voters. What is it Browning says? It's in Bishop Blougram, I believe. 'When the fight begins within himself, a man's worth something.' It's an intellectual fight, of course."

His words were spoken quietly, but I realized suddenly that the mysterious force which had drawn me to him now, against my will, was an *intellectual* rather than apparently sentimental one, an intellectual force seeming to comprise within it all other human attractions. And yet I felt a sudden contrition.

"See here, Krebs," I said. "I didn't come here to bother you about these matters, to tire you. I mustn't stay. I'll call in again to see how you are—from time to time."

"But you're not tiring me," he protested, stretching forth a thin, detaining hand. "I don't want to rot, I want to live and think as long as I can. To tell you the truth, Paret, I've been wishing to talk to you—I'm glad you came in."

"You've been wishing to talk to me?" I said.

"Yes, but I didn't expect you'd come in. I hope you won't mind my saying so, under the circumstances, but I've always rather liked you, admired you, even back in the Cambridge days. After that I used to blame you for going out and taking what you wanted, and I had to live a good many years before I began to see that it's better for a man to take what he wants than to take nothing at all. I took what I wanted, every man worth his salt does. There's your great banker friend in New York whom I used to think was the arch-fiend. He took what he wanted, and he took a good deal, but it happened to be good for *him.* And by piling up his corporations, Ossa on Pelion, he is paving the way for a logical economic evolution. How can a man in our time find out what he does want unless he takes something and gives it a trial?"

"Until he begins to feel that it disagrees with him," I said. "But then," I added involuntarily, "then it may be too late to try something else, and he may not know what to try." This remark of mine might have surprised me had it not been for the feeling—now grown definite—that Krebs had something to give me, something to pass on to me, of all men. Indeed, he had hinted as much, when he acknowledged a wish to talk to me. "What seems so strange," I said, as I looked at him lying back on his pillows, "is your faith that we shall be able to bring order out of all this chaos—your belief in Democracy."

"Democracy's an adventure," he replied, "the great adventure of man-kind. I think the trouble in many minds lies in the fact that they persist in regarding it as something to be made *safe.* All that can be done is to try to make it as safe as possible. But no adventure is safe—life itself is an adventure, and neither is that safe. It's a hazard, as you and I have found out. The moment we try to make life safe we lose all there is in it worth while."

I thought a moment.

"Yes, that's so," I agreed. On the table beside the bed in company with two or three other volumes, lay a Bible. He seemed to notice that my eye fell upon it.

"Do you remember the story of the Prodigal Son?" he asked. "Well, that's the parable of democracy, of self-government in the individual and in society. In order to arrive at salvation, Paret, most of us have to take our journey into a far country."

"A far country!" I exclaimed. The words struck a reminiscent chord.

"We have to leave what seem the safe things, we have to wander and suffer in order to realize that the only true safety lies in development. We have first to cast off the leading strings of authority. It's a delusion that we can insure ourselves by remaining within its walls—we have to risk our lives and our souls. It *is* discouraging when we look around us to-day, and in a way the pessimists are right when they say we don't see democracy. We see only what may be called the first stage of it; for democracy is still in a far country eating the husks of individualism, materialism. What we see is not true freedom, but freedom run to riot, men struggling for themselves, spending on themselves the fruits of their inheritance; we see a government intent on one object alone—

exploitation of this inheritance in order to achieve what it calls prosperity. And God is far away."

"And—we shall turn?" I asked.

"We shall turn or perish. I believe that we shall turn." He fixed his eyes on my face. "What is it," he asked, "that brought you here to me, to-day?"

I was silent.

"The motive, Paret—the motive that sends us all wandering into a far country is divine, is inherited from God himself. And the same motive, after our eyes shall have been opened, after we shall have seen and known the tragedy and misery of life, after we shall have made the mistakes and committed the sins and experienced the emptiness—the same motive will lead us back again. That, too, is an adventure, the greatest adventure of all. Because, when we go back we shall not find the same God—or rather we shall recognize him in ourselves. Autonomy is godliness, knowledge is godliness. We went away cringing, superstitious, we saw everywhere omens and evidences of his wrath in the earth and sea and sky, we burned candles and sacrificed animals in the vain hope of averting scourges and other calamities. But when we come back it will be with a knowledge of his ways, gained at a price,—the price he, too, must have paid—and we shall be able to stand up and look him in the face, and all our childish superstitions and optimisms shall have burned away."

Some faith indeed had given him strength to renounce those things in life I had held dear, driven him on to fight until his exhausted body failed him, and even now that he was physically helpless sustained him. I did not ask myself, then, the nature of this faith. In its presence it could no more be questioned than the light. It *was* light; I felt bathed in it. Now it was soft, suffused: but I remembered how the night before in the hall, just before he had fallen, it had flashed forth in a smile and illumined my soul with an ecstasy that yet was anguish. . . .

"We shall get back," I said at length. My remark was not a question— it had escaped from me almost unawares.

"The joy is in the journey," he answered. "The secret is in the search."

"But for me?" I exclaimed.

"We've all been lost, Paret. It would seem as though we have to be."

"And yet you are—saved," I said, hesitating over the word.

"It is true that I am content, even happy," he asserted, "in spite of my wish to live. If there is any secret, it lies, I think, in the struggle for an open mind, in the keeping alive of a desire to know more and more. That desire, strangely enough, hasn't lost its strength. We don't know whether there is a future life, but if there is, I think it must be a continuation of this." He paused. "I told you I was glad you came in—I've been thinking of you, and I saw you in the hall last night. You ask what there is for you—I'll tell you,—the new generation."

"The new generation."

"That's the task of every man and woman who wakes up. I've come to see how little can be done for the great majority of those who have reached our age. It's hard—but it's true. Superstition, sentiment, the habit of wrong thinking—or of not thinking at all have struck in too deep, the habit of unreasoning acceptance of authority is too paralyzing. Some may be stung back into life, spurred on to find out what the world really is, but not many. The hope lies in those who are coming after us—we must do for them what wasn't done for us. We really didn't have much of a chance, Paret. What did our instructors at Harvard know about the age that was dawning? what did anybody know? You can educate yourself—or rather reeducate yourself. All this"—and he waved his hand towards his bookshelves—"all this has sprung up since you and I were at Cambridge; if we don't try to become familiar with it, if we fail to grasp the point of view from which it's written, there's little hope for us. Go away from all this and get straightened out, make yourself acquainted with the modern trend in literature and criticism, with modern history, find out what's being done in the field of education, read the modern sciences, especially biology, and psychology and sociology, and try to get a glimpse of the fundamental human needs underlying such phenomena as the labour and woman's movements. God knows I've just begun to get *my* glimpse, and I've floundered around ever since I left college. . . . I don't mean to say we can ever see the whole, but we can get a clew, an idea, and pass it on to our children. You have children, haven't you?"

"Yes," I said. . . .

He said nothing—he seemed to be looking out of the window.

"Then the scientific point of view in your opinion hasn't done away with religion?" I asked presently.

"The scientific point of view *is* the religious point of view," he said earnestly, "because it's the only self-respecting point of view. I can't believe that God intended to make a creature who would not ultimately weigh his beliefs with his reason instead of accepting them blindly. That's immoral, if you like—especially in these days."

"And are there, then, no 'over-beliefs'?" I said, remembering the expression in something I had read.

"That seems to me a relic of the method of ancient science, which was upside down,—a mere confusion with faith. Faith and belief are two different things; faith is the emotion, the steam, if you like, that drives us on in our search for truth. Theories, at a stretch, might be identified with 'over-beliefs' but when it comes to confusing our theories with facts, instead of recognizing them as theories, when it comes to living by 'over-beliefs' that have no basis in reason and observed facts,—that is fatal. It's just the trouble with so much of our electorate to-day—unreasoning acceptance without thought."

"Then," I said, "you admit of no other faculty than reason?"

"I confess that I don't. A great many insights that we seem to get from what we call intuition I think are due to the reason, which is unconsciously at work. If there were another faculty that equalled or transcended reason, it seems to me it would be a very dangerous thing for the world's progress. We'd come to rely on it rather than on ourselves—the trouble with the world is that it has been relying on it. Reason is the mind—it leaps to the stars without realizing always how it gets there. It is through reason we get the self-reliance that redeems us."

"But you!" I exclaimed. "*You* rely on something else besides reason?"

"Yes, it is true," he explained gently, "but that Thing Other-than-Ourselves we feel stirring in us is power, and that power, or the Source of it, seems to have given us our reason for guidance—if it were not so we shouldn't have a semblance of freedom. For there is neither virtue nor development in finding the path if we are guided. We do rely on that power for movement—and in the movements when it is withdrawn we are helpless. Both the power and the reason are God's."

"But the Church," I was moved by some untraced thought to ask "you believe there is a future for the Church?"

"A church of all those who disseminate truth, foster open-mindedness, serve humanity and radiate faith," he replied—but as though he were speaking to himself, not to me. . . .

A few moments later there was a knock at the door, and the woman of the house entered to say that Dr. Hepburn had arrived. I rose and shook Krebs's hand: sheer inability to express my emotion drove me to commonplaces.

"I'll come in soon again, if I may," I told him.

"Do, Paret," he said, "it's done me good to talk to you—more good than you imagine."

I was unable to answer him, but I glanced back from the doorway to see him smiling after me. On my way down the stairs I bumped into the doctor as he ascended. The dingy brown parlour was filled with men, standing in groups and talking in subdued voices. I hurried into the street, and on the sidewalk stopped face to face with Perry Blackwood.

Reading 20

Joe Hill

Wallace Stegner

Many Americans were ready to accept the conservative approach of the Progressive reformers, who sought to correct the ills of society with a patch-work quilt of legislation. But nearly one million voters chose the Socialist Presidential candidate, Eugene V. Debs, in 1912. The Industrial Workers of the World (IWW), or Wobblies, represented another, more radical alternative to the Progressives. Using passive resistance tactics and appealing to the lower-class itinerant workers, they challenged the capitalist system itself. Joe Hillstrom (Hill), one of their organizers, became a folk hero. In this fictional exchange with a missionary friend he expounds some of his philosophy.

Now when the mission doors are closed for the night and the last stew-bum steered off to a cot in the dormitory, protesting all the way his shame before Jesus for his unclean life, a preacher who has long since lost his illusions about his ability to reweave the unmeshed character of the defeated may relax in half-amused communion with himself, and in the bare clean kitchen may examine the justifications of a clean bare life.

There is a ritual to coffee at midnight, and whatever reflections Lund may have, however the day may have tried his patience or his faith, however his private catechism may run, it is a ritual that calms him. He is a Swede, one of those for whom coffee softens the stiff fibers of the mind. He drinks twenty cups a day, strong as lye and hot enough to crack tooth enamel, but this last cup of the day is the best, the most leisurely. In this hour of privacy and meditation his feet sound hollow and pleasantly lonely on the linoleum. The room contains nothing but himself; for a while there is no fretfulness in his mind. Though he may indulge his scepticism, he doubts without bitterness; though he may debate the premises of his whole existence, he confronts himself without heat or self-accusation. For this short while he can afford to be a puttery philosopher, as quiet within and without as trees dripping in the stillness after a rain.

Coffee at midnight is a Low Mass performed without deacon or incense; a ritualistic laying-out of mug, spoon, sugar bowl, milk can, with something

like a genuflection and a wordless intonation as the big pot, never empty or
cool through the long day, is pushed onto the gas ring. There are formal
movings and stoopings as before an altar, the pouring, the measuring of milk
and sugar, are liturgically deliberate; and when the mug is finally held between
the hands, warming them, the lips approach it as if it might contain the Host.
To move through the ritual itself is one sort of pleasure; to contemplate it in
these mildly terms is another. A man trained for the ministry acquires a respect
for ritual; a man conducting a mission on the waterfront has little enough
opportunity to practice it.

Into this compline service one night, coming after canonical hours and
tapping with his knuckles on the kitchen door that opened on the alley, came
Joe Hillstrom, sailor, longshoreman, common worker, IWW organizer and
composer of labor songs. He wore corduroys and a blue work shirt and a gray
and red coat sweater, and as Lund put out a surprised and inquiring head he
slipped in sideways to stand faintly smiling while Lund shut and bolted the
door.

"What's up?"

"Nothing. I saw your light still on."

"You'll get shot sometime, sliding up alleys like a burglar," Lund said.
He waved at the table and pulled out a chair. "I was just having a cup of
coffee."

Joe sat down at the oilcloth-covered table. He seemed to Lund little
changed by three years in the labor wars. A little tighter in the mouth, perhaps
—a little tighter in every way, as if an inner tension strung the rather flat voice,
sharpened the eyes, screwed up the cords of the muscled neck, pulled and
stretched the whole face so that it looked older, colder, less responsive. He sat
loosely, slumping in the chair, and his big workman's hands were quiet on the
oilcloth. He sipped, and grinned, and for a second he was boyish.

"You still haven't learned how to make coffee," he said.

"What's the matter with it?"

"I was just trying to make up my mind. Something you put in it, or wash
the pot in. Varnish, or turpentine, or something."

"Well, there's only a dash of turpentine," Lund said. "For flavor."

Joe emptied his cup into the sink. "I better make you some fresh as an
antidote."

"You're a fine Swede," Lund said. Amused, he watched Joe dump and
rinse the pot and fill it again with water and coffee. In the midst of measuring
the coffee Joe turned.

"You weren't planning to go to bed, were you?"

"What if I had been?"

"That'd be too bad," Joe said. He lighted the gas and stood with the curling black match in his hand, listening for a moment, head bent, his attention far off. Then he snapped the match at the rubbish pail and stared with hard concentration at Lund.

"How many hours a day do you put in in this place?"

"I don't know," Lund said, surprised. "I live here. It's not like working on a job."

"Eight or nine in the morning till after midnight," Joe said. "Seven days a week."

"I tried once to get you as my helper," Lund said. "If I'm sweated, you're responsible."

But he could not catch and hold Joe's eye for the mutual amusement he intended. Joe tipped the coffeepot and looked in, went to the back door and stood straddle-legged, his head tilted, looking the length of the kitchen at Lund. As if he had not intended to, he fell to listening again, and Lund watched him curiously, thinking that he had the air of not paying attention to what he himself said.

"Quiet," he said, and shook his head slightly and came back to sit down.

"The best time of day," Lund said. "Souls all saved, sheep all brought into the fold, everything snug."

Including the whole mission with a circular jerk of the head, Joe asked, "Who pays for this?"

"The mission?"

"Yes."

"Mainly the synod. I get some help now and then from two churches in Los Angeles, and the one here. Once a year we get a contribution from the old country."

"Rich church members."

"No. Mostly just ordinary people giving a few dollars. We're always in the hole."

"Who makes up the deficit, you?"

"Why do you want to know?"

"I'm trying to figure out why you bury yourself in a place like this. It ties you down, it costs you money, and you don't really believe you're saving any souls. What are you in it for?"

The direct blue stare was challenging, the face sharp and intent as if much hinged on Lund's answer. The missionary said mildly, "What are you in the IWW for? Are you making your fortune out of that?"

"No," Joe said impatiently, and struck Lund's words away with his hand. "I'm asking you now."

Eventually Lund had to shrug. "A lot of people need a helping hand."

The coffee boiled over and put out the fire, filling the room with the stink of burning grounds. Joe pulled the pot off the ring, turned off the gas, reached to the sink and got a half-cup of cold water which he poured into the pot. After a half-minute's wait for the grounds to settle he filled Lund's cup and his own.

"That sounds kind of smug," he said unexpectedly.

Lund was stung. If there was one thing he feared it was the thing he had seen too often in his own profession, the self-righteousness that could creep up on a man like fat or baldness, greasing the mind and clouding the vision and making a good man over into something almost detestable. In an unappreciated profession it was so easy to take comfort and justification from one's own sense of blamelessness. A hot retort jumped into his mind, but he held it back, glaring across the table into Joe's narrowed eyes. He saw the amusement there, and after a moment he could laugh. He was being baited again, and by one who knew how to find the tender spot.

"Self-righteousness is the vice of the meek," Lund said. "I'm not that meek. I'd just rather do this than be pastor in some Minnesota town."

But oddly Joe seemed already to have lost interest in exploiting the advantage he had gained. The argument that Lund was now prepared for died away before it was begun, and Joe eyed Lund over the rim of his coffee mug. His adam's apple moved as he swallowed. "You know you're an enemy of the working class, don't you, not really a helper?" he said, and set the cup down.

"I hadn't been informed," Lund said politely.

"Then I'll inform you."

Across from the missionary he sat and pursed his mouth, thinking—a complicated and difficult young man with a mind that could never quite be predicted. He was tough, ironical, sharp, intolerant, full of stereotypes and tired revolutionary clichés and yet prickly with unexpected observations and the echoes of unexpected books, sometimes soggy with sentimentality and self-pity and sometimes as unyielding and hostile as a row of bayonets. In the slight pause Lund shifted, mentally on his toes, trying to anticipate where the attack was coming and in what tone. For one clean instant, as Joe looked at him, he remembered something he had read as a boy in some book of western adventure. A white man and a Ute Indian, to settle a difficulty that had arisen between their respective groups, tied their left wrists together and fought with knives. He remembered now how unexpectedly that argument had been settled: instead of stabbing for his enemy's breast or throat the white man made one quick slash across the Ute's bound wrist, dropped his knife and seized the Ute's knife hand and held him until he bled to death. Lund was mentally protecting his wrists as well as his throat while he watched Joe and waited.

"All right," Joe said, "let me tell you about preachers. Preachers and politicians. You can't be either one and be on the side of the workingman. You can talk and preach and pray and say come to Jesus, but you're still part of the system, and the system is against the worker. It's made special just to keep him down, and there are a lot of ways. One is the way Engels talks about, the armed men. That's all the state is, a body of armed men hired by the bosses. It doesn't matter what armed men, Deputies, cops, National Guard, Pinkertons, they're all part of it. They slam it on the worker or the down-and-outer and they tip their hats to the boys in the high collars . . ."

"Now just a minute," Lund said.

"Or the politicians. They're part of the system too. They come around on Election Day with butter oozing out their pores, with their secret Australian ballot and their manhood suffrage and all the rest. Holy smoke! That's a pretty bum joke. You don't elect your representatives. You swap masters. Fire one and get another one just like him, and this should make you feel fine. What good is the ballot box? A workingman gets freedom from it just about the way he gets protection from the law."

Cramming his pipe while he watched the intent thin face, Lund saw that what he was talking about meant something to him. It was something he had thought about and wanted to say out. The vagueness, the wandering of his attention, were gone. He talked seriously and a little pompously, as if reciting a lesson.

"I don't own a single ballot box," Lund said, to give him the proper amount of irritating prod.

Joe did not smile. "You're part of the system, just the same. Armed men to hold the oppressed class down, politicians to promise them everything and pull wool over their eyes and make them think they're controlling their own business, and then preachers to make heaven so wonderful a man will stand for anything down below. It's a thimblerigger's game. The pea isn't under any of the shells."

"So I shouldn't feed a hungry man or give a bed to a bum?"

"I didn't say that," Joe said slowly. "But just the same, if you didn't the slaves might get mad quicker and rise up and take the rights they've been done out of."

"Let's be practical," said Lund. "These are down-and-outers, stew-bums, derelicts, a lot of them. If somebody doesn't take care of them they'll probably not live to rise up."

The wide stare was oddly hard to meet, pale and intense. "The down-and-outers are licked anyway," Joe said. "They're the casualties of the system, and they wind up scabbing on their real friends. Once they take the handout they're gone. It'd be better they had to die off than hang around taking scraps and licking the masters' hands and beating down wages with their scabbing. It's the handout that does it. In the old country they oppress labor with bayonets, but here we do it with handouts. That's where you come in."

"Is this part of some soapbox spiel?" Lund said, not really meaning the sneer.

Joe was abstracted, thinking. "I go down to the docks a lot when I'm in Pedro. I take down a piece of bread or something and sit on the dock and after while the rats come out and start nosing around. In about two days I can have the toughest old rat on the waterfront eating out of my hand in broad daylight like a squirrel."

Lund was silent, sloshing his mug around on the oilcloth and studying the circles like a penmanship exercise that it made. He laughed. "Well, I'm sorry for all the souls I've bribed over onto the boss's side with coffee and doughnuts." He was disappointed in Joe. The power to discriminate was no longer there; the hard uncompromising arrogance of the self-righteous was in his voice and in the sterile doctrines he preached. It was as if he looked out on the world through a set of ideas as rigid as the bars on a jail window, and everything he saw was striped in the same pattern. For a moment Lund was tempted to toss back at him the word "smug," but just then Joe looked up slily and smiled and pulled down his mouth.

"Bad coffee, too," he said. Somehow that one remark took the insistent pressure out of what he had been saying. Lund found himself thinking that Joe could be absurd, as the intelligent but under-educated could always be absurd, and he could perhaps be dangerous, a really deadly partisan, but he would also be something of a seeker always, and something of an artist.

He continued to look smilingly into Joe's face. Finally he said, "Life is a battleground to you."

"It's always been a battleground. It's taken the working class hundreds of years to get to the point where they can fight with a chance of winning."

"But you think they'll win."

"It's inevitable."

"And after they've won, then what? After they've thrown the bosses off their backs and broken up this system, what do they erect in its place?"

"Then the workers will own the instruments of production and will operate industry for the good of all. After the class war is won there is no more need for the state. The armed men and the ballot boxes and all the rest of it will wither away, and we get a classless and stateless society."

Lund knocked hot ash into his palm and held it there till it grew too hot to hold, when he dumped it in the trash bucket. The hope. The unshakable piety! He whistled a moment between his lips and then said, "And you attack me for being a Heaven-monger."

"What?"

"Let it go, let it go." He thought to himself ruefully that he had taken up the wrong mythology. His own had led him to scepticism and humanitari-

anism. Joe had a faith that would have shamed a Christian martyr, and it led
him to crusades, blood-letting and head-knocking in lofty causes, an assurance
that could let the whole lost world of down-and-outers go because their decline
would be a mark of the coming millennium.

There was no reaching him, no communication possible between a sceptic
and a zealot, a dubious Christian and a militant IWW. The Wobbly program,
what made it attractive to men like Joe Hillstrom, was that it was no program
at all. It was as reflexive as a poke in the nose, and about as constructive. We
are oppressed; fight back. The other side uses any means to hold us down; use
any means to get up. There went the whole weary round, the new hatreds
begotten on the bodies of the old. The master class has gobbled the earth;
throw it out and put in its place a new master class of workers in the expecta-
tion that under its benign rule government and class struggle and injustice will
wither away. Wonderful. All it needed was harps and wings.

Suppose just once, he said to Joe Hillstrom's thick contentious skull, that
men tried to *whittle* their world into change and progress instead of blasting
it. Suppose we didn't try to blast them out and burn them and kill them but
whittled at them, replacing evil with lesser evil, forcing a concession here and
an improvement there and substituting for good a greater good. Suppose we
tried overcoming the old sins that have been with us since Adam, and have
never left us because we have always elected in our hostility and eagerness and
ignorance to fight fire with fire, violence with violence, oppression with oppression? Suppose you fought evil and injustice with your whole might but refused
to adopt their methods? Would any more, in the long run, die? Don't you know
that violence is unslaked lime that burns the hands throwing it as well as the
flesh it is thrown upon?

You apostle of hostility and rebellion, I could read you a sermon in
brotherly interdependence, I could show you how you and I are both everybody's servant and everybody's master, I could demonstrate to you that your
way of righting wrongs may cure these wrongs but will surely create others.
I could be eloquent to show you that there is no way but the way of peace.
You sneer at peace, but I could show you that peace is not quietude, not
meekness, not weakness, not fear. It need no more accept current evils than
you and your fellows in the violent crusade. It doesn't even demand what
Christianity has been demanding for centuries. It doesn't demand love, necessarily. It demands only reasonable co-operation, for which men have a genius
when they try.

All the arts are arts of peace. Don't give me your Jack London Darwinism
and your philosophy of progress by class war. Talk to me about class peace
and I'll talk to you. Come to me as a man and I'll talk to you. But don't come
to me as a partisan with bloody hands and talk about the cleansing and

purifying that arises from violence. A partisan is no man any more; he is a man whittled to a sharp point, every humane quality in him, all his compassion and talent and intelligence and common sense and sense of justice pared away in the interest of striking power. The partisan is hooded like a hawk, kept on the wrist at all times except when the quarry is flushed, except when there is enemy blood to let.

But he did not say this. Neither did he say what he had often thought, and what he thought, almost irrelevantly, now: that humanity moves both ways on a street with a double dead-end, and that Vengeance sits with an axe at one end and Mercy sits in weak tears at the other, and that only Justice, which sits in the middle and looks both ways, can really choose.

Chapter 4

Empire and War

Reading 21

The Rough Riders

Hermann Hagedorn

The Spanish-American War (1898) was largely a product of the sensational-
ist yellow press, which aroused American public opinion against Spain and
for Cuba so that the McKinley administration felt compelled to bow to the
popular demand for war. The immediate cause, however, was the destruction of the American battleship *Maine* in Havana harbor. The atmosphere of
hysteria created by this disaster is captured in the following selection. Note
especially the role of Theodore Roosevelt and his reaction to the crisis.

That day, New York is in a fever. In the hotels, banks, business houses, clubs,
restaurants, lawyer's offices; in the trolley-cars, on the platforms of the ele-
vated, in the jingling, swaying horse-cars; on the ferry-boats; in the dingy
ferry-houses, the smoky, crowded Grand Central; on the Brooklyn Bridge,
belching its struggling masses in City Hall Square; in the streets—everywhere
on the streets—one theme, the *Maine!*

"Uxtra! Read 'e uxtra! *Maine* sunk! Hundreds massacred! Uxtra! President preparing for war! Uxtra! Uxtra!"

Newsboys are doing a land-office business.

"The *Maine!* My God, what d'you make of it? On a peaceful visit! And
blown up without warning! This will mean war, sure's you're born. No nation
can stand for that. We've stood by long enough. Now we'll go in and clean
up! Business? Business be damned! We've got some business to take care of in
Cuba. Those people at our door, kicked and beaten by a tottering, mediaeval
aristrocracy! We'll wipe the whole outfit clean off the map, clean off the map!"

On the Stock Exchange there is frantic going and coming. The ticker
catches the fever and becomes delirious; prices drop and struggle up a few
points and drop farther than before. There are conferences and more conferences; telegrams, reporters; anxious speculators; a rush of emissaries to Washington.

"My God, what a crime! . . . now that business was just getting started
again. Wire Senator Peyton. Get him to see the President at once. Who can
line up the New York congressmen? We can't let the President go into a war
now!"

The newspaper offices are madhouses. But the yellow sheets are in heaven. Edition after edition. What a killing! Once in a lifetime you made a killing like this. "If there were a war! There's been no war in America since journalism got up from the dead and began to be journalism. If there was a war! What a God-awful killing you could make! Jesus Christ! . . ."

In the offices of the soberer journals, gray-haired editors, pencils in hand, sit staring at the wall. "National honor. Yes. It's worth fighting for. It is the only thing that *is* worth fighting for. But has it been attacked? Really? Suppose it was an internal explosion? Grant that it was a mine, or a torpedo—who was responsible? An individual fanatic? Or was it the Spanish government? Is it not incredible that it should be the Spanish government? It might have been a crazy Cuban, trying to rouse the United States against Spain. But even if it was a Spanish sympathizer, if Spain behaves decently and tries to find the fanatic—in what way is our honor involved, except as we smirch it ourselves by intemperate action? We are just coming of age as a nation. Are we going to conduct our foreign relations in the mood of a drumhead court under the cottonwoods? Quiet, brothers, quiet! There shall be a reckoning! We will require an accounting! But we will be just, we will be honorable, we will be self-controlled. Not a rabble, but men! Good God, give us steady heads in Washington!"

But in the yellow sheets—*headlines*—HEADLINES!

SPAIN GUILTY!

WAR IMMINENT!

EXTERNAL EXPLOSION PROVED!

McKINLEY VACILLATING!

NATIONAL HONOR IMPERILED BY DELAY!

From Havana, the voice of a captain and a gentleman, the last to leave his shattered, burning ship:

"Public opinion should be suspended until further report. In such cases it is best not to think but to know."

SIGSBEE.

Washington is bewildered with excitement—a hotbed of startling reports and sensational rumors. The cruiser *New York* has been ordered to Havana. Fitzhugh Lee, the American consul-general in Havana, has been assassinated. There has been an emergency meeting of the Cabinet. The President has gone to the Capitol. Congress will declare war tonight or at the latest tomorrow.

All lies.

But there is an air of suppressed excitement among the employees at the White House, and the corridors of the Senate and House are like the trading pit during a wild, upward market. Twenty men have resolutions all ready to present—fiery words of righteous indignation—national honor.

In the Senate, Hoar of Massachusetts, Lodge of Massachusetts, Platt of Connecticut, Hanna of Ohio, have difficulty in checking the almost overpowering sentiment for immediate action. In the House, "Czar" Reed, the Speaker, has need of all his parliamentary resources to prevent impulsive action. The dogs of war are straining at their chains with a vengeance.

Public business is almost at a standstill. Eager and excited citizens hover about the Executive Mansion, crowd into the office of the President's private secretary, seek out officials in the State, War and Navy Building. Every item of information, true or false, is dissected, talked over, enlarged upon.

"Accident?" That was no accident! It was a submarine mine. That's what it was. With the wire running to Morro Castle. They say the Secretary of the Navy has a telegram from Captain Sigsbee saying it was a mine."

A newsboy—another extra: "CONVINCING EVIDENCE! SAILOR SAW FATAL TORPEDO!" A story told by an imaginative Jackie to a hungry reporter. It is pondered and analyzed. Could a torpedo be seen? If seen, why did the sailor not instantly report it? Was it after all a torpedo that caused the disaster, or a mine? And if a mine, was it a fixed mine or a floating mine? *Ad infinitum.*

Meanwhile, one item of truth emerges from the welter of rumors and inventions: the Secretary of the Navy has appointed a Naval Board of Inquiry, headed by Captain William T. Sampson, to proceed at once to Havana, accompanied by divers and all necessary equipment to make a thorough investigation of the wreck.

In the Secretary's office, meanwhile, the emotions and the imagination are more controlled than in the solemn and ornate ante-room or in the corridors, but the excitement is no less sharp. The solemn portraits of former Secretaries look down upon a roomful of naval officers in uniform, and congressmen, and an army officer or two; and a few favored correspondents. The naval officers are of the opinion that the explosion was accidental, resulting from the spontaneous combustion of a coal bunker or the overheating of the partitions between the boilers and the powder magazines. A correspondent points out that the coal bunkers are separated from the forward magazine which was the only one which exploded; and that Captain Sigsbee has cabled that the regular inspection, held an hour and a half before the disaster, showed the temperature of the magazines to have been normal.

One of the naval officers throws up his hands in an unhappy gesture.

"If you want to know my private opinion, not for publication," says another, "it's that somebody blew her up. Either a hot-blooded Spaniard venting his rage, or a cold-blooded Cuban trying to force a war. One guess is as good as another."

Secretary Long with his large, rather round face and wideset benignant eyes, is calm, almost placid. Having no guile in his own soul, he is unable to believe that there is any in the Spaniard's.

"An act of God, gentlemen!" exclaims an old admiral with feeling, "not an act of Spain!"

Peter Ingles, down from New York on the rush to hear what there is to hear for the benefit of the New York *Sun*, turns to Hayden Cusack on the leather-covered settee beside him. "If we can prove it," he whispers irreverently behind his hand, "will we declare war on God, or merely demand an apology?"

The impressive ante-room of the office of the Secretary of the Navy is livelier this morning than it has been for a half dozen administrations; but the centre of energy is not the room where Mr. Long is pouring oil upon the perturbed waters, but the adjoining quarters of his Assistant Secretary. It is illuminating to watch the door (under the spreadeagle and the flags) leading from the marble-tiled corridor into the office. Men go in and men go out, in two steady streams—a varied assortment of men, naval officers, army officers, principally, but politicians also, of every shade, the whole spectrum from the ultra-violet of statesmanship to the infra-red of ward-heeling. Among them, a little uneasy at finding themselves in such strange company, are one or two scholarly-looking individuals, a naturalist, a historian. A foreign diplomat comes, smiles and engages an army officer in conversation. The *Maine!* The *Maine!* The word is like a bee humming here, there and everywhere. "Has he got any news? He'll know what's what if anybody does! I'll betcha if he had his way . . . !"

The swinging door seems never to be still. The men go in and come out; go in oppressed with the sense of disaster, worried, divided in mind, come out, clarified, somehow strengthened; go in like the dull people most of them are, come out with springy steps and faces alight with interest and resolution. There is evidently an unusual person on the other side of that swinging door. His radiations seem to pierce the wall.

"Extraordinary creature!" exclaims a stately individual as he returns to the hall. "Such energy, such force!"

"Knew me after fifteen years!" booms a backwoodsman. "Don't that beat hell? If there's war an' he goes. . . ."

"I tell you," cries a politician to his companion, "you tie up to that fella an' you'll wear diamonds. Don't let Tom Platt or Ed Lauterbach or them other fellas fool ye. That man's goin' to be. . . ."

The contrast between the heavy going in of these people and their dynamic coming out is almost comic.

A general comes, a minister plenipotentiary, an English nobleman, a noted preacher who looks like Job.

Peter Ingles watches it all with a faint smile under the blond moustache and thinks of the congregating of the jungle-folk at dusk about a water-hole.

The colored doorkeeper at his little table is up and down, up and down, all smiles: "Yassir, yassir," he says, "it sure am a busy day, yassir, ebery day's a busy day here, sir, yassir. Dey sure all do grabitate to de office o' Mister Rosyvelt. Dey sure do grabitate, yassir."

Ingles turned to Cusack. "Going to see T. R.?"

"No, I guess not," answered the older man slowly, breathing on his glasses and gently rubbing them. "I'm waiting for Jerkins, the steel man, who's gone to see Long about a contract. Anyway, I haven't fallen under the spell."

"What have you got against Teddy?"

"Nothing, except that he's a blatant egotist and a windjammer; all talk."

"He wasn't all talk on the New York Police Commission."

"What did he *do*?" queried the other, irritably.

"He cleaned up the Force, for one thing. I happen to know something about that. The *Messenger* sent me on his trail to show him up and then wouldn't print my article because the record was too good. He's not all talk down here either. Any of the correspondents 'll tell you: he's really the whole show in the Navy Department and he's more than half the show in agitating intervention in Cuba."

"Oh, I don't like him! He irritates me. He's always talking as though he'd discovered Virtue, and she had made him her press-agent."

"He's a hell of a feller, Cusack. Really. Funny combination of idealist and practical man, scholar and adventurer. Knows an awful lot, reads all the time, works like a demon and plays like a thirteen-year-old. Afraid of nothing. Takes jobs no one else wants, where it's all sweat and no credit, and handles 'em so damn well the whole country sits up and takes notice."

"He has an instinct for drama," Cusack admitted, drily. "Oh, sure enough. And he likes to make a racket wherever he goes. But the racket always advertises something which needs advertising—some good cause blushing unseen, or some pile of garbage that needs to be carted to the town dump. He likes the limelight all right. It isn't for any petty gratification of his vanity, though, but for the added power the limelight gives him."

Cusack adjusted his glasses and smiled at his neighbor from the elevation of a fifteen years' seniority. "I thought hero-worship was out of date."

Ingles grinned. "Go ahead. Lay it on. I'll admit everything. I think he's great, and I'll lay you a dinner that if you were in a room alone with him for three-quarters of an hour, you would too. He's a human being. And contrary to the census reports, human beings are rare. I love him."

"Now, you've said something," said Cusack. "When a newspaperman loves a politician, Gabriel is tuning up his trump."

The room of the Assistant Secretary of the Navy was less stately—and less orderly—than the ante-room or the office of the head of the Department; books and maps and papers were scattered over the broad, hideously carved walnut desk; papers and maps and books were stacked on the mantelpiece, reaching up toward the engraving of Oliver Hazard Perry. There was an old-fashioned wall-clock between two fine old engravings of battle scenes, and a model of the U.S.S. *Olympia* stood under glass where the Assistant Secretary, sitting at his desk, could receive from it what stimulation he needed whenever the suggestion came from Secretary Long that Commodore Dewey out in Hongkong really did not need her. Amid all these symbols of belligerency stood, strode, exclaimed, gesticulated, adjured, excoriated, Theodore Roosevelt.

There were six or eight men in the room with him, in groups of twos and threes, talking earnestly. The *Maine,* the *Maine,* the *Maine!* Always, everywhere, the *Maine.* The Assistant Secretary was talking now to this group, now to that; now to all the groups at once; now, as emphatically, to a single individual. Peter Ingles stood in the window and listened, and looked happy, being in a congenial atmosphere.

Roosevelt was speaking, his head forward, his teeth gleaming, his eyes intense. "For three years I have been saying that we should put an end to Spanish misrule in Cuba! But the peace-at-any-price people—pitiful creatures! —said that what was happening in Cuba was no concern of ours! What has happened to the *Maine* may be different in external details from what has been happening to the Cubans, but Spanish arrogance and Spanish cruelty are behind both." He gave a quick toss of his head. "And for the *victims,* the *result* is the same!"

For a moment he stood erect, composed. "They call me a jingo. I am *not* a jingo. I am for peace. But I am for justice before I am for peace. I put peace very high as an agent for bringing about justice. But when peace fails to bring justice, I am, if necessary, for war."

Ingles lifted his head, and smiled gently. "What is the administration going to do, Mr. Roosevelt?"

The Assistant Secretary's mood semmed instantly to change; he looked at the handsome young adventurer with a quizzical look, squinting, his head tilted; then he thrust out his jaw, and grinned, unctuously. "Are you asking that foolish question in your public capacity as a purveyor of information, mainly erroneous, or as a fellow literary cuss with a talent for reticence?"

Ingles laughed. "Have it your own way, Mr. Roosevelt."

"Very *good!*" The voice went into a slight falsetto. "To you in your public capacity, I am glad to state that the Administration will do its utmost to see that the facts regarding the *Maine* are brought to light."

Ingles gave a gay snort. "I can't get a scoop on the yellows with that."

"But to you, as a discreet young friend of mine," Roosevelt proceeded, "I will add that I expect that there will be three months of *ab-so-lutely* futile conversation, at the end of which the issues will have become so blurred that no one will know black from white; and another hundred thousands Cubans will be dead." The teeth flashed; then slowly the lips were drawn shut over them, as a diaphragm is drawn shut over a lens; he leaned forward; his cheeks were flushed. "We will probably never find out what destroyed the *Maine*. Officially, it will go down as an accident. Personally, I believe the *Maine* was sunk by an act of dirty treachery, and I would give anything I possess if President McKinley would order the fleet to Cuba tomorrow."

Everybody in the room had turned to listen; there were murmurs of assent; of dissent.

An open, lifted hand went smashing into an open palm, "We will come to it, gentlemen! But probably not until the rains and fevers begin in the territory where we will have to fight. Nine-tenths of wisdom is being wise in time! And the price of delay in matters of this sort is always in terms of human life!"

"But, Theodore!—"

"My dear sir!——"

"War is out of the question!"

"Cuba—the *Maine*—Cuba—accident—forward magazines—Admiral Belcher declares—Spain—the *Maine*. . . ."

"Gentlemen, America's duty—America's honor——!"

Peter Ingles did not choose to contribute any sparks to the conflagration. He was looking at Theodore Roosevelt; and with a smile, softly, very softly, humming Old Hundred. . . .

The *Maine!*

The news flies over the land. Boston, Buffalo, Chicago, St. Louis, Kansas City, Denver, San Francisco, are for once at one in their emotions with Washington and New York. Iowa, Kansas, Nevada, Colorado, Montana, forget the bitterness of 1896, the sharp divisions of the fight for free silver, the "imperial East," the "enslaved West." Bryan, the boy orator of the Platte, has only words of cordial support for the man in the White House whom he excoriated as the first of a new line of Caesars. There is no East and West.

Broad Street in Richmond speaks the words that Broad Street in New York is speaking. Atlanta cries, "*We*'ll show 'em!" New Orleans shouts, "*We* won't stand it," thinking not of a section but of the nation. Confederate captains and majors and colonels and generals take down the old swords. Wiry old Joe Wheeler, the South's comet on horseback in the late unpleasantness, dreams of new cavalry charges. For the first time in fifty years there is no North and South.

At country stores in Maine, in Alabama, in Oregon and Texas and Delaware, there are indignation meetings of local sages gathered about the wood stove. Wherever men congregate in post-offices, on railroad platforms, in smoking-cars, there is discussion, orating, pounding of fists; and everywhere women flutter mightily.

REMEMBER THE MAINE!

Riders carry the tidings—and the slogan—from ranch to ranch in Montana, Arizona, Wyoming, Utah Texas.

The cabin, half hidden in the snow, the shack, burning in the desert heat, are shaken from sleep by the news.

Children, hearing of the *Maine*, in the post-office or the schoolroom, rush home breathless.

Milling crowds in front of billboards. Excited crowds in theatres. Orators —everywhere orators. And emotion!

> *Remember the Maine!*
> *To hell with Spain!*

It is only February, but the temperature of the national blood is well above the delirium point.

But Matthew Kerdie, dreamer and writer of tales, stretches his legs in front of an open fire in a room on West Twenty-third Street, in New York, and turns to Hallsmith—he of the bushy hair and heavy moustache and the round face and the childlike heart—and says. "All this talk of Spain blowing up the *Maine* is nonsense. Spaniards didn't blow her up and Cubans didn't blow her up. And she didn't blow herself up."

"I don't see that you've got much left."

"Nothing but destiny. Unless I misread all the signs, destiny has some large plans for these United States in this new century we're moving toward. And destiny, if she wants to, can operate without conspirators."

Reading 22

Lower than the Angels

Walter Karig

The beginning of World War I found the United States with virtually no army. The immense task was to make soldiers out of the six million recruits and four million draftees as quickly as possible. The process was a painful one for the usually undisciplined American boy but was somehow accomplished. The typical trials of a draftee in the new army are the subject of the following passage.

The line got under way, Marvin somewhere near the middle among strangers. A frozen dirt road underfoot, many trees all about, lights winking in the distance. Lights close by as the road turned and a gate, a sentry, bayonet fixed and gleaming. Marvin felt a thrill from coccyx to occiput. The men who had saved their little flags began pulling them out, and Marvin did too. The staff had broken.

"Fa God's sakes put them goddam flags away, ya look like a bunch a immigrunts!"

The sergeant's admonition was hastily obeyed. Marvin casually dropped his gift of the D.A.R. into the road.

The column passed low wooden buildings, all illuminated. A few soldiers were about. Mostly they watched the draft pass by silently. A few jeered:

"Caught cha, hah?"

"Got caught inna draft, an dont they look sick!"

"I want my mommer."

"You're in the army now ya not behind the plow ya sonuvabitch ye'll never get rich ya inna army now."

Across a wide field. Another barbed-wire barrier and gate and overcoated sentry, bayonet agleam. Lights, like those around ammunition plants, and two-story buildings in a row a hundred yards away.

"Colyum halt. Raff-fess. Raffess, goddammit! Cantcher unnerstand English? Right—face. Toin right."

A longish wait again while officers and noncoms conferred.

"Count off!"

After two or three attempts sandwiched between explanations, the line was successfully enumerated by individuals. In sections of two hundred the men were marched through the lights and through the gates. Marvin was in the second lot, had to stand in the cold, feeling for once in his conscious life acutely insignificant and helplessly dependent, his every thought and emotion alien to surroundings. It was worse than any new job, worse than school even. He envied the soldiers striding past in heavy boots, envied them not only their freedom of motion but their ability to salute with snap, turn corners sharply.

Commands at last and the gang stepped forward, into glare, through a gate, to a vast, barnlike building smelling of camphor, pine, and wood smoke. In single file the men shuffled past a long counter, received each a canvas cot, folded and tied; two blankets, a crackling tablet of pillow; checked off by name and number again; lined up in the darkness once more; at last, marched up to and into one of the big buildings.

"This colyum upstairs, this un right isside."

Marvin was on the ground floor. A vast room of raw lumber, naked wiring fruited at intervals with light bulbs. Warmer than outdoors, but not much.

"Line up in the middle, there. Now count off by fours—one, two, three, four. Ready? Count off . . . Okay. Odd men to the left, evens to the right. Now men, set up your cots. We seem short of mattresses and pillows but you wont be here long. Fold your blankets and put them at the end of the cot."

A baby-faced young officer talking, standing at the door.

"Dont lose your cards and papers. As soon as you're ready you eat."

One man raised his hand, schoolboy fashion, waving violently.

"Do you want to ask a question?"

"Please, mister, where's the terlet?"

Groans and laughter from the double line. The lieutenant conferred with the sergeant.

"Right to the end of the street. Ya cant miss it." The sergeant.

"Are you in a hurry? Very well, make it snappy. And, men, you will please learn to regulate the calls of nature so they will not interfere with duty," said the apple-cheeks, seriously. "Now get those cots up."

Marvin untied the bleached khaki cords of his cot, straightened out the contraption, legs up, pulled apart and adjusted the braces, turned the job right side up and folded his blankets at the foot, his suitcase on top of them. The lieutenant walked past, nodded, and smiled at Marvin.

"Good work, soldier."

Marvin gulped, tried to salute, was overcome by a sudden stage fright. Good work, soldier! Jesus, maybe he'd be a sergeant himself soon.

They lined up again, marched out, were led to another building mostly open shed, where fires glowed and the smell of food expanded every nostril, contracted every gut. Tin plate and aluminum mug; strong black coffee in the mug here; hash on the plate there, and mashed turnips and rice. Big wooden boxes filled with white bread cut in thick slices. Marvin took three. Trestle tables and benches. The men ate animally.

Two in blue overalls poured more coffee from big pots slung on a stick; from a bushel basket another tossed every man a doughnut.

"Boy, this is livin high."

"Please passa cream, sweetheart."

"White meat or dark?"

Back to the barracks. "Lights out in ten minutes."

Marvin took off his shoes, his overcoat, coat and pants. He spread his blankets, topped them with his overcoat, folded his pants to supplement the pillow. Shoes off, he climbed under the blankets. Across the way one man was on his knees, praying. One guy was putting on pajamas, for God's sakes.

Blip, and the lights went out.

It was goddam cold. The cold air came up through the canvas of the cot. Marvin got up and put a blanket beneath him. Snores were already beginning.

A soft thud.

"Jeezt, I fell outa bed."

"Lissen, youse guys! Pipe down an shut your goddam mouths. You're in the army now an by Jesus you cant cut up no jack while I'm ridin herd on youse, you lousy yellerbelly sons of bitches. Quiet now or by God I'll make you sweat for it termorrer."

That was the sergeant. That guy had guts. That guy was-s-s . . .

"Now cough."

"Now lean over and pull your cheeks apart. Okay."

A long line of naked men, shuffling on tender feet over rough floor boarding, posturing and cutting obscene capers at the orders of half a dozen crisp, curt army surgeons, booted and spurred, reflectors on foreheads and stethoscopes looped around necks.

"Stand on your left foot. On your right foot. Say a-a-ah."

Tap-a-ap on chest, insult of cold metal on ribs.

"Open your mouth. Tsk-tsk. Ever go to a dentist?"

"Yes, sir, to get some rottin teeth—"

"You need fixing up. Get this now, sergeant . . . "

Shivering on a chalk mark. "How far down can you read? Now hold the card over the other eye. Can you hear this watch ticking . . . ?"

A long line of naked men on tender feet. Some with deadwhite corns on cramped pink toes; some furred like the beast; some smooth and milky-white as girls. Some with tanned arms and shoulders; some tattooed and some circumcised. Some pimpled, some scarred.

"One hat, six an seven."

"Six an seven, ri!"

"One blouse, thurry-six."

"Thoidy-six, ri!"

But no gun, no bayonet. Marvin wasnt a soldier yet. He looked something like one, talked like one surely. He wore the itching trappings from heel to head, hide to overcoat. He walked stridingly, saluted elaborately, smoked Camels and called bread "punk"; Tuesday's stringy viand, "corn willy," and Friday's prandial gesture to the fast, "goldfish." He learned squads left and right; the about-face cunningly executed by a locking of instep with Achilles tendon; by the numbers; as you were. He arose in the dark and cold and went to bed earlier than he had ever the last half of his life.

After the evening meal he went to the Y hut, center for Christian good times and weak five-cent cocoa. HAVE YOU WRITTEN YOUR MOTHER TO-DAY?

Cigarette smoke, songs, almond bars, ruled writing paper with the red triangle. Magazines without covers.

Then Marvin was a soldier with a gun, gun, gun. He had a number too. His civilian clothes went home, cutting the navel cord that bound him to $80 a week, pickups, midnight suppers and silk shirts. He wrote the first news-bearing letter of his life. He kept his gun clean as instructed, and learned to right shoulder, port, ground and stack arms.

He had new buddies, for the men had been graded according to size, and Birnbaum was rarely seen; then, when seen, he wore a corporal's stripes and was exercising a typewriter instead of a rifle, goddam office worker.

"Them guys shouldnt be let to wear uniforms as if they was soldiers. A buncha male stenogerfers an male cooks an all wearin uniforms like they was fightin men, for cripe's sake."

He wrote home that the army wasnt bad but the food was lousy and the underwear itched and there were no sheets and the hours were long and the work hard and did anybody buy the Saxon yet the war would last ten years but wait till the Americans got over there Over There and it wouldnt last a month and the pay was $30 a month but he'd assigned half of it to Mom and he was paying $5 on a Liberty bond so please send some cigarettes and stuff.

Mother wrote slantingly and pale blue that Marvin was terribly missed and that he should take care of himself, not get his feet wet, and the store was doing pretty good considering everything was regulated and she was sending a package.

Reading 23

Mademoiselle from Armentières

As the Civil War became a distant memory, the American people forgot the horrors of war and tended to glamorize it. Secretary of State John Hay even commented about the Spanish-American War, "It wasn't much of a war but it was the best one we could get at the time." (This idea is repeated in the following selection.) World War I occasioned many songs and parades which reflected the popular enthusiasm for war and the lack of understanding of the suffering brought by war. "Mademoiselle from Armentieres", the most famous of the songs of the American Expeditionary Force, was popular with British soldiers before it became the American favorite. It was sung by the doughboy to ease the tedium of long marches. The doings of the mademoiselle were recorded in hundreds of verses, often spontaneously composed by unknown bards while on the march. Unfortunately, most of them are unprintable.

"Oh farmer, have you a daughter fair, parlee-voo,
Oh farmer, have you a daughter fair, parlee-voo,
Oh farmer, have you a daughter fair,
Who can wash a solider's underwear, hinky dinky dinky, parlee-voo."

"Oh, yes, I have a daughter fair,
With lily-white hands and golden hair."

Mademoiselle from Armentières
She ain't even heard of underwear.

If you never wash your underwear,
You'll never get the Croix de Guerre.

Mademoiselle from Armentières
She hasn't been kissed in forty years.

She may have been young for all we knew,
When Napoleon flopped at Waterloo.

The French, they are a funny race,
They fight with their feet and save their face.

The cootie is the national bug of France,
The cootie's found all over France,
No matter where you hang your pants.

The officers get all the steak,
And all we get is the belly-ache.

The general got a Croix de Guerre,
The son-of-a-gun was never there.

My Froggie girl was true to me,
She was true to me, she was true to you,
She was true to the whole damn army, too.

You might forget the gas and shell,
But you'll never forget the mademoiselle.

There's many and many a married man,
Wants to go back to France again.

'Twas a hell of a war as we recall,
But still 'twas better than none at all.

Reading 24

East of Eden

John Steinbeck

After the United States entered World War I, the overwhelming majority of American people supported the war with complete enthusiasm, convinced that this was truly "the war to end all wars." Unfortunately, this all-out war effort resulted in widespread violations of civil rights on the home front. In many communities Americans of German ancestry were discriminated against and even persecuted. Some "patriots" aided the war effort by stoning dachshunds to death, barring the music of Bach and Beethoven, and even banning the teaching of German in the high schools. The events in Salinas, California depicted in the following account were duplicated in thousands of communities throughout the land.

Sometimes, but not often, a rain comes to the Salinas Valley in November. It is so rare that the *Journal* or the *Index* or both carry editorials about it. The hills turn to a soft green overnight and the air smells good. Rain at this time is not particularly good in an agricultural sense unless it is going to continue, and this is extremely unusual. More commonly, the dryness comes back and the fuzz of grass withers or a little frost curls it and there's that amount of seed wasted.

The war years were wet years, and there were many people who blamed the strange intransigent weather on the firing of the great guns in France. This was seriously considered in articles and in arguments.

We didn't have many troops in France that first winter, but we had millions in training, getting ready to go.

Painful as the war was, it was exciting too. The Germans were not stopped. In fact, they had taken the initiative again, driving methodically toward Paris, and God knew when they could be stopped—if they could be stopped at all. General Pershing would save us if we could be saved. His trim, beautifully uniformed soldierly figure made its appearance in every paper every day. His chin was granite and there was no wrinkle on his tunic. He was the epitome of a perfect soldier. No one knew what he really thought.

We knew we couldn't lose and yet we seemed to be going about losing. You couldn't buy flour, white flour, any more without taking four times the quantity of brown flour. Those who could afford it ate bread and biscuits made with white flour and made mash for the chickens with the brown.

In the old Troop C armory the Home Guard drilled, men over fifty and not the best soldier material, but they took setting-up exercises twice a week, wore Home Guard buttons and overseas caps, snapped orders at one another, and wrangled eternally about who should be officers. William C. Burt died right on the armory floor in the middle of a push-up. His heart couldn't take it.

There were Minute Men too, so called because they made one minute speeches in favor of America in moving-picture theaters and in churches. They had buttons too.

The women rolled bandages and wore Red Cross uniforms and thought of themselves as Angels of Mercy. And everybody knitted something for someone. There were wristlets, short tubes of wool to keep the wind from whistling up soldiers' sleeves, and there were knitted helmets with only a hole in front to look out of. These were designed to keep the new tin helmets from freezing to the head.

Every bit of really first-grade leather was taken for officers' boots and for Sam Browne belts. These belts were handsome and only officers could wear them. They consisted of a wide belt and a strap that crossed the chest and passed under the left epaulet. We copied them from the British, and even the

British had forgotten their original purpose, which was possibly to support a heavy sword. Swords were not carried except on parade, but an officer would not be caught dead without a Sam Browne belt. A good one cost as much as twenty-five dollars.

We learned a lot from the British—and if they had not been good fighting men we wouldn't have taken it. Men began to wear their handkerchiefs in their sleeves and some foppish lieutenants carried swagger sticks. One thing we resisted for a long time, though. Wristwatches were just too silly. It didn't seem likely that we would ever copy the Limeys in that.

We had our internal enemies too, and we exercised vigilance. San Jose had a spy scare, and Salinas was not likely to be left behind—not the way Salinas was growing.

For about twenty years Mr. Fenchel had done hand tailoring in Salinas. He was short and round and he had an accent that made you laugh. All day he sat cross-legged on his table in the little shop on Alisal Street, and in the evening he walked home to his small white house far out on Central Avenue. He was forever painting his house and the white picket fence in front of it. Nobody had given his accent a thought until the war came along, but suddenly we knew. It was German. We had our own personal German. It didn't do him any good to bankrupt himself buying war bonds. That was too easy a way to cover up.

The Home Guard wouldn't take him in. They didn't want a spy knowing their secret plans for defending Salinas. And who wanted to wear a suit made by an enemy? Mr. Fenchel sat all day on his table and he didn't have anything to do, so he basted and ripped and sewed and ripped on the same piece of cloth over and over.

We used every cruelty we could think of on Mr. Fenchel. He was our German. He passed our house every day, and there had been a time when he spoke to every man and woman and child and dog, and everyone had answered. Now no one spoke to him, and I can see now in my mind his tubby loneliness and his face full of hurt pride.

My little sister and I did our part with Mr. Fenchel, and it is one of those memories of shame that still makes me break into a sweat and tighten up around the throat. We were standing in our front yard on the lawn one evening and we saw him coming with little fat steps. His black homburg was brushed and squarely set on his head. I don't remember that we discussed our plan but we must have, to have carried it out so well.

As he came near, my sister and I moved slowly across the street side by side. Mr. Fenchel looked up and saw us moving toward him. We stopped in the gutter as he came by.

He broke into a smile and said, "Gut efning, Chon. Gut efning, Mary."

We stood stiffly side by side and we said in unison, "Hoch der Kaiser!"

I can see his face now, his startled innocent blue eyes. He tried to say something and then he began to cry. Didn't even try to pretend he wasn't. He just stood there sobbing. And do you know?—Mary and I turned around and walked stiffly across the street and into our front yard. We felt horrible. I still do when I think of it.

We were too young to do a good job on Mr. Fenchel. That took strong men—about thirty of them. One Saturday night they collected in a bar and marched in a column of fours out Central Avenue, saying, "Hup! Hup!"in unison. They tore down Mr. Fenchel's white picket fence and burned the front out of his house. No Kaiser-loving son of a bitch was going to get away with it with us. And then Salinas could hold up its head with San Jose.

Of course that made Watsonville get busy. They tarred and feathered a Pole they thought was a German. He had an accent.

We of Salinas did all of the things that are inevitably done in a war, and we thought the inevitable thoughts. We screamed over good rumors and died of panic at bad news. Everybody had a secret that he had to spread obliquely to keep its identity as a secret. Our pattern of life changed in the usual manner. Wages and prices went up. A whisper of shortage caused us to buy and store food. Nice quiet ladies clawed one another over a can of tomatoes.

It wasn't all bad or cheap or hysterical. There was heroism too. Some men who could have avoided the army enlisted, and others objected to the war on moral or religious grounds and took the walk up Golgotha which normally comes with that. There were people who gave everything they had to the war because it was the last war and by winning it we would remove war like a thorn from the flesh of the world and there wouldn't be any more such horrible nonsense.

There is no dignity in death in battle. Mostly that is a splashing about of human meat and fluid, and the result is filthy, but there is a great and almost sweet dignity in the sorrow, the helpless, the hopeless sorrow, that comes down over a family with the telegram. Nothing to say, nothing to do, and only one hope—I hope he didn't suffer—and what a forlorn and last-choice hope that is. And it is true that there were some people who, when their sorrow was beginning to lose its savor, gently edged it toward pride and felt increasingly important because of their loss. Some of these even made a good thing of it after the war was over. That is only natural, just as it is natural for a man whose life function is the making of money to make money out of a war. No one blamed a man for that, but it was expected that he should invest a part of his loot in war bonds. We thought we invented all of it in Salinas, even the sorrow.

Reading 25

Black River

Carleton Beals

In the 1920s the American imperialism of earlier years was continued. This was especially true in Latin America, where American businessmen steadily expanded their influence. In the following selection an oil company in Mexico employs a special staff to foment revolution to protect its investment. Officials of petroleum firms did in fact plan such escapades and used well-financed propaganda agencies in the United States to gain support for their misdeeds or obtain the backing of prominent politicians.

One day, through a roundabout source, Bartlett received a communication from Yarza. Unless the oil companies paid him $100,000 a month he would begin burning wells.

Barlett was closeted with Sadler over the matter. "The situation comes down to this. Whichever gang we play with we've got to shell out. There's no doubt Yarza is in a position to burn our wells, perhaps to destroy most of the field. If he gives us his word not to commit such depredations he'll keep it. The Federals can only give us halfway protection. Tomorrow we may need a leverage in Yarza against the Federals themselves. The new constitutional provisions will ruin us. We're not going to stand for them one minute. We'll fight and fight to the last ditch."

Sadler stiffened his lean body. "You people, if I have anything to do with it, will have the complete backing of the Department in whatever you decide to do. These are abnormal times."

"The companies have decided to pay the demanded $100,000."

"Probably wisest. The State Department will back you. If that constitution goes into effect it means no end of trouble."

"It means so much trouble," said Bartlett, wriggling his small bulky frame furiously in his chair, "that the U.S. may have to intervene in this cock-eyed country."

Sadler shook his head mournfully. "If I had my way we'd march in tomorrow. Pershing should go on to Mexico City at once. But there's still too much oppoisition sentiment in our country for such a step."

Bartlett raged. "We backed Carranza. Now look at his pronouncements, his anti-American attitude. By George, we'll take over the oil region—by force if necessary. If the American government can't get up backbone enough to do it why we'll do it ourselves."

"Did you ever hear of Signor Cavour, Minister of the House of Savoy?" asked Mr. Sadler. "He's one of my heroes."

"So!" Bartlett concealed his ignorance.

"Do you remember his remarks as to how he was going to unify Italy: 'I'll eat it, leaf by leaf, like an artichoke'."

"Ha, Ha! Not bad."

"Perhaps we can apply that nearer home. 'Leaf by leaf.' "

"An artichoke plan! Bartlett brought his fist down. "You're right. You've hit on the idea I've been working on for some time. The oil region must be split off from Mexico. Suppose the United States is engaged in a world-struggle tommorow. An unfriendly government here—and where are we at? Are we going to let some ragged General stand in our way? We can't permit the oil-supply to be cut off under any circumstances. I'm a patriot, Sadler. Constantly. I have my country's needs in mind. Won't it be better to settle the whole problem beforehand? See what's coming, Sadler, and help us out. CEMOC will *always* take care of you. Sound out your friends in the service. Find out who is with us and let me know—everything in your usual discreet way, of course."

"I'll do everything I can."

"That's why we'll need Yarza. If we set up an oil republic under the protection of Washington he could be guaranteed the first presidency of the new government. We would have a sort of Platt Amendment so American marines could land at any time to protect American property."

"The Cuban venture has worked well."

"Exactly. If necessary, such an oil republic could be annexed. In the southeast we could stir up the Maya districts and unite them to Central America where they logically belong. And in the center of the country—what would still be Mexico—we could back a friendly president. I suggest we choose a man who is well-known, one of the former Díaz Científicos, a man of probity, who is a great admirer of the United States."

"You have someone in mind?"

"Yes. For instance, Señor Agustín Sotomayor is a man who would command universal respect—except of course from these ragged revolutionists. But he could be kept in office until the independence or annexation of the oil region was definitely determined beyond revocation. Then what is left of Mexico could be left to stew in its own juice."

"It sounds feasible."

"It is. The only solution."

"You'll have to swing enough public sentiment behind you."

"Easy. Once the thing is under way people will fall in line. You can put anything over on the American public, the easiest led congregation of human beings in the world. Concerted propaganda in the press, schools, over the radio, by paid lobbyists and university professors, and you can swing the country to any point of view over night."

"That's true."

"The oil companies are already considering the establishment of a powerful propaganda-bureau in New York. The State Department will always listen. And if you, Sadler, are with us you could count on a high position when the scheme is put through, either with us or in an official capacity."

"What do you expect me to do?"

"Your reports on the situation here are implicitly believed by the State Department. I suggest that you keep the entire ramifications of this scheme in mind, that you sound out our high officials, also our consuls in Yucatán and Guatemala. We should have copies of all your correspondence in our secret CEMOC files so we can keep track of every phase of the negotiations. As for me, I'm leaving for Washington immediately, and am getting in touch with my old Arizona friend, Senator Eddie Caddington; and something will be started —soon. Are you with us?"

"To the last ditch."

"Guard will handle Yarza."

"And I'll follow out all your ideas."

"Hunkey-dory. Full steam ahead. Faint heart never won fair lady."

Chapter 5

Between the Wars

Reading 26

Revelry

Samuel Hopkins Adams

Warren G. Harding, the small-town Ohio newspaper editor who became President of the United States in 1921, expressed the spirit of the decade in his demand that the nation "return to normalcy." Unfortunately, this friendly, easy-going, Rotarian-type Chief Executive presided over one of the most corrupt and scandal-ridden administrations in the nation's history. Several of his appointees, including two cabinet members, were eventually sent to prison. The following selection is from a very popular novel of the day and accurately describes how graft was carried on. The main character, Willis Markham is a thinly disguised President Harding.

Amazement had been the reaction of Washington when Handy Andy Gandy was appointed Secretary of Public Health. It was just a little too raw. That he would land a fat job was to be expected. Hadn't he been a chum of Willis Markham's in the Senatorial days? Wasn't he a regular attendant at the Crow's Nest whist parties? But how did he, with his fake degree from the shadiest of diploma factories, qualify for the highest medical office in the government? And, even more puzzling, what did he figure on getting out of it?

The new Secretary answered neither question. He simply sawed wood. First he set forth his plan to combine all medical activities of the Federal government, a project so dear to the profession that it almost forgave his appointment. The Secretaries of War and Navy surrendered their hospitals and equipment without protest, being politicians of too much tact to oppose the President's move on behalf of his friend, Gandy; and though the United States Public Health Service entered a spirited objection, it was helpless, being a mere appendage of the Treasury Department, ruled and overruled by Maxson, the frail high priest of high finance, whose interest in matters scientific was nil.

Against Secretary-Doctor Gandy's second great innovation, there could be no reasonable cavil, the establishment of a chain of tuberculosis hospitals across the country. As economy and efficiency had commended the first project, so humanity supported the second. A bill conferring upon the new department the right to condemn and occupy land for hospital purposes was passed, after word had gone around that President Markham desired this great humanitarian work to stand as a monument to his administration, by a Congress still subservient in spirit to the impressive Markham plurality. Nobody was particularly surprised when Charles M. Madrigal went into Gandy's office as his right-hand man, for Charley was another pal of the President's. Shrewdly judging that wherever Handy Andy settled there would be molasses, Madrigal had prevailed upon his friend, Bill, to put him there. His first stroke of genius was to institute a triple inventory comprehending all supplies and equipment of the three services to be absorbed. The final figures, in shining millions, imparted their glow to his eyes and even lighted up the dull orbs of his superior when presented to that able gentleman.

"We'll sell 'em," said the Secretary.

Madrigal goggled. "All?"

"Clean sweep."

"Gee! But, look here, Doc! Isn't there a lot of that stuff that could be used?"

"Unfit," said Secretary Gandy. "Condemned."

Madrigal whistled in impressible admiration. Business on this scale was beyond even his dreams. But there was a fly in the ointment. "They'll have to be put up for competitive bidding."

"Will they?"

"That's the law."

"There's a way around most laws."

"What way?"

"What are you here for?" asked the Secretary with chill finality.

The blithe Madrigal began to perceive that he was expected to earn his money. "I'll look into it," he undertook.

"About these sheets, now, at the Millvale Stores." The Secretary examined the list prepared by his subordinate. "How badly damaged are they?"

Madrigal stared. "Damaged? They're new. Not unboxed yet."

"How—badly—damaged—are—they?"

"Oh!" Madrigal gulped, swallowing the idea. "Pretty poor shape, I expect." He had an inspiration. "Some of the storerooms leak."mm

"Exactly. According to this tally sheet they are inventoried at $1.23 apiece. Excessive," pronounced the Hon. Anderson Gandy severely.

"Oh, abslootly!" Madrigal was getting his clue.

"What would you consider a fair selling price, in view of the—er—damage?"

"You tell me and I'll tell you," chirped Madrigal brightly, hoping to cover his comprehensive ignorance of the cotton goods business.

"I am calling upon you for an estimate."

"Well, haffa dollar."

"M-m-m! Rather high on a bulk sale."

Make it a quarter," said the surbordinate with desperate generosity.

"At such a price I know of a vurry reliable firm in Detroit that might be interested. Here is their card. Now, blankets. M-m-m! Five thousand pairs at Keggston Landing, I see."

"Moth-eaten," Madrigal improvised.

"How unfortunate"' The Honorable Secretary grinned. "But some value remains, I suppose."

"Not more than $1.12 a pair," said the pupil firmly.

"Cost $3.88. Yes: that would be about right. You might try these people." He wrote a name and address on a card. "Keeping me quite out of it, of course."

"Abslootly"' repeated Charley Madrigal.

They passed on to surgical gauze, toothbrushes, floor cleaner in thousands of cans, mosquito wire, drugs, iron cots, and as the list grew and the enthusiasm of Mr. Madrigal warmed, the Secretary was obliged several times to check his too-apt pupil and suggest that there was such a thing as moderation in the bargain counter appeal.

"You get the idea," said he.

"I'll say I do!" Obviously the idea was to buy dear and sell cheap, a new and prodigiously profitable principle in economics. The weasel brain of Madrigal perceived that by clever juggling of prices he could hold out for himself quite as much as he turned over to his superior. Why not? Wasn't fifty-five a fair cut? He had all the work to do: all the risk to take. Risk? That didn't count, in his dollar-dazzled vision. Who was going to kick? And if they did kick, what would that get 'em? Bill Markham would show the soreheads where they got off. Trust Old Bill to take care of his pals.

Later there was born of these shrewd negotiations that flood of "Army Sales," "Navy Sales," "Government Supply Stores" and fly-by-night merchandising which offered to the public real values at the expense of legitimate retail trade, unable to compete with such bargains. The immediate effect was that Charley Madrigal in his enthusiasm went out and ordered the highest priced car on the market.

Satisfied that these operations were in safe hands, the Secretary of Public Health now turned his attention to another source of emolument. Hospitals were to be dotted here and there across the map. Hospitals must have land to stand on, and his department was empowered to purchase the land or even to acquire it by condemnation, though this was another phase which the astute Dr. Gandy, with his knowledge of western oil and mineral values, meant to put to another use. Real estate operators could be found who would not be insensible to opportunities of quick sales to a generous buyer, nor impenetrable to the suggestion of a modest split. Uncle Sam could afford the money in a

humanitarian cause such as this. A broad view of the enterprise was indicated. The Hon. Anderson Gandy went to the Crow's Nest to see his pal, Daniel Lurcock. Him he found shooting craps with Jeff Sims for quarters. Gandy did not wholly trust Lurcock, the scope of whose unofficial power and influence made him uneasy, and Lurcock did not really like Gandy, whom he considered a bit of a tightwad; but they worked together well enough when their interests ran parallel.

"I want to talk to you, Dan," said the Secretary of Public Health.

"Talk," returned Lurcock caressing the "bones" proffessionally between his palms before releasing them. Rattling, they fell, rolled, stopped. "Hell's bells! Twelve again."

"Privately."

"Jeff is in on all my business."

"I'll go mix a drink. You can't hurt my feelings," said the factotum with his grin of pudgy good-humor.

"You've got friends out through the country that can be trusted with inside business, haven't you?" said the visitor as the door closed.

"In every state," was the positive affirmation. No mere boastfulness, this. Daniel Lurcock's political strength lay in the fact that he had become by virtue of psychological as well as financial gifts, a consulting lobbyist of national fame. Wherever there was a difficult or dangerous official stiutation, a shady deal to put over, a threatening scandal to suppress, a row imminent between politics and the business interests which might spill the beans and put good men in wrong, this Ulysses of the political underworld, knowing cities and the hearts of men, was urgently summoned. Thus he had established important and confidential connections everywhere and had bestowed and received favors which constituted a debt and a bond between himself and his allies all over the country, a series of notes payable on demand in good faith, service, and helpfulness.

"In every state," repeated the Secretary with appreciation. "I can use 'em. If they're right."

"They're right. What's up?"

"Purchase of hospital sites."

The other nodded. "Thought so. Where do you start?"

"Massachusetts."

Lurcock briefly consulted his remarkable memory. "I've got a firm for you," he announced. "Who'll handle it on your end?"

"I thought of Duke Forrest."

"What's the big idea?" asked the suddenly suspicious Lurcock, and added, as if answering himself; "He's got a hell of a good-looking wife."

"Nothing like that," disclaimed Gandy virtuously.

"Charley Madrigal was giving her a whirl for a time."

"He and Forrest are pretty thick."

"Think the Duke is safe?"

"Safe as anybody. He knows the ground there. Operated through New England with those booze release permits."

"I know all about that. He did his job. But, say, why not give Jeff, here" (he jerked his head toward the inner room) "a look-in on some of this?"

("He wants to get his bit from both ends," reflected the outraged Gandy; but this was no time to haggle.) "Certainly," he agreed. "Later on. There'll be enough to go around. The Old Man's taken quite a fancy to Forrest, too," he added. Thus they habitually referred to the President who was ten years younger than either of them. It marked the respect due his high office and the affection evoked by his amiable personality.

"You wanta keep it dark from the Old Man," warned Lurcock.

"That's easy."

"He's had a change of heart."

"How's that?" demanded the other, his ever wakeful suspicions startled.

"Since he's worked into this job of being President, he's off the old stuff."

"Sure! Of course. For publication."

"I'm telling you," insisted Lurcock. "Bill understands the game; he's no lily-finger. He knows that guys don't go into politics for their health and he never blamed the other fellow for getting his bit; he'd even give a friendly shove now and again, when, as, and if needed, provided it wasn't too raw. Bill was always broad-minded and practical, even though he never touched money himself, not even when it was slipped to him under cover. But now he's got religion."

"Jeest!" interjected the other, appalled. "What d'you mean?"

"Oh, not psalm-singing. Religion about his job. Read me a regular sermon the other day, all about what the Party expects of us and pulling together and playing the game on the level, now that we're in the Big League. Meant it, too."

"Second term stuff. That's what's biting him."

"Maybe. But as far as our little operations go, what he don't know won't hurt him."

"But isn't he liable to think it's queer that Forrest——"

"He's going to be too busy to think," prophesied Lurcock grimly. "Too busy with his job. The Old Man has developed a hunch for hard work. That's another angle of his change of heart."

"Start up the chariot and we'll all go to heaven together," chanted Gandy sardonically.

Lurcock raised his voice. "Hey, Jeff! Where are those damn drinks?"

"Right here, boss." Jeff Sims reappeared bearing a tray full of pleasant clinkings. It was he who gave them a toast in his thick, cheery accents.

"Here's to small risks and big profits."

"How are things on the Hill?" inquired Lurcock after drinking. Gandy was supposed to keep tabs on the Senate for the operators at the Crow's Nest, which he was able to do effectually through his former connections there.

"Quiet enough just now. There's always a little talk."

"Who's doing it?"

"The jay-walkers mostly."

"We've got that bunch where we want 'em under this administration," said Lurcock with satisfaction. "Every time one of 'em tries to insurge he gets a crack over the beezer with the gavel."

"They don't dare peep, them S. O. B's," cackled Jeff Sims.

"There's not so many that the Secret Service hasn't got something on."

"Can you blame 'em for not exactly loving you up on the Hill?" said the other with a short laugh.

"Me?" The unofficial potentate seemed innocently surprised. "What have I got to do with it?"

"That's what they want to know in the coat room."

"They've got nothing on me, anyway," reflected the other comfortably. "Anything I do, I do as a private citizen. I'm not a government official. Now, with you," he added spitting out the remains of a dead and mangled cigar, "it's different."

"What are you getting at?" Andy glared.

"Not a thing."

"I can take care of myself."

"I'll bet on it. And you've landed in the right place to do it."

"Look here, Dan Lur—"

But the other had raised a hamlike hand. "Now don't you get het up, Doc. I'm only telling you for your own good."

"Go on and tell me, then. Come down to cases," said the other in sulky defiance.

"Well, since you press me, I'd suggest that you go slow with your deals for a while. There's no harm in that, is there? It don't pay to advertise in some lines."

"What deals?" demanded Gandy.

Lurcock waved his hand. "Not inside the Department. I wouldn't question that. But anything outside that might be traceable. There was a rumor of some real estate in Califorina that you've been looking into."

"It's a God-damned lie, and you can mind you own business."

"All right, all *right*!" returned Lurcock, unruffled. "You needn't get peeved. You'll be around to the party to-morrow?"

The Secretary of Public Health hesitated. "Sure," he answered more amiably. "Send me a memo of that Detroit firm, will you?" He left.

Said Lurcock: "He's up to something."

"Sure, he is. What is the deal?"

"I don't just exactly know. I'm afraid of that guy, Jeff. His mouth waters when he talks business. That's a bad sign. He'll spill the beans so wide we'll all get scalded if we don't watch him."

Jeff Sims nodded solemnly. "Them damn amateurs!" he growled.

Reading 27

Main Street

Sinclair Lewis

Perhaps the greatest novelist of the 1920s was Sinclair Lewis. In his writings Lewis attacked many aspects of American life. His most famous novel was *Main Street*, in which he portrayed life in the small town as dull and suffocating for the creative individual. One critic claimed that "*Main Street* gave the country the whole inept, frustrated struggle of a period toward imitation culture." To a certain extent, this popular novel was an effective study of the standing clash between rural and urban values in American life, a theme which many writers have developed throughout the years. In this novel Carol, a doctor's wife, suffers from the sterility of life in the small town of Gopher Prairie.

In reading popular stories and seeing plays, asserted Carol, she had found only two traditions of the American small town. The first tradition, repeated in scores of magazines every month, is that the American village remains the one sure abode of friendship, honesty, and clean sweet marriageable girls. Therefore all men who succeed in painting in Paris or in finance in New York at last become weary of smart women, return to their native towns, assert that cities are vicious, marry their childhood sweethearts and, presumably, joyously abide in those towns until death.

The other tradition is that the significant features of all villages are whiskers, iron dogs upon lawns, gold bricks, checkers, jars of gilded cat-tails, and shrewd comic old men who are known as "hicks" and who ejaculate "Waal I swan." This altogether admirable tradition rules the vaudeville stage, facetious illustrators, and syndicated newspaper humor, but out of actual life it passed forty years ago. Carol's small town thinks not in hoss-swapping but in cheap motor cars, telephones ready-made clothes, silos, alfalfa, kodaks, phonographs, leather-upholstered Morris chairs, bridge-prizes, oil-stocks, motion-pictures, land-deals, unread sets of Mark Twain, and a chaste version of national politics.

With such a small-town life a Kennicott or a Champ Perry is content, but there are also hundreds of thousands, particularly women and young men, who are not at all content. The more intelligent young people (and the fortunate widows!) flee to the cities with agility and, despite the fictional tradition, resolutely stay there, seldom returning even for holidays. The most protesting patriots of the towns leave them in old age, if they can afford it, and go to live in California or in the cities.

The reason, Carol insisted, is not a whiskered rusticity. It is nothing so amusing!

It is an unimaginatively standardized background, a sluggishness of speech and manners, a rigid ruling of the spirit by the desire to appear respectable. It is contentment . . . the contentment of the quiet dead, who are scornful of the living for their restless walking. It is negation canonized as the one positive virtue. It is the prohibition of happiness. It is slavery self-sought and self-defended. It is dullness made God.

A savorless people, gulping tasteless food, and sitting afterward, coatless and thoughtless, in rocking-chairs prickly with inane decorations, listening to mechanical music, saying mechanical things about the excellence of Ford automobiles, and viewing themselves as the greatest race in the world.

She had inquired as to the effect of this dominating dullness upon foreigners. She remembered the feeble exotic quality to be found in the first-generation Scandinavians; she recalled the Norwegian Fair at the Lutheran Church, to which Bea had taken her. There, in the *bondestue,* the replica of a Norse farm kitchen, pale women in scarlet jackets embroidered with gold thread and colored beads, in black skirts with a line of blue, green-striped aprons, and ridged caps very pretty to set off a fresh face, had served *rommegrod og legse* —sweet cakes and sour milk pudding spiced with cinnamon. For the first time in Gopher Prairie Carol had found novelty. She had reveled in the mild foreignness of it.

But she saw these Scandinavian women zealously exchanging their spiced puddings and red jackets for fried pork chops and congealed white blouses, trading the ancient Christmas hymns of the fjords for "She's My Jazzland Cutie," being Americanized into uniformity, and in less than a generation losing in the grayness whatever pleasant new customs they might have added to the life of the town. Their sons finished the process. In ready-made clothes and ready-made high school phrases they sank into propriety, and the sound American customs had absorbed without one trace of pollution another alien invasion.

And along with these foreigners, she felt herself being ironed into glossy mediocrity, and she rebelled, in fear. The respectability of the Gopher Prairies, said Carol, is reinforced by vows of poverty and chastity in the matter of knowledge. Except for half a dozen in each town the citizens are proud of that achievement of ignorance which it is so easy to come by. To be "intellectual" or "artistic" or, in their own word, to be "highbrow," is to be priggish and of dubious virtue.

Large experiments in politics and in co-operative distribution, ventures requiring knowledge, courage, and imagination, do originate in the West and Middlewest, but they are not of the towns, they are of the farmers. If these heresies are supported by the townsmen it is only by occasional teachers, doctors, lawyers, the labor unions, and workmen like Miles Bjornstam, who are punished by being mocked as "cranks," as "half-baked parlor socialists." The editor and the rector preach at them. The cloud of serene ignorance submerges them in unhappiness and futility.

Here Vida observed, "Yes—well—Do you know, I've always thought that Ray would have made a wonderful rector. He has what I call an essentially religious soul. My! He'd have read the service beautifully! I suppose it's too late now, but as I tell him, he can also serve the world by selling shoes and—I wonder if we oughtn't to have family-prayers?"

Doubtless all small towns, in all countries, in all ages, Carol admitted, have a tendency to be not only dull but mean, bitter, infested with curiosity. In France or Tibet quite as much as in Wyoming or Indiana these timidities are inherent in isolation.

But a village in a country which is taking pains to become altogether standardized and pure, which aspires to succeed Victorian England as the chief mediocrity of the world, is no longer merely provincial, no longer downy and restful in its leaf-shadowed ignorance. It is a force seeking to dominate the earth, to drain the hills and sea of color, to set Dante at boosting Gopher Prairie, and to dress the high gods in Klassy Kollege Klothes. Sure of itself, it bullies other civilizations, as a traveling salesman in a brown derby conquers the wisdom of China and tacks advertisements of cigarettes over arches for centuries dedicated to the sayings of Confucius.

Such a society functions admirably in the large production of cheap automobiles, dollar watches, and safety razors. But it is not satisfied until the entire world also admits that the end and joyous purpose of living is to ride in flivvers, to make advertising-pictures of dollar watches, and in the twilight to sit talking not of love and courage but of the convenience of safety razors.

And such a society, such a nation, is determined by the Gopher Prairies. The greatest manufacturer is but a busier Sam Clark, and all the rotund senators and presidents are village lawyers and bankers grown nine feet tall.

Though a Gopher Prairie regards itself as a part of the Great World, compares itself to Rome and Vienna, it will not acquire the scientific spirit, the international mind, which would make it great. It picks at information which will visibly procure money or social distinction. Its conception of a community ideal is not the grand manner, the noble aspiration, the fine aristocratic pride, but cheap labor for the kitchen and rapid increase in the price of land. It plays at cards on greasy oil-cloth in a shanty, and does not know that prophets are walking and talking on the terrace.

If all the provincials were as kindly as Champ Perry and Sam Clark there would be no reason for desiring the town to seek great traditions. It is the Harry Haydocks, the Dave Dyers, the Jackson Elders, small busy men crushingly powerful in their common purpose, viewing themselves as men of the world but keeping themselves men of the cash-register and the comic film, who make the town a sterile oligarchy.

She had sought to be definite in analyzing the surface ugliness of the Gopher Prairies. She asserted that it is a matter of universal similarity; of flimsiness of construction, so that the towns resemble frontier camps; of neglect of natural advantages, so that the hills are covered with brush, the lakes shut off by railroads, and the creeks lined with dumping-grounds; of depressing sobriety of color; rectangularity of buildings; and excessive breadth and straightness of the gashed streets, so that there is no escape from gales and from sight of the grim sweep of land, nor any windings to coax the loiterer along, while the breadth which would be majestic in an avenue of palaces makes the low shabby shops creeping down the typical Main Street the more mean by comparison.

The universal similarity—that is the physical expression of the philosophy of dull safety. Nine-tenths of the American towns are so alike that it is the completest boredom to wander from one to another. Always, west of Pittsburg, and often, east of it, there is the same lumber yard, the same railroad station, the same Ford garage, the same creamery, the same box-like houses and two-story shops. The new, more conscious houses are alike in their very attempts at diversity: the same bungalows, the same square houses of stucco or tapestry brick. The shops show the same standardized, nationally advertised wares; the newspapers of sections three thousand miles apart have the same "syndicated features"; the boy in Arkansas displays just such a flamboyant ready-made suit as is found on just such a boy in Delaware, both of them iterate the same slang phrases from the same sporting-pages, and if one of them is in college and the other is a barber, no one may surmise which is which.

If Kennicott were snatched from Gopher Prairie and instantly conveyed to a town leagues away, he would not realize it. He would go down apparently the same Main Street (almost certainly it would be called Main Street); in the same drug store he would see the same young man serving the same ice-cream soda to the same young woman with the same magazines and phonograph records under her arm. Not till he had climbed to his office and found another sign on the door, another Dr. Kennicott inside, would he understand that something curious had presumably happened.

Finally, behind all her comments, Carol saw the fact that the prairie towns no more exist to serve the farmers who are their reason of existence than do the great capitals; they exist to fatten on the farmers, to provide for the townsmen large motors and social preferment; and, unlike the capitals, they do not give to the district in return for usury a stately and permanent center, but only this ragged camp. It is a "parasitic Greek civilization"—minus the civilization.

Reading 28

Babbitt

Sinclair Lewis

In *Babbitt* Sinclair Lewis depicted the promotional-minded, go-getter real estate man who could only think in terms of profit. Babbitt reveals not only his lack of depth but also the fact that when he is outside his area of professional competence he is a functional illiterate. Although the author sought in this novel to satirize the business mentality of the 1920s, he created a stereotype for all ages.

Babbitt spoke well—and often—at these orgies of commercial righteousness about the "realtor's function as a seer of the future development of the community, and as a prophetic engineer clearing the pathway for inevitable changes"—which meant that a real-estate broker could make money by guessing which way the town would grow. This guessing he called Vision.

In an address at the Boosters' Club he had admitted, "It is at once the duty and the privilege of the realtor to know everything about his own city and its environs. Where a surgeon is a specialist on every vein and mysterious cell of the human body, and the engineer upon electricity in all its phases, or every bolt of some great bridge majestically arching o'er a mighty flood, the realtor must know his city, inch by inch, and all its faults and virtues."

Though he did know the market-price, inch by inch, of certain districts of Zenith, he did not know whether the police force was too large or too small, or whether it was an alliance with gambling and prostitution. He knew the means of fire-proofing buildings and the relation of insurance-rates to fire-proofing, but he did not know how many firemen there were in the city, how they were trained and paid, or how complete their apparatus. He sang eloquently the advantages of proximity of school-buildings to rentable homes, but he did not know—he did not know that it was worth while to know—whether the city schoolrooms were properly heated, lighted, ventilated, furnished; he did not know how the teachers were chosen; and though he chanted "One of the boasts of Zenith is that we pay our teachers adequately," that was because he had read the statement in the *Advocate-Times*. Himself, he could not have given the average salary of teachers in Zenith or anywhere else.

He had heard it said that "conditions" in the County Jail and the Zenith City Prison were not very "scientific;" he had, with indignation at the criticism of Zenith, skimmed through a report in which the notorious pessimist Seneca Doane, the radical lawyer, asserted that to throw boys and young girls into a bull-pen crammed with men suffering from syphilis, delirium tremens, and insanity was not the perfect way of educating them. He had controverted the report by growling, "Folks that think a jail ought to be a bloomin' Hotel Thornleigh make me sick. If people don't like a jail, let 'em behave 'emselves and keep out of it. Besides, these reform cranks always exaggerate." That was the beginning and quite completely the end of his investigations into Zenith's charities and corrections; and as to the "vice districts" he brightly expressed it, "Those are things that no decent man monkeys with. Besides, smatter fact, I'll tell you confidentially: it's a protection to our daughters and to decent women to have a district where tough nuts can raise cain. Keeps 'em away from our own homes."

As to industrial conditions, however, Babbitt had thought a great deal, and his opinions may be coordinated as follows:

"A good labor union is of value because it keeps out radical unions, which would destroy property. No one ought to be forced to belong to a union, however. All labor agitators who try to force men to join a union should be hanged. In fact, just between ourselves, there oughtn't to be any unions allowed at all; and as it's the best way of fighting the unions, every business man ought to belong to an employers'-association and to the Chamber of Commerce. In union there is strength. So any selfish hog who doesn't join the Chamber of Commerce ought to be forced to."

In nothing—as the expert on whose advice families moved to new neighborhoods to live there for a generation—was Babbitt more splendidly innocent than in the science of sanitation. He did not know a malaria-bearing mosquito from a bat; he knew nothing about tests of drinking water; and in the matters of plumbing and sewage he was as unlearned as he was voluble. He often referred to the excellence of the bathrooms in the houses he sold. He was fond of explaining why it was that no European ever bathed. Some one had told him, when he was twenty-two, that all cesspools were unhealthy, and he still denounced them. If a client impertinently wanted him to sell a house which had a cesspool, Babbitt always spoke about it—before accepting the house and selling it.

When he laid out the Glen Oriole acreage development, when he ironed woodland and dipping meadow into a glenless, orioleless, sunburnt flat prickly with small boards displaying the names of imaginary streets, he righteously put in a complete sewage-system. It made him feel superior; it enabled him to sneer privily at the Martin Lumsen development, Avonlea, which had a cesspool; and it provided a chorus for the full-page advertisements in which he announced the beauty, convenience, cheapness, and supererogatory healthfulness of Glen Oriole. The only flaw was that the Glen Oriole sewers had insufficient outlet, so that waste remained in them, not very agreeably, while the Avonlea cesspool was a Waring septic tank.

The whole of the Glen Oriole project was a suggestion that Babbitt, though he really did hate men recognized as swindlers, was not too unreasonably honest. Operators and buyers prefer that brokers should not be in competition with them as operators and buyers themselves, but attend to their clients' interests only. It was supposed that the Babbitt-Thompson Company were merely agents for Glen Oriole, serving the real owner, Jake Offutt, but the fact was that Babbitt and Thompson owned sixty-two per cent of the Glen, the president and purchasing agent of the Zenith Street Traction Company owned twenty-eight per cent, and Jake Offutt (a gang-politician, a small manufacturer, a tobacco-chewing old farceur who enjoyed dirty politics, business diplomacy, and cheating at poker) had only ten per cent, which Babbitt and the Traction officials had given to him for "fixing" health inspectors and fire inspectors and a member of the State Transportation Commission.

But Babbitt was virtuous. He advocated, though he did not practise, the prohibition of alcohol; he praised, though he did not obey, the laws against motor-speeding; he paid his debts; he contributed to the church, the Red Cross, and the Y.M.C.A.; he followed the custom of his clan and cheated only as it was sanctified by precedent; and he never descended to trickery—though, as he explained to Paul Riesling:

"Course I don't mean to say that every ad I write is literally true or that I always believe everything I say when I give some buyer a good strong selling-spiel. You see—you see it's like this: In the first place, maybe the owner of the property exaggerated when he put it into my hands, and it certainly isn't my place to go proving my principal a liar! And then most folks are so darn crooked themselves that they expect a fellow to do a little lying, so if I was fool enough to never whoop the ante I'd get the credit for lying anyway! In self-defense I got to toot my own horn, like a lawyer defending a client—his bounden duty, ain't it, to bring out the poor dub's good points? Why, the Judge himself would bawl out a lawyer that didn't, even if they both knew the guy was guilty! But even so, I don't pad out the truth like Cecil Rountree or Thayer or the rest of these realtors. Fact, I think a fellow that's willing to deliberately up and profit by lying ought to be shot!"

Babbitt's value to his clients was rarely better shown than this morning, in the conference at eleven-thirty between himself, Conrad Lyte, and Archibald Purdy.

Reading 29

This Side of Paradise

F. Scott Fitzgerald

The 1920s was marked by a cynical attitude on the part of youth. Disillusioned by the results of World War I, young people questioned the basic values of American life. The result was a new permissiveness in sexual mores, skepticism toward materialism, and the doubting of established religion. F. Scott Fitzgerald was one of the most articulate interpreters of the state of mind of this so-called "lost generation," as the following selection shows.

Once he had been miraculously able to scent evil as a horse detects a broken bridge at night, but the man with the queer feet in Phoebe's room had diminished to the aura over Jill. His instinct perceived the fetidness of poverty, but no longer ferreted out the deeper evils in pride and sensuality.

There were no more wise men; there were no more heroes; Burne Holiday was sunk from sight as though he had never lived; Monsignor was dead. Amory had grown up to a thousand books, a thousand lies; he had listened eagerly to people who pretended to know, who knew nothing. The mystical reveries of saints that had once filled him with awe in the still hours of night, now vaguely repelled him. The Byrons and Brookes who had defied life from mountain tops were in the end but flaneurs and poseurs, at best mistaking the shadow of courage for the substance of wisdom. The pageantry of his disillusion took shape in a world-old procession of Prophets, Athenians, Martyrs, Saints, Scientists, Don Juans, Jesuits, Puritans, Fausts, Poets, Pacifists; like costumed alumni at a college reunion they streamed before him as their dreams, personalities, and creeds had in turn thrown colored lights on his soul; each had tried to express the glory of life and the tremendous significance of man; each had boasted of synchronizing what had gone before into his own rickety generalities; each had depended after all on the set stage and the convention of the theatre, which is that man, in his hunger for faith will feed his mind with the nearest and most convenient food.

Women—of whom he had expected so much; whose beauty he had hoped to transmute into modes of art; whose unfathomable instincts, marvellously incoherent and inarticulate, he had thought to perpetuate in terms of experience—had become merely consecrations to their own posterity. Isabelle, Clara, Rosalind, Eleanor, were all removed by their very beauty, around which men had swarmed, from the possibility of contributing anything but a sick heart and a page of puzzled words to write.

Amory based his loss of faith in help from others on several sweeping syllogisms. Granted that his generation, however bruised and decimated from this Victorian war, were the heirs of progress. Waving aside petty differences of conclusions which, although they might occasionally cause the deaths of several millions of young men, might be explained away—supposing that after all Bernard Shaw and Bernhardi, Bonar Law and Bethmann-Hollweg were mutual heirs of progress if only in agreeing against the ducking of witches— waiving the antitheses and approaching individually these men who seemed to be the leaders, he was repelled by the discrepancies and contradictions in the men themselves.

There was, for example, Thorton Hancock, respected by half the intellectual world as an authority on life, a man who had verified and believed the code he lived by, an educator of educators, an adviser to Presidents—yet Amory knew that this man had, in his heart, leaned on the priest of another religion.

And Monsignor, upon whom a cardinal rested, had moments of strange and horrible insecurity—inexplicable in a religion that explained even disbelief in terms of its own faith: if you doubted the devil it was the devil that made you doubt him. Amory had seen Monsignor go to the houses of stolid philistines, read popular novels furiously, saturate himself in routine, to escape from that horror.

And this priest, a little wiser, somewhat purer, had been, Amory knew, not essentially older than he.

Amory was alone—he had escaped from a small enclosure into a great labyrinth. He was where Goethe was when he began "Faust"; he was where Conrad was when he wrote "Almayer's Folly."

Amory said to himself that there was essentially two sorts of people who through natural clarity or disillusion left the enclosure and sought the labyrinth. There were men like Wells and Plato, who had, half unconsciously, a strange, hidden orthodoxy, who would accept for themselves only what could be accepted for all men—incurable romanticists who never, for all their efforts, could enter the labyrinth as stark souls; there were on the other hand sword-like pioneering personalities, Samuel Butler, Renan, Voltaire, who progressed much slower, yet eventually much further, not in the direct pessimistic line of speculative philosophy but concerned in the eternal attempt to attach a positive value to life. . . .

Amory stopped. He began for the first time in his life to have a strong distrust of all generalities and epigrams. They were too easy, too dangerous to the public mind. Yet all thought usually reached the public after thirty years in some such form: Benson and Chesterton had popularized Huysmans and Newman; Shaw had sugar-coated Nietzche and Ibsen and Schopenhauer. The man in the street heard the conclusions of dead genius through some one else's clever paradoxes and didactic epigrams.

Life was a damned muddle . . . a football game with every one off-side and the referee gotten rid of—every one claiming the referee would have been on his side. . . .

Progress was a labyrinth . . . people plunging blindly in and then rushing wildly back, shouting that they had found it . . . the invisible king—the *élan vital*—the principle of evolution . . . writing a book, starting a war, founding a school. . . .

Amory, even had he not been a selfish man, would have started all inquiries with himself. He was his own best example—sitting in the rain, a human creature of sex and pride, foiled by chance and his own temperament of the balm of love and children, preserved to help in building up the living consciousness of the race.

In self-reproach and loneliness and disillusion he came to the entrance of the labyrinth.

Another dawn flung itself across the river; a belated taxi hurried along the street, its lamps still shining like burning eyes in a face white from a night's carouse. A melancholy siren sounded far down the river.

. . .

The afternoon waned from the purging good of three o'clock to the golden beauty of four. Afterward he walked through the dull ache of a setting sun when even the clouds seemed bleeding and at twilight he came to a graveyard. There was a dusky, dreamy smell of flowers and the ghost of a new moon in the sky and shadows everywhere. On an impulse he considered trying to open the door of a rusty iron vault built into the side of a hill; a vault washed clean and covered with late-blooming, weepy watery-blue flowers that might have grown from dead eyes, sticky to the touch with a sickening odor.

Amory wanted to *feel* "William Dayfield, 1864."

He wondered that graves ever made people consider life in vain. Somehow he could find nothing hopeless in having lived. All the broken columns and clasped hands and doves and angels meant romances. He fancied that in a hundred years he would like having young people speculate as to whether his eyes were brown or blue, and he hoped quite passionately that his grave would have about it an air of many, many years ago. It seemed strange that out of a row of Union soldiers two or three made him think of dead loves and dead lovers, when they were exactly like the rest, even to the yellowish moss.

Long after midnight the towers and spires of Princeton were visible, with here and there a late-burning light—and suddenly out of the clear darkness the sound of bells. As an endless dream it went on; the spirit of the past brooding over a new generation, the chosen youth from the muddled, unchastened world, still fed romantically on the mistakes and half-forgotten dreams of dead statesmen and poets. Here was a new generation, shouting the old cries, learning the old creeds, through a revery of long days and nights; destined finally to go out into that dirty gray turmoil to follow love and pride; a new generation dedicated more than the last to the fear of poverty and the worship of success; grown up to find all Gods dead, all wars fought, all faiths in man shaken. . . .

Amory, sorry for them, was still not sorry for himself—art, politics, religion, whatever his medium should be, he knew he was safe now, free from all hysteria—he could accept what was acceptable, roam, grow, rebel, sleep deep through many nights. . . .

There was no God in his heart, he knew; his ideas were still in riot; there was ever the pain of memory; the regret for his lost youth—yet the waters of disillusion had left a deposit on his soul, responsibility and a love of life, the faint stirring of old ambitions and unrealized dreams. But—oh, Rosalind! Rosalind! . . .

"It's all a poor substitute at best," he said sadly.

And he could not tell why the struggle was worth while, why he had determined to use to the utmost himself and his heritage from the personalities he had passed. . . .

He stretched out his arms to the crystalline, radiant sky.

"I know myself," he cried, "but that is all."

Reading 30

Appearance of a Man

George Backer

The unprecedented prosperity of the decade, which some observers had assumed would banish poverty from the land, ended with the stock market crash of October 1929. In a matter of days more than $30 billion in stock values were lost, as the average price of leading securities more than halved. Thousands of individuals were immediately affected by the stock market debacle, most of them businessmen. This selection deals with the way the disaster was felt by one group of men.

"The governors of the Exchange will be meeting at two this afternoon to decide whether to open tomorrow morning. There are too many transactions that can't be cleared, and if they do open, it will almost certainly be disorderly."

Skeffington paused—the next bit of news relieved him of any shadow of responsibility or right to take part in further discussion of Keating's scheme. "The necessity for the decision is being communicated to Washington."

"Then the Exchange is to close? Until when?" Bromley was relieved. This was the responsible alternative to Jim's proposal. The market would get the chance it needed to recover. Things were to be as they had been. It should be kept shut for several days.

"The formal decision hasn't been taken, but I would rely on its being decided at two."

What did "communicated to Washington" mean? This was an element Keating knew nothing about, a new dimension to the problem for which he was not prepared. He felt naked, all of him exposed to danger. "What has Washington to do with it?"

Silence gave the answer before Skeffington said, "Perhaps nothing. I don't know."

Sargent's reaction was instant. Nuts! Washington was being called in to make the price the Skeffingtons got for an orderly opening respectable. His quick conviction brought clarity. His euphoria was over; he was in the jungle that was the reality from which he had emerged and which he had forgotten, and Skeffington and his Bank were the enemy. Here Sargent could function best, for the rules of this fight he fully understood. So that's why Skeffington wouldn't agree to joint support of the five and a half's because he actually thought he'd be able to take over Mid-American. Now Sargent wanted Keating, a fool and unimportant, to get out so that he could have Skeffington alone, face to face. He turned to Keating. "What it means to you is that you'd better forget about your consortium."

Skeffington took up the theme, "Yes, Mr. Keating, your idea came too late. Besides, it was impossible. Now, if you will, we can get to our business. The tentative agreement you have with Mr. Sargent for an exchange of stock —I think we can all agree that it should be forgotten."

The baldness and the tone horrified Bromley. Skeff wanted to punish Keating as if he were responsible for the market's actions.

Sargent did not let Keating answer. "That's a question for Jim and me." Skeffington mustn't get the impression that he could dictate. He turned to Keating. "Have you any stock left to exchange? I ask because you said the market couldn't hurt you."

Keating had hardly followed what they were saying; he was too aware that a moment ago he had been so sure because the future could be decided in this room. And now it couldn't, and not he but Washington, as unknown as chance, was to affect the future and his destiny. He looked at Skeffington, waiting for an answer, then at Sargent. These were figures at Bradley's calling "banco" in their small world that suddenly had only the power to decide the destiny of clerks and stock options. It wasn't his world. But why hadn't he known? And where was he supposed to go? What was he? But he must answer Sargent in their terms, until he knew more than that to be part of this now —of Mid-American—would be to be defeated. "What I said was true. My shares cost me exactly nothing. How was I to be hurt? If you remember, it was the directorship that brought about the question of the exchange of shares. If I was no longer interested in that"—that dead world, powerless, unattractive —"there'd be no question of a merger, would there?"

As long as it was Keating's decision, not Skeffington's, Sargent didn't care. "You mean you're no longer interested?"

Keating was standing now, ready to leave. "Roly, that went down the drain about three minutes ago." He nodded to Stephen. "Mr. Skeffington, do you want a letter to that effect for your files?"

It seemed to Keating that in the hour he had been out of the office every man in his business life had wanted to speak to him. Miss Thomas' list was in two columns of local and long-distance calls. It was wonderful how everyone wanted to tell him the market had gone to hell! Next to "Mr. H. Stein" was the number "3." Keating looked up. "Three times in an hour?"

Miss Thomas nodded. "The last was only a few minutes ago. And I didn't put it on the list, but Mr. Royce asked for you just after you left. Miss Swaine said it was awfully important, and would you go in as soon as you got back. I told her you'd gone to Mr. Bromley's."

"Thanks." He took the names and went into his own office to leave his coat. What Royce had on his mind was about as important to him as Skeffington's Mid-American business had been. They were the same type. They *looked* good—and that was all. These tall, gray-haired—and Sargent was only the tallest and grayest.

Coming out of his room, Keating stopped at Miss Thomas' desk. "I'll be in Royce's office if there's anything important, but don't put through anyone who's called already. Those are for later." If at all.

Royce was bending over the ticker in the classic pose when Keating came in. He looked up, but what had happened since he had tried to reach Keating had made a mockery of the warning and order he had proposed to give his partner. Now no rebuke to Keating, no order which would establish his authority could wipe out the utterly helpless feeling the last hour of cascading numbers on the tape had brought. He was almost glad to see his partner; he could at least ask him the question he had been unable to stop asking himself. What did this mean? Benson had told him that half their accounts were closed out. Not that that mattered much. "Have you had a look at the prices?"

"Not since I left Bromley's. The ticker was too far behind to mean anything then."

"And it hasn't caught up. Did they have anything to say?"

"The market won't open tomorrow. The excuse is that time is needed to clear today's transactions." That's just what it was: an excuse by the frightened.

"Isn't that a good idea?" Somebody had decided something. Royce felt less alone.

"Not as good as opening a strong recovery market." What power might really do! If only he'd been given the chance! Again the intimation of completion—the goal of substance he had been striving for—tightened his body.

"Would that be possible?"

"It could be if . . ." And the "if" made him see, as he stared at this nervous, shaken old man, that "they" did not have the power to let him save them—and himself. That was the truth he would have to learn to live with.

Royce was comforted somehow. Keating didn't seem to have an answer either. "No. I think no market and a strong statement from the President— but it must be *very* strong—can turn the corner."

Washington . . . the President. Keating remembered what he had said to Dan Kennedy about the primacy of industry with its right of ultimate decision, and the realization of how far from the truth he had been shook him. "Miss Swaine said there was a particular reason you wanted to see me." He had to get out of sight of this ugly old man before his control gave way.

"Yes. That was this morning. I thought then we ought to agree that on our own offerings we wouldn't be tempted to begin supporting them because they look cheap. That's academic now. Did you see the last price for Vir-Penn?"

"I didn't know it had opened." His remoteness from Vir-Penn, from participation in anything taking place anywhere, made the statement mechanical. But in his stomach was the warning of crisis.

"There was a sale of three thousand—came through about noon—at one-half the issue price."

"Do you know who got them?" Whoever the buyer was, he was fooling himself. All he was getting was three thousand shares, not last month's dream at half the price.

Royce shook his head, and Keating said, "I've got a long list of calls waiting."

Royce nodded agreement and dismissal. It had been a good meeting; he had learned a lot. And with the Exchange closed, there'd be time enough tomorrow to do what was necessary. Keating's back was that of a beaten man, but now that they'd had the sense to close the Exchange, Keating's back was no cause for anxiety. Tomorrow would be time enough even for his problems.

The worst was over. If the President and the Secretary of the Treasury—no, just the President—made a very strong statement . . . But suppose it wasn't enough? Suppose when they opened again there was another day like this? Half their accounts were gone already; prices *couldn't* come back. And if it went any further . . . After they'd closed down the Exchange once, what else could they do? Royce was conscious of being tired—so tired. If it didn't end today, there was no telling what would happen.

Reading 31

All the Best People

Sloan Wilson

The stock market collapse of 1929 triggered a catastrophic depression that spread throughout the land. One-third of the wage earners were soon out of work and almost everyone suffered in some way. Especially hard-hit were the businessmen who had never suffered want and were thus ill-prepared to meet the new situation. Men like Captain Stauffer in the following selection were used to living beyond their means, and they had difficulty understanding that money even for life's necessities was not available. Although many men in Stauffer's circumstances did go ahead and commit suicide, note his return to frontier American values as he sought to solve his problems.

Captain Stauffer was completely wiped out on Wall Street that terrible fall. The idea that he had no money, that is to say, no money at all except a few hundred dollars in the bank at Lake George Village, was bewildering. He could no longer pay the rent on his apartment in Washington, and could not afford the tuition of his children's schools. He could not make the last payment on the schooner he had built, and would lose the $50,000 he had already put into it. He no longer could get credit, even at small stores where he had traded for decades. Panicked by the thought that before long he might even be unable to feed his family, he called a friend in Washington to see if he could go back on active duty with the Navy, but the Navy too was cutting down and they were trying to get rid of officers rather than hire them. He had always thought that if he ever needed a civilian job, he could qualify as an expert on marine salvage work, but companies specializing in that were not employing anyone immediately after the crash. When the captain started to drive back to Lake George after his disastrous trip to New York, he had barely enough money to pay his hotel bill and to buy gasoline for his big Packard phaeton.

As he drove over the winding roads through Albany and Saratoga, the captain tried to formulate some plan with which to placate the panic he knew his wife would suffer when he told her what had happened. If she suggested that they could borrow on his life insurance, he would have to tell her that he already had done that in his last attempts to hang onto his falling stock, and that money had gone with the rest. Their only big asset was their cottage at Paradise Point and their share in the association which he had been unable to mortgage because of the complications of group ownership. If he sold the *Lady of the Lake* and his other boats and his cars, they might have enough cash to eat for many months and to rent some very small apartment. In Glens Falls the captain stopped at the garage of the dealer who had sold him his car a few months ago for $3,500. To his astonishment he was offered only $300, and that was to be paid with a note instead of cash. In such times it probably would be extremely difficult to sell a luxurious boat like the *Lady of the Lake* for any price soon, he realized, despite the fact that she was almost new and had cost $12,000 to convert into a fancy little yacht.

"What are we going to do?" Mary would ask, and with a terrible feeling in the pit of his stomach, Captain Stauffer realized that he had no answer. Recent headlines about men jumping out of windows on Wall Street flashed into his mind. For another month his life insurance would remain in effect without further payments, and despite the fact that he had been able to borrow only $30,000 on it, would pay close to $300,000 in the event of his death. There was a suicide clause in the policy, but a hunting accident would not be questioned if he left no note. The thought that for almost thirty days he would have this last desperate option open calmed the captain. Even worse than the fear of being unable to support his family was the guilt for having talked his wife out of the money she had inherited, and the thought of self-punishment was almost comforting.

Despite the chaos of his thoughts, Captain Stauffer's outward appearance had not changed at all when he drove his gleaming phaeton back to Paradise Point that fall. A meticulous dresser all his life, he had by habit sent his suits to the cleaner, and carefully knotted his tie under his stiff collar every morning during the panic. Although he normally was a fairly heavy drinker all through the days of Prohibition, he hadn't touched a drop since, as he thought of it, the floor had started to fall away under him. When he stepped from the car to tell his wife that he had lost all their money, he looked dapper and self-confident as ever.

"Hello, Harry," she said, giving him a kiss on the check. "Is it as bad as the papers say?"

"It's pretty bad," he replied, and taking her arm, led her into the house.

"Run outside and play," Mary said to Caroline who with Martha's aid was sewing a doll's dress on her mother's machine.

The daughter of a lawyer who considered himself a Virginia gentleman, Mary had been brought up to believe herself a lady of quality, one characteristic of which is the ability to take adversity well. She did not scream when her husband gave her the bad news, she did not cry, and she did not indulge in any recriminations. Feeling herself the heroine in a drama, she drew herself up and said, "We will survive somehow, even if we have to take in boarders. My grandparents did that after the Civil War."

Of course that wasn't a very practical plan because they were part owners of an inn next door which might well have a hard time finding enough boarders to survive, Captain Stauffer realized, but an impossible plan was better than none or the dark last resort he carried in the back of his mind.

"Yes, dear, we can always take in boarders," he said.

"You mustn't worry about this being your fault," Mary continued. "After all, it's happening all over the country to everybody."

Her words were correct according to her code, but after speaking them, Mary went into her bedroom and lay down. That night she had a terrible attack of asthma, a disease she had not suffered since childhood, and for months after she spent hours lying awake late at night staring into the darkness and gasping for breath.

The panic was affecting great numbers of people all over the country, as Mary had said, but Captain Stauffer found it maddening to note that it was actually improving the fortunes of his immediate neighbors, Laura Hoffman and Charles Campbell, whose incomes remained virtually stable while the price of almost everything fell. Part of the code of these people of course was a rule against discussing money even with close friends. Aware that in the elation of making millions on paper, he had often broken this rule, Captain Stauffer was now grateful for it. On the afternoon of his return from the wreckage of Wall Street, Laura Hoffman stopped in at his cottage with the gift of a giant puffball she had found in the woods, and her conversation consisted entirely of directions about how to cook it and make it taste like eggplant. That evening Charles and Christina stopped in with the news that several lead musket balls had been found near the center of a large oak tree the workmen had cut up for firewood, and Charles gave one to Caroline. Just before leaving Charles said, "Don't worry about the Point, Harry. The association is in fine shape, and we won't have to make any payments this year. We may be able to finish the wing for less than the estimates. I've stopped everything until the dust settles."

"I think that's wise," Captain Stauffer said. "I'm afraid you won't be able to count on me financially for some time."

"This storm will blow over," Charles said, slapping him on the back. "After all, they always do."

The fact that storms always blow over is of little help to drowned sailors, Captain Stauffer reflected morbidly the next week. The first snow had fallen the night before, and to prevent the pipes from freezing, all the water had been shut off. Laura Hoffman had gone back to Philadelphia, and the Campbells returned to Daytona Beach, where houses were renting for practically nothing, Charles said.

"How much is that?" Captain Stauffer asked.

"Big mansions that used to bring a thousand dollars a month are going for anything that will pay the taxes."

That of course would be beyond his reach, Captain Stauffer knew. He had listed his boats for sale, but the yacht broker had told him there was no action that fall at any price. When he paid his immediate bills in the village, Captain Stauffer figured he would be down to less than a hundred dollars of cash, and he still had no plans about where to go for the winter. With the water shut off and the cold winds beginning to rattle the many big windows of a cottage designed for coolness, not warmth, it was becoming abundantly clear that something had to be done soon. Weakened by the insomnia caused by her nightly bouts with asthma, Mary stayed almost all day in her room, uncomplaining but also without the ability to give comfort. The children huddled around the fireplace, still startled by the fact that Martha had gone. The day after he had returned from New York, the Captain had told Martha and his three other servants that he could no longer afford to pay or even to feed them, and had put them all on a train to Albany, where presumably they could find other jobs.

Captain Stauffer figured that his insurance would be good until November 21, but that it would be suspicious if he shot himself in a hunting accident on the last day it was in effect, or even on one of the very last days. On the dawn of November 16, after a night of hearing his wife's tortured attempts to breathe, Captain Stauffer said to her, "I think I'll go out and try to get a deer. I saw some tracks on the path up the mountain yesterday."

"That would be nice," she said. "Be careful."

"One thing I know is how to handle a gun," he said with a grim laugh, kissed her on her moist, wrinkled forehead and put on a heavy sheepskin jacket. From a rack in the study where his many graphs still showed his stocks heading for the moon, he took a Springfield rifle. The bullets were in the drawer of a fine old Chippendale cabinet he had inherited from his mother whose forefathers had brought it on a sailing vessel from England. Slipping a handful of the heavy brass cartridges into his pocket, he caught sight of a silver flask he had bought at Tiffany's the year before. Shaking it and finding it about half full, he put that in his pocket before picking up the gun and striding out to the path leading up the mountain.

It was not a day suited to his mood of despair, for bright sunshine was sparkling on the untrodden snow and the foliage on the sides of the mountains was as brilliant and varied in pattern as a Turkish rug. His boots made a pleasant sound as they crunched through the thin crust of snow on the path, and as he started to breathe hard from the exertion of climbing, the cold air stabbing into his lungs felt good. There actually were many deer tracks, and he decided to follow a set that looked fresh. To avoid giving suspicion of suicide, he wanted to make the hunting expedition look legitimate.

The tracks led Captain Stauffer away from the path, but they circled back to the top of the mountain. Remembering the time he and his friends had climbed there in evening dress to celebrate his latest triumph, he sat down, leaning the rifle against a tree, and unscrewed the top of his flask. He certainly had been a damn fool for many years, maybe all his life, he reflected, and if he had to commit suicide he wished he could leave a note which would make Mary grateful for the insurance. It was damn annoying, he thought, for a professional military man to have to leave his family with the impression that he was stupid enough to shoot himself by accident. With a grimace of disgust he loaded his gun. Stretching away to the narrows beneath him, the lake was an intense cobalt blue flecked with whitecaps, and he thought it might be fun to take one last sail out there, riding the bitter winds all the way up to Ticonderoga, perhaps, but all the Star boats had been laid up for the winter, and he didn't have time to launch and rig one, not unless he wanted to crowd his insurance deadline suspiciously close. The snow had turned the unforested land on Paradise Point white. Looking down at his cottage there, which had smoke pouring from its fieldstone chimney, Captain Stauffer was reminded of a Currier and Ives print of a pioneer's log house in the winter wilderness. His own forefathers had built farms in the virgin forest of Massachusetts long ago, and some of them in more recent times had moved west, building their own houses and growing most of their own food. If they had been able to survive without money in the wilderness, why couldn't he? What horrible weakness had suffused his blood, making him his own murderous enemy? His forefathers had been hunters capable of finding better targets. They would have thought it easy to survive on the banks of Lake George in an era when no Indians were stalking them, when the wars were all over, when there was really nothing important to worry about at all.

What would his pioneer forefathers have done? First they would board up the windows of the Cottage, and find some way of beefing up the walls of one room, at least, to keep out the winter winds. They would carry what water they needed in buckets from the lake. Instead of sitting here on the mountaintop preparing to murder themselves, they would be actively hunting deer, raccoons, hedgehogs, squirrels, rabbits, anything they could eat, and their children would be out fishing. They would be raising chickens, sheep, and hogs, and in the spring they would plant corn and other vegetables instead of roses and peonies in the formal gardens of Paradise Point.

While he was thinking all this, the deer which Captain Stauffer had been following circled back and entered a clearing almost a hundred yards away from him. Hearing the dainty click of hooves on the icy rock, Captain Stauffer looked up and saw that it was a good-sized stag. As the captain grabbed his rifle, the stag bounded over the trunk of a fallen oak, but Stauffer had always been an expert marksman, and the bullet he had meant for himself found its mark in the animal's heart. Stretched out on the snow, the stag kicked convulsively in the center of a growing pool of blood. Staring down into its fear-crazed eyes, Captain Stauffer decided not to shoot himself yet. That night he concluded that suicide should never be necessary for a man strong enough to carry a young stag home from the mountaintop and to drop it triumphantly at his children's feet.

That fall Captain Stauffer insulated the walls of his cottage with tarpaper and straw. Mary borrowed $2,000 from a sister in Virginia, and the children went to the public school in Lake George Village. Mary's asthma did not improve, and the children had constant colds, but as he labored with a bucksaw cutting firewood and hammered away at a large chicken coop in the top of his fancy new boathouse, Captain Stauffer realized he had probably never been healthier in his life.

Reading 32

Poor No More

Robert Ruark

The Depression had its impact upon all people but the lower strata of society were hardest hit. The South, which had never been really prosperous in the first place, felt the economic debacle quickly. This reading presents the impact of hard times upon a high school boy and his family in a North

From *Poor No More* by Robert C. Ruark. Copyright © 1959 by Robert C. Ruark. Reprinted by permission of Holt, Rinehart and Winston, Inc.

Carolina town. He has to sacrifice his dogs and gun, little enough compared
to what his elders are forced to do.

It was 1929, and the banks busted, and most folks followed the banks. It was
1929, and the wholesale groceries, having been gradually absorbed by the huge
chain stores, went bankrupt. It was 1929, and Richard Price, Craig's father,
had a nervous breakdown that further fruited into pneumonia and tuberculosis. It was 1929, and Sam Price died of cancer, and Caroline Price died of a
heart attack. Old Sam's house in New Truro was sold up for taxes, and Richard
Price lost his big square brick house in Kensington for the simple inability to
pay. Craig Price's mother, Lilian, caught adult measles, which left her with
an incurable heart weakness. And Craig Price, then a chubby sophomore in
high school, failed to make the Hi-Y Club, largely because of a shy unsociabil-
ity that approached surliness.

The events blurred in the boy's mind. Catastrophe piled on catastrophe,
until catastrophe became almost meaningless. Mills closed, banks sent their
respected presidents to jail for embezzlement, small stores filed bankruptcy
petitions, and a few people, hopelessly strangled by financial entanglement,
mustered up sufficient courage to shoot themselves, even in such a small
metropolis as Kensington. The economic downfall of the nation struck the
South with special impact, because this was feudal society in which nearly
everyone, except the poor folks, played Mr. Micawber and persisted in expect-
ing that Something Would Turn Up. The dream was over, but nobody cared
to wake up.

In one noble house on Front Street the stiff-necked owners burnt ancient
fine furniture during a harsh winter. Possibly they would not have sold the
furniture, out of pride, even had there been a buyer. Richard Price, after two
years' absence from his big brick house in the suburbs, moved back in as a
tenant because nobody else could afford to buy it. He built a partition in the
back hall, and converted the upstairs into separate apartments, which were
rented to schoolteachers and nurses. Craig was beginning to smoke cigarettes,
and to take an active interest in girls. Suddenly, thirteen-year-old Craig Price
sped to a knowledge of sex which his mother had not been able to impart from
her score of glossily graphic books and more vocally graphic lectures. The girls
upstairs had frequent visitors. At puberty, it occurred to Craig that the laughter and the later departures were not entirely of a cultural nature, especially
when he blundered upstairs one afternoon on some aimless errand and encoun-
tered one of the paying guests buck-naked in the presence of the family dentist,
who was equally unhampered by garment. His scientific experiment with
Eunice suddenly reformed in his mind, and he realized in one searing flash that

the business of baby production was not without its pleasurable diversion. The naked lady, decently clad once more, cornered him next day.

"Craig," she said, "I know you were upstairs yesterday. I'll give you a dollar not to tell your mother what you saw."

"Keep your goddamn dollar," he said. "I won't tell her anyway. But I *saw* you, and you *know* I saw you. I saw you naked in my house. You're a bad woman."

"Not a *bad* woman, Craig. Just a woman. You'll understand when you get older."

"I don't have to get older to understand," Craig said. "I don't ever want to see you again." Craig didn't know it, but he was incipiently in love, and had received his first wound.

The formerly naked lady shrugged. "All right, little boy," she said. "Go and tattle to your mother." Shortly thereafter she moved out. Craig never mentioned the matter to Lilian.

Seen through Craig's retrospective eyes, the years before he graduated from high school comprised almost pure fantasy. One year, when his mother was selling insurance—not life insurance, but the other kind, fire and theft, because his father was selling life insurance—he was left almost completely alone for most of his waking hours. This was still in the rooming house stage, as opposed to several other stages, such as when they later moved to a small house out-of-town so that Mother Lilian could run the kitchen in a suburban hotel. Late in the afternoon several merry gentlemen, obviously quite drunk, rapped on the back door which led to the upstairs apartments, and Craig answered.

"What's a little boy like you doing here in a place like this?" one of the soberer of the merry gentlemen asked.

"I live here," Craig said. "What do you want?"

The most-nearly-sober gentleman looked at his less sober companions. "But the manicurist in the hotel said that this was a . . ." He broke it off sharply, as he saw the boy's expression. "Come on, gents," he said. "Let's go. There's been a mistake somewhere. Sorry, son. Be seein' you."

Craig heard a roar of a motor as the wheels spun in the back yard. Then, a voice from upstairs: "Who was that, just left?"

"It's me, Craig. Some men came knocking on the door. They must of got the wrong house. They went away."

The voice from upstairs said, in a lower tone, to somebody else. "Goddammit, there goes dinner. Betsy called from the hotel and she . . ." the shrill voice dwindles to an angry buzz.

Shortly the phone rang, a taxi arrived, and two of the paying guests bustled out of the house.

It was almost impossible for the boy Craig to comprehend what was going on during the years from 1929 to 1931, while he completed his high school years, fell in love, was spurned, and lost his confidence in kissing games. He had seen his family go from two big cars to one ramshackle Ford without emotion. Sam had died finally of the cancer which possessed him, leaving Craig with a sense almost of relief that it was over. Miss Caroline's passing bothered him not at all. He didn't truly understand the failures of the banks; and the bankruptcy of his father's firm was past his knowledge, since the firm continued, but under a new management, and without his father. Food appeared on the table at regular intervals no matter where the family lived. He was warm in winter, well-clothed, and did tolerably well in high school, and did not object to riding a bicycle three miles a day to get there. But it was always a blur, the actual events that knuckled themselves into the floury whole. And the events were always staccato.

One day he came back from high school and was not met, as usual, by the dogs. He whistled and no dogs answered, to leap against him and give him the daily wet slap of eager tongue across the face. He went to look for his gun, and it was missing from its rack. Desperately he walked the fields, and searched the woods. When his father arrived that night Craig was panic-stricken.

"Somebody's stolen the dogs and my gun!" he cried. "I've looked everywhere, and . . ."

Richard Price's face was gray and deeply bitten by lines around the mouth.

"You may as well know," he said. "I had to sell the dogs. I got a good offer, and I had to make a turn. The man that wanted the dogs wanted a gun, too. He'll sell everything back to me if I can raise the money when the bird season's finished."

"You won't raise the money," Craig said. "You always say you will but you won't. What *right* have you got to sell my dogs and my gun?"

"I'm your *father*," Richard Price said very gently. "And I sold my own gun some time back."

Father and son looked at each other, and both turned away. Thereafter there was very little more to say.

With Grandpa Sam the parting had been different. The old man came back from his last trip North, where he had been taking radium treatments for an indisputable cancer which strangled him like an evilly flourishing weed. His skin was translucently waxen, and he was in unremitting pain. He managed a sickly grin when he got off the train, and as soon as he arrived at his son's now-rented house in Kensington he called Craig aside.

"Let's you and me walk down to the cowlot," he said, "and get away from the strangers."

The cow had gone from the cowlot—sold—and the pony had gone—sold —and the billy goat had gone, but the quail still whistled sweetly to each other, and the hollow croak of the rain crows could be heard in the patch of forest which braced the cowlot from behind. The cornstalks were sere and liver-spotted on the yellowed shucks, and a rabbit started, sat, and leisurely ran, as the old man and the boy walked along the path, time-trodden through the cornfield. Sam Price grunted from his pain, but walked the last hundred yards to the Jimson weed-choked cowlot and sat down on a split-rail fence.

"Ain't no need for me to tell you I'm going to die," he said. "And the sooner the better. I'm rotten with this thing. It's spread from my mouth up, and from my neck down. Even the doctors quit fooling me, up at Hopkins."

"But Grandpa, why? They must be able to do something, they got to be able to do something!"

"Nope, they can't do a dod-limbed thing. And anyhow, everybody's got to do it sometime—even you, my boy. One way's as good as the other when it comes time. In a way I'm glad. I never amounted to nothin', and what's more I didn't seem to care. I ploughed through seventy-odd years like a fieldhand who don't care if the crop makes or don't make."

The old man stopped for a moment, as pain knifed at him and slashed his face.

Reading 33

The Grapes of Wrath

John Steinbeck

The farmers of the Great Plains were hit by two disasters during the Depression. First, farm prices dropped 61 percent from 1929 to 1933. Secondly, a long drought created a dust bowl. Many farmers who lost their land through foreclosure made their way to California to work as migrant laborers. These "Okies" and "Arkies" often lived on the verge of starvation in squalid camps, while their children died of malnutrition. This famous selection from Steinbeck's *The Grapes of Wrath* indicts a society which has perfected advanced techniques to increase agricultural production but which destroys fruits and vegetables while people starve.

Along the rows, the cultivators move, tearing the spring grass and turning it under to make a fertile earth, breaking the ground to hold the water up near the surface, ridging the ground in little pools for the irrigation, destroying the weed roots that may drink the water away from the trees.

And all the time the fruit swells and the flowers break out in long clusters on the vines. And in the growing year the warmth grows and the leaves turn dark green. The prunes lengthen like little green bird's eggs, and the limbs sag down against the crutches under the weight. And the hard little pears take shape, and the beginning of the fuzz comes out on the peaches. Grape blossoms shed their tiny petals and the hard little beads become green buttons, and the buttons grow heavy. The men who work in the fields, the owners of the little orchards, watch and calculate. The year is heavy with produce. And men are proud, for of their knowledge they can make the year heavy. They have transformed the world with their knowledge. The short, lean wheat has been made big and productive. Little sour apples have grown large and sweet, and that old grape that grew among the trees and fed the birds its tiny fruit has mothered a thousand varieties, red and black, green and pale pink, purple and yellow; and each variety with its own flavor. The men who work in the experimental farms have made new fruits: nectarines and forty kinds of plums, walnuts with paper shells. And always they work, selecting, grafting, changing, driving themselves, driving the earth to produce.

And first the cherries ripen. Cent and a half a pound. Hell, we can't pick 'em for that. Black cherries and red cherries, full and sweet, and the birds eat half of each cherry and the yellowjackets buzz into the holes the birds made. And on the ground the seeds drop and dry with black shreds hanging from them.

The purple prunes soften and sweeten. My God, we can't pick them and dry and sulphur them. We can't pay wages, no matter what wages. And the purple prunes carpet the ground. And first the skins wrinkle a little and swarms of flies come to feast, and the valley is filled with the odor of sweet decay. The meat turns dark and the crop shrivels on the ground.

And the pears grow yellow and soft. Five dollars a ton. Five dollars for forty fifty-pound boxes; trees pruned and sprayed, orchards cultivated—pick the fruit, put it in boxes, load the trucks, deliver the fruit to the cannery—forty boxes for five dollars. We can't do it. And the yellow fruit falls heavily to the ground and splashes on the ground. The yellowjackets dig into the soft meat, and there is a smell of ferment and rot.

Then the grapes—we can't make good wine. People can't buy good wine. Rip the grapes from the vines, good grapes, rotten grapes, wasp-stung grapes. Press stems, press dirt and rot.

But there's mildew and formic acid in the vats.

Add sulphur and tannic acid.

The smell from the ferment is not the rich odor of wine, but the smell of decay and chemicals.

Oh, well. It has alcohol in it, anyway. They can get drunk.

The little farmers watched debt creep up on them like the tide. They sprayed the trees and sold no crop, they pruned and grafted and could not pick the crop. And the men of knowledge have worked, have considered, and the fruit is rotting on the ground, and the decaying mash in the wine vats is poisoning the air. And taste the wine—no grape flavor at all, just sulphur and tannic acid and alcohol.

This little orchard will be a part of a great holding next year, for the debt will have choked the owner.

This vineyard will belong to the bank. Only the great owners can survive, for they own the canneries too. And four pears peeled and cut in half, cooked and canned, still cost fifteen cents. And the canned pears do not spoil. They will last for years.

The decay spreads over the State, and the sweet smell is a great sorrow on the land. Men who can graft the trees and make the seed fertile and big can find no way to let the hungry people eat their produce. Men who have created new fruits in the world cannot create a system whereby their fruits may be eaten. And the failure hangs over the State like a great sorrow.

The works of the roots of the vines, of the trees, must be destroyed to keep up the price, and this is the saddest, bitterest thing of all. Carloads of oranges dumped on the ground. The people came for miles to take the fruit, but this could not be. How could they buy oranges at twenty cents a dozen if they could drive out and pick them up? And men with hoses squirt kerosene on the oranges, and they are angry at the crime, angry at the people who have come to take the fruit. A million people hungry, needing the fruit—and kerosene sprayed over the golden mountains.

And the smell of rot fills the country.

Burn coffee for fuel in the ships. Burn corn to keep warm, it makes a hot fire. Dump potatoes in the rivers and place guards along the banks to keep the hungry people from fishing them out. Slaughter the pigs and bury them, and let the putrescence drip down into the earth.

There is a crime here that goes beyond denunciation. There is a sorrow here that weeping cannot symbolize. There is a failure here that topples all our success. The fertile earth, the straight tree rows, the sturdy trunks, and the ripe fruit. And children dying of pellagra must die because a profit cannot be taken from an orange. And coroners must fill in the certificates—died of malnutrition —because the food must rot, must be forced to rot.

The people come with nets to fish for potatoes in the river, and the guards hold them back; they come in rattling cars to get the dumped oranges, but the kerosene is sprayed. And they stand still and watch the potatoes float by, listen to the screaming pigs being killed in a ditch and covered with quicklime, watch the mountains of oranges slop down to a putrefying ooze; and in the eyes of the people there is the failure; and in the eyes of the hungry there is a growing wrath. In the souls of the people the grapes of wrath are filling and growing heavy, growing heavy for the vintage.

Chapter 6

World War II

Reading 34

The Winds of War

Herman Wouk

World War II came to Europe in September 1939, when the British and French supported Poland against Nazi aggression. Most Americans believed that the nation could stay out of the conflict. But after France fell in June 1940, and Britain faced powerful Germany alone, many reluctantly accepted the idea that the United States had to provide some assistance to the British. Despite the fact that he was preparing to run for an unprecedented third term, President Roosevelt pushed Congress for a draft bill in 1940 and for appropriations for rearmament. In addition, he aided Britain by trading what were termed "obsolete" ships, planes, and guns. In the following the President discusses some of the problems he faced with his Berlin naval attaché, Victor Henry, a career Navy man, who had a ringside seat at all of the major events preceding and during World War II.

It was a shock for Victor Henry to see Franklin Roosevelt out from behind the desk in a wheelchair. The shirt-sleeved President was massive and power-ful-looking down to the waist; below that, thin seersucker trousers hung piti-fully baggy and loose on his fleshless thigh bones and slack lower legs. The crippled man was looking at a painting propped on a chair. Beside him stood the Vice Chief of Naval Operations for Air, whom Victor Henry knew well: a spare withered little naval aviator, one of the surviving pioneers, with a lipless mouth, a scarred red face, and ferocious tangled white eyebrows.

"Hello there!" The President gave Victor Henry a hearty handshake, his grip warm and damp. It was a steamy day, and though the windows of the oval study were open, the room was oppressively hot. "You know Captain Henry, of course, Admiral? His boy's just gotten his wings at Pensacola. How about this picture, Pug? Like it?"

Inside the heavy ornate gold frame, a British man-o'-war under full sail tossed on high seas beneath a storm-wracked sky and a lurid moon. "It's fine, Mr. President. Of course I'm a sucker for sea scenes."

"So am I, but d'you know he's got the rigging wrong?" The President accurately pointed out the flaws, with great relish for his own expertise. "Now how about that, Pug? All the man had to do was paint a sailing ship—that was his whole job—and he got the rigging wrong! It's positively *unbelievable* what people will do wrong, given half a chance. Well, that thing's not going to hang in here."

During all this, the admiral was training his eyebrows like weapons at Victor Henry. Years ago, in the Bureau of Ordnance, they had violently disagreed over the deck plating on the new carriers. Junior though he was, Henry had carried his point, because of his knowledge of metallurgy. The President now turned his chair away from the painting, and glanced at a silver clock on his desk shaped like a ship's wheel. "Admiral, what about it? Are we going to put Pug Henry to work on that little thing? Will he do?"

"Well, if you assigned Pug Henry to paint a square-rigger, Mr. President," the admiral replied nasally, with a none too kind look at Pug, "you might not recognize it, but he'd get the rigging right. As I say, a naval aviator would be a far more logical choice, sir, but—" He gestured reluctant submission, with an upward chop of a hand.

The President said, "We went through all that. Pug, I assume somebody competent is tending shop for you in Berlin?"

"Yes, sir."

Roosevelt gave the admiral a glance which was a command. Picking his white hat off a couch, the admiral said, "Henry, see me at my office tomorrow morning at eight."

"Aye aye, sir."

Victor Henry was left alone with the President of the United States. Roosevelt sighed, smoothed his thin rumpled gray hair, and rolled himself to his desk. Victor Henry now noticed that the President did not use an ordinary invalid's wheelchair, but an odd piece of gear, a sort of kitchen chair on wheels, in and out of which he could easily slide himself. "Golly, the sun's going down, and it's still sweltering in here." Roosevelt sounded suddenly weary, as he contemplated papers piled on the desk. "Isn't it about time for a drink? Would you like a martini? I'm supposed to mix a passable martini."

"Nothing better, sir."

The President pressed a buzzer. A grizzled tall Negro in a gray gabardine jacket appeared and deftly gathered papers and folders out of various trays, while Roosevelt pulled wrinkled papers from one pocket and another, made quick pencilled notes, jabbed papers on a spike and threw others in a tray. "Let's go," he said to the valet. "Come along, Pug."

All down one long hall, and in the elevator, and down another hall, the President glanced at papers and scrawled notes, puffing at the cigarette holder in his teeth. His gusto for the work was evident, despite the heavy purple fatigue smudges under his eyes and the occasional deep coughs racking his chest. They arrived in a small dowdy sitting room hung with sea paintings. "That thing isn't going to end up in here either," said the President. "It's going in the cellar." He handed all the papers to the valet, who wheeled a chromium-stripped bar beside his chair and left.

"Well, how was the wedding, Pug? Did your boy get himself a pretty bride?" said the President in chatty and warm, if faintly lordly tones, measuring out gin and vermouth like an apothecary. Henry thought that perhaps the cultured accent made him sound more patronizing than he intended to be. Roosevelt wanted to know about the Lacouture house, and wryly laughed at Victor Henry's account of his argument with the congressman. "Well, that's what we're up against here. And Ike Lacouture's an intelligent man. Some of them are just contrary and obstinate fools. If we get Lacouture in the Senate, he'll give us real trouble."

A very tall woman in a blue-and-white dress came in, followed by a small black dog. "Just in time! Hello there, doggie!" exclaimed the President, scratching the Scottie's head as it trotted up to him and put its paws on the wheelchair. "This is the famous Pug Henry, dear."

"Oh? What a pleasure." Mrs. Roosevelt looked worn but energetic: an imposing, rather ugly woman of middle age with fine skin, a wealth of soft hair, and a smile that was gentle and sweet, despite the protruding teeth stressed in all the caricatures. She firmly shook hands, surveying Pug with the astute cool eyes of a flag officer.

"The Secret Service has an unkind name for my dog," Roosevelt said, handing his wife a martini. "They call him The Informer. They say he gives away where I am. As though there were only one little black Scottie in the world. Eh, Fala?"

"What do you think of the way the war's going, Captain?" said Mrs. Roosevelt straight off, sitting in an armchair and holding the drink in her lap.

"It's very bad, ma'am, obviously."

Roosevelt said, "Are you surprised?"

Pug took a while to answer. "Well, sir, in Berlin they were mighty sure that the western campaign would be short. Way back in January, all their government war contracts had a terminal date of July first. They thought it would all be over by then and they'd be demobilizing."

Roosevelt's eyes widened. "That fact was never brought to my attention. That's extremely interesting."

Mrs. Roosevelt said, "Meantime, are they suffering hardships?"

Victor Henry described the "birthday present for the Führer" drive, collecting household tin, copper, and bronze; the newsreel of Göring adding busts of himself and Hitler to a mountain of pots, pans, and irons, and washtubs; the death penalty announced for collectors caught taking anything for their own use; the slogan, *One pan per house; ten thousand tons for the Führer.* He talked of snowbound Berlin, the lack of fuel, the food rationing, the rule that a spoiled frozen potato had to be bought with each good one. It was against the law, except for foreigners and sick people, to hail a taxi in Berlin. Russian food deliveries were coming in slowly, if at all, so the Nazis were wrapping butter from Czechoslovakia in Russian-printed packages to foster the feeling of Soviet support. The "war-time beer," a uniform brew reduced in hops and alcohol content, was undrinkable, but the Berliners drank it.

"They've got a 'wartime soap' too," Pug said. "*Einheitsseife.* When you get into a crowded German train it's not much in evidence."

Roosevelt burst out laughing. "Germans are getting a bit ripe, eh? I love that. *Einheitsseife!*"

Pug told jokes circulating in Berlin. In line with the war effort speed-up, the Führer had announced that the period of pregnancy henceforth would be three months. Hitler and Göring, passing through conquered Poland, had stopped at a wayside shrine. Pointing to the crucified Christ, Hitler asked Göring whether he thought that would be their final fate. "*Mein Führer,* we are perfectly safe," Göring said. "When we are through there will be no wood or iron left in Germany."

Roosevelt guffawed at the jokes and said that there were far worse ones circulating about himself. He asked animated questions about Hitler's mannerisms in the meeting at Karinhall.

Mrs. Roosevelt interjected in a sharp serious tone, "Captain, do you think that Mr. Hitler is a madman?"

"Ma'am, he gave the clearest rundown on the history of central Europe I've ever heard. He did it off the cuff, just rambling along. You might think his version entirely cockeyed, but it all meshed together and ticked, like a watch."

"Or like a time bomb," said the President.

Pug smiled at the quick grim joke, and nodded. "This is an excellent martini, Mr. President. It sort of tastes like it isn't there. Just a cold cloud."

Roosevelt's eyebrows went up in pride and delight. "You've described the *perfect* martini! Thank you."

"You've made his evening," said Mrs. Roosevelt.

Roosevelt said, "Well, my dear, even the Republicans would agree that as a President, I'm a good bartender."

It wasn't much of a jape, but it was a presidential one, so Pug Henry laughed. The drink, the cosiness of the room, the presence of the wife and the dog, and the President's naïve pleasure in his trivial skill, made him feel strangely at home. The little black dog was the homiest touch; it sat worshipping the crippled President with a bright stare, now and then running a red tongue over its nose or shifting its look inquiringly to Pug.

Sipping his martini, his pose in the wheelchair as relaxed as before, but the patrician tones subtly hardening for business, Roosevelt said, "Do you think the British will hold out, Pug, if the French collapse?"

"I don't know much about the British, sir."

"Would you like to go there for a spell as a naval observer? Possibly after you've had a month or so back in Berlin?"

Hoping that Franklin Roosevelt was in as pleasant a mood as he seemed, Victor Henry took a plunge. "Mr. President, any chance of my not going back to Berlin?"

Roosevelt looked at the naval captain for an uncomfortable five or ten seconds, coughing hard. His face sobered into the tired gravity of the portraits that hung in post offices and naval stations.

"You go back there, Pug."

"Aye aye, sir."

"I know you're a seafaring man. You'll get your sea command."

"Yes, Mr. President."

"I'd be interested in your impressions of London."

"I'll go to London, sir, if that's your desire."

"How about another martini?"

"Thank you, sir, I'm fine."

"There's the whole question of helping the British, you see, Pug." The President rattled the frosty shaker and poured. "No sense sending them destroyers and planes if the Germans are going to end up using them against us."

Mrs. Roosevelt said with a silvery ring in her voice, "Franklin, you know you're going to help the British."

The President grinned and stroked the Scottie's head. Over his face came the look of complacent, devilish slyness with which he had suggested buying the Allied ocean liners—eyebrows raised, eyes looking sidewise at Pug, mouth corners pulled far up. "Captain Henry here doesn't know it yet, but he's going to be in charge of getting rid of those old, useless, surplus Navy dive bombers. We badly need a housecleaning there! No sense having a lot of extra planes cluttering up our training stations. Eh, Captain? Very untidy. Not shipshape."

"Is that definite at last? How wonderful," said Mrs. Roosevelt.

"Yes. Naturally the aviators didn't want a 'black shoe' to handle it." Roosevelt used the slang with self-conscious pleasure. "So naturally I picked one. Aviators all stick together and they don't like to part with planes. Pug will pry the machines loose. Of course it may be the end of me if word gets out. *That'll* solve the third-term question! Eh? What's your guess on that one, Pug? Is that man in the White House going to break George Washington's rule and try for a third term? Everybody seems to know the answer but me."

Victor Henry said, "Sir, what I know is that for the next four years this country is going to need a strong Commander-in-Chief."

Roosevelt's mobile pink face turned grave and tired again, and he coughed, glancing at his wife. He pressed a buzzer. "Somebody the people aren't bored with, Pug. A politician exhausts his welcome after a while. Like an actor who's been on too long. The good will ebbs away and he loses his audience." A Navy lieutenant in dress blues with gold shoulder loops appeared in the doorway. Roosevelt offered his hand to Victor Henry. "That Sumner Welles thing didn't come to anything, Pug, but our conscience is clear. We made the effort. You were very helpful."

"Aye aye, sir."

"Welles wasn't as impressed with Hitler as you evidently were."

"Sir, he's more used to being around great men."

A peculiar flash, not wholly pleasant, came and went in the President's tired eyes. "Good-bye, Pug."

Reading 35

From Here to Eternity

James Jones

On Sunday, December 7, 1941, "a date which will live in infamy," Secretary of State Cordell Hull was receiving in his office Japanese envoys with their latest answer in a long series of diplomatic exchanges, when he was advised of the attack on Pearl Harbor. Thus, the decision for war or peace was made by the Japanese. Although the signs of approaching war were numerous and some journalists had predicted its coming, most Americans were shocked when it finally came and were horrified that war had been initiated by a sneak attack while diplomatic efforts were still in progress. Before the day was over, 19 of 94 naval vessels at Pearl Harbor were sunk or disabled and 150 planes were destroyed. Military dead totalled 2,335, and civilian deaths exceeded 1200. The following describes the reaction of a group of soldiers who were on the scene when the war began.

It was a typical Sunday morning breakfast, for the first weekend after payday. At least a third of the Company was not home. Another third was still in bed asleep. But the last third more than made up for the absences in the loudness of their drunken laughter and horseplay and the clashing of cutlery and halfpint milk bottles.

Warden was just going back for smconds on both hotcakes and eggs, with that voracious appetite he always had when he was drunk, when this blast shuddered by under the floor and rattled the cups on the tables and then rolled on off across the quad like a high wave at sea in a storm.

He stopped in the doorway of the KP room and looked back at the messhall. He remembered the picture the rest of his life. It had become very quiet and everybody had stopped eating and looked up at each other.

"Must be doin some dynamitin down to Wheeler Field," somebody said tentatively.

"I heard they was clearin some ground for a new fighter strip," somebody else agreed.

That seemed to satisfy everybody. They went back to their eating. Warden heard a laugh ring out above the hungry gnashings of cutlery on china, as he turned back into the KP room. The tail of the chow line was still moving past the two griddles, and he made a mental note to go behind the cooks' serving table when he bucked the line this time, so as not to make it so obvious.

That was when the second blast came. He could hear it a long way off coming toward them under the ground; then it was there before he could move, rattling the cups and plates in the KP sinks and the rinsing racks; then it was gone and he could hear it going away northeast toward the 21st Infantry's football field. Both the KPs were looking at him.

He reached out to put his plate on the nearest flat surface, holding it carefully in both hands so it would not get broken while he congratulated himself on his presence of mind, and then turned back to the messhall, the KPs still watching him.

As there was nothing under the plate, it fell on the floor and crashed in the silence, but nobody heard it because the third groundswell of blast had already reached the PX and was just about to them. It passed under, rattling everything, just as he got back to the NCOs' table.

"This is it," somebody said quite simply.

Warden found that his eyes and Stark's eyes were looking into each other. There was nothing on Stark's face, except the slack relaxed peaceful look of drunkenness, and Warden felt there must not be anything on his either. He pulled his mouth up and showed his teeth in a grin, and Stark's face pulled up his mouth in an identical grin. Their eyes were still looking into each other.

Warden grabbed his coffee cup in one hand and his halfpint of milk in the other and ran out through the messhall screen-door onto the porch. The far door, into the dayroom, was already so crowded he could not have pushed through. He ran down the porch and turned into the corridor that ran through to the street and beat them all outside but for one or two. When he stopped and looked back he saw Pete Karelsen and Chief Choate and Stark were all right behind him. Chief Choate had his plate of hotcakes-and-eggs in his left hand and his fork in the other. He took a big bite. Warden turned back and swallowed some coffee.

Down the street over the trees a big column of black smoke was mushrooming up into the sky. The men behind were crowding out the door and pushing those in front out into the street. Almost everybody had brought his bottle of milk to keep from getting it stolen, and a few had brought their coffee too. From the middle of the street Warden could not see any more than he had seen from the edge, just the same big column of black smoke mushrooming up into the sky from down around Wheeler Field. He took a drink of his coffee and pulled the cap off his milk bottle.

"Gimme some of that coffee," Stark said in a dead voice behind him, and held up his own cup. "Mine was empty."

He turned around to hand him the cup and when he turned back a big tall thin red-headed boy who had not been there before was running down the street toward them, his red hair flapping in his self-induced breeze, and his knees coming up to his chin with every step. He looked like he was about to fall over backwards.

"Whats up, Red?" Warden hollered at him. "Whats happening? Wait a minute! Whats going on?"

The red-headed boy went on running down the street concentratedly, his eyes glaring whitely wildly at them.

"The Japs is bombing Wheeler Field!" he hollered over his shoulder. "The Japs is bombing Wheeler Field! I seen the red circles on the wings!"

He went on running down the middle of the street, and quite suddenly right behind him came a big roaring, getting bigger and bigger; behind the roaring came an airplane, leaping out suddenly over the trees.

Warden, along with the rest of them, watched it coming with his milk bottle still at his lips and the twin red flashes winking out from the nose. It came over and down and up and away and was gone, and the stones in the asphalt pavement at his feet popped up in a long curving line that led up the curb and puffs of dust came up from the grass and a line of cement popped out of the wall to the roof, then back down the wall to the grass and off out across the street again in a big S-shaped curve.

With a belated reflex, the crowd of men swept back in a wave toward the door, after the plane was already gone, and then swept right back out again pushing the ones in front into the street again.

Above the street between the trees Warden could see other planes down near the smoke column. They flashed silver like mirrors. Some of them began suddenly to grow larger. His shin hurt from where a stone out of the pavement had popped him.

"All right, you stupid fucks!" he bellowed. "Get back inside! You want to get your ass shot off?"

Down the street the red-haired boy lay sprawled out floppy-haired, wild-eyed, and silent, in the middle of the pavement. The etched line on the asphalt ran up to him and continued on on the other side of him and then stopped.

"See that?" Warden bawled. "This aint jawbone, this is for record. Thems real bullets that guy was usin."

The crowd moved reluctantly back toward the dayroom door. But one man ran to the wall and started probing with his pocketknife in one of the holes and came out with a bullet. It was a .50 caliber. Then another man ran out in the street and picked up something which turned out to be three open-end metal links. The middle one still had a .50 caliber casing in it. The general movement toward the dayroom stopped.

"Say! Thats pretty clever," somebody said. "Our planes is still usin web machinegun belts that they got to carry back home!" The two men started showing their finds to the men around them. A couple of other men ran out into the street hurriedly.

"This'll make me a good souvenir," the man with the bullet said content-edly. "A bullet from a Jap plane on the day the war started."

"Give me back my goddam coffee!" Warden hollered at Stark. "And help me shoo these dumb bastards back inside!"

"What you want me to do?" Chief Choate asked. He was still holding his plate and fork and chewing excitedly on a big bite.

"Help me get em inside," Warden hollered.

Another plane, on which they could clearly see the red discs, came skidding over the trees firing and saved him the trouble. The two men hunting for metal links in the street sprinted breathlessly. The crowd moved back in a wave to the door, and stayed there. The plane flashed past, the helmeted head with the square goggles over the slant eyes and the long scarf rippling out behind it and the grin on the face as he waved, all clearly visible for the space of a wink, like a traveltalk slide flashed on and then off of a screen.

Warden, Stark, Pete and the Chief descended on them as the crowd started to wave outward again, blocking them off and forcing the whole bunch inside the dayroom.

The crowd milled indignantly in the small dayroom, everybody talking excitedly. Stark posted himself huskily in the doorway with Pete and the Chief flanking him. Warden gulped off the rest of his coffee and set the cup on the magazine rack and pushed his way down to the other end and climbed up on the pingpong table.

"All right, all right, you men. Quiet down. Quiet down. Its only a war. Aint you ever been in a war before?"

Reading 36

Harvest of Hate

Georgia Day Robertson

On the home front World War II was fought without the hysteria and the
suspension of civil liberties so common in World War I. The one exception
was in the treatment on the West Coast of Americans of Japanese ancestry.
More than 110,000 such persons (of whom some 70,000 were American-
born) were forced to leave their homes, farms, and businesses with little
advance warning and often at great financial loss. They were sent to reloca-
tion camps away from the Coast. The federal government ultimately com-
pensated them in some small part for the monetary losses they suffered, but
nothing could repay them for the insult to human dignity they endured, as
this passage documents.

There was a mountainous heap of baggage on the platform beside the train,
where men were busily loading the baggage car. More people were arriving all
the time struggling with their bags and bundles of bedding, some brought to
the station by friends, some who came by streetcar.

There were young and old, rich and poor, weak and strong. The fifteen
hundred persons brought together by Army orders were from all stations of
life. There were humble peasant farmers in dark suits and white shirts and
wives in chain store dresses. There were the well-to-do and sophisticated city
dwellers with all the style and savoir faire of the elite. There was a small group
of college girls in bright sweaters and sleek slacks, one with her identification
tag and her Phi Beta Kappa key mingling with ironic intimacy on her sweater
front. There were high school boys, scowling and angry over the stupidity of
it all, and young men from the University cut deep by the knife thrusts of
suspicion aimed at them. There were babies in baskets, and a bride and groom
who had married at the last minute to keep from being sent to different camps.

There were the old. And the crippled. And the blind. There was an old
man dying of cancer. And one on crutches barely able to stand. Some crippled
with rheumatism and others worn out from age and hard work. Pathetic
figures.

There were little tots toddling on their first uncertain steps, already tired
and fretful, reflecting in their unhappy faces the strain under which their

parents had labored the past few days. Anxious lines around the eyes of tired fathers and mothers as they tried to comfort their children and wondered what was in store for them. Would there be good food, or any food? Milk? Would there be medical care? What would happen to their little ones now the parents were no longer able to look to their welfare?

There were quiet, acquiescent little women. Issei women. What flight of the imagination would be required to regard them as dangerous!

The military dragnet had been no respecter of persons. It had been drawn through the designated area with merciless efficiency, into the sanctuary of the old and infirm as well as the able, and had dragged them forth from the comfort and warmth of their firesides and beds. Here they stood, many with difficulty, desolate and shivering in the chill evening air from the sea, waiting to entrain for internment—and, for some, eventual death. Pullman accommodations had been provided for the sick and aged, and they were being put on board as rapidly as possible.

The swarming people who filled the platform to overflowing were unusually orderly for such a large number under difficult circumstances; and there was something incongruous in the presence of military police stationed at intervals the entire length of the platform. Towering over this throng of subdued little people, they looked as much out of place as stage settings inadvertently left from a previous act. The young people eyed these guards with unbelief and resentment.

There was a veteran of World War I limping about on an ill-fitting artificial foot; he had left his own in France a quarter of a century before. He was wearing a worn and faded overseas cap at a jaunty angle and was stumping about talking to everyone, trying to bolster morale.

"Heh! Where you going, Charley?" someone yelled.

"Military secret," the vet retorted with a resounding laugh which brought some smiles where scowls had been.

There was Mr. Imoto, dressed in new tweeds and flashy tan oxfords, looking very much as if he were starting on a world tour. His expensive new cowhide luggage stood out among the worn suitcases and lumpy bundles like "a Nisei at a meeting of the Native Sons," Tad quipped when he saw it. Tad had found Bill Harada who, in a neat gray suit and navy tie with tiny white dots, was leaning comfortably against the station, smoking a cigarette. Although the two were worlds apart in their opinion and reaction to what was happening to them, they liked each other and the University was a common bond between them. They would see much of each other in the months ahead.

Reading 37

The War Lover

John Hersey

In attaining victory in Asia and Europe some 15 million American boys entered the Armed Forces. To many of them their military career was the high point of their lives, and later they looked back upon their military service with fondness. This was especially true of those who saw little combat. Some men, however, as has been true in all wars, loved combat and after distinguishing themselves on the battlefield could never again adjust to the peacetime world. The probing of the psyche of a war lover, a bomber pilot in the European theater, is the subject of the following.

"There it was, Bo. What I'd come, through agony, to know about Dugger, and what I'd thought all along about your pilot. The stuffing came right out of him." Daphne stood up, and she was angry in a way I'd never seen her. "Why do you men have a conspiracy of silence about this part of war, about the pleasure of it?" She was unusually disturbed. She said men pretended that battle was all tragedy—separation, terrible living conditions, fear of death, diarrhea, lost friends, wounds bravely borne, sacrifice, patriotism. "Why do you keep silent about the reason for war? At least, what *I* think is the reason for war: that some men enjoy it, some men enjoy it too much." She said she didn't mean just the life of campaigns, getting away from everything humdrum, from responsiblities, from having to take care of others. "More than that," she said, "I mean, the pleasure your pilot gets." She said something about the gratification that wells up out of "the dark slimy place of toads and snakes and hairy men"—from deep, deep down. At one point she said, "I think we ought to worry less about the future life, in peacetime, of the ones who break down in battle, and more about what's going to come of those who enjoy it too much. They're going to inflict their curse on the rest of us in peacetime. . . . Knives, billies; all that . . . They're going to pass it on to their children. We'll have other wars. Oh, Bo, I don't know what we can do about these men, how you can educate this thing out of them, or stamp it out, or heal it out— or whether you can get rid of it at all." She just had a feeling, a woman's feeling, that this was where all the trouble came from. We couldn't have a real peace while these men still had that drive in them. "Diplomacy won't make peace; diplomacy's just a mask." And she said, "Economic systems, ideologies —excuses."

But I wasn't ready, yet, to think about all this that Daphne was so vehemently pouring out. I was feeling bruised and sullen, and I said, "If he's so horrible, why did you undress for him?"

Daphne blushed; a hot red glow of shame burned her face. At least I thought at first it was shame. Partly it was, I still believe. But partly it was anger.

"Because I have a life to live," she said. "Life goes on. You men in a war think the war's all there is, you mistake risking your lives for taking responsibility, and you think that having taken that responsibility—which incidentally you never do by deliberate choice; you claim someone has forced it on you— you think then you can abandon all others: to your families, to your conscience, to women. Women aren't made to sleep around."

"Then why do you do it?"

A funny little smile curled Daphne's lips. "I want to be fought over," she said. "*I* want to cause a war."

Her sudden elusiveness made me sarcastic, for my first and only time with Daphne. "The face that launched a thousand Flying Fortresses?"

In a small voice Daphne said, "Bo, your tour's almost over."

"So you were willing to get in bed with Marrow because my tour was almost over? His tour's almost over, too, you know. I don't get it."

"Do you remember that Sunday of the bank holiday, when I didn't come up to London? That was the same thing, Bo. I was looking around; don't you see that I have to look around, now that your tour's almost over?"

"You can look. You don't have to get into bed with a guy's pilot, do you?"

"I got into bed with you, Bo, the first night I went out with you. I didn't hear you criticize me for that."

That line slowed me down.

"You see, my Bo, I was forced to realize, you forced me to realize, as your tour went along, that you didn't really want me very much more than Marrow does—though there was a big difference, darling, darling; you gave me a lot. But you see, you didn't want me, a woman; you just wanted a camp follower, a stop-gap till your tour was over and you could go home to your other life. You just wanted a war girl. Isn't that right?"

I didn't feel like facing quite so much quite so fast, and I lashed out again. "How come you loved this Dugger character if he was so repulsive, like Marrow?"

"I was a child, Bo. It was during the Blitz. It's so chancy, the kind of people you meet."

"Yeah," I said, "but how could you think you loved a guy like that?"

"You had your Janet. You've told me all about her, Bo. We shouldn't have to account to each other for our educations, should we?"

Touché, but I didn't say so.

"And besides, darling, I broke off with Dugger as soon as I realized that he didn't love me, he only loved war."

"And you've been breaking off with me because . . ." I thought of Doc Randall's report of Daphne—how she had cried on the phone with him and had said that she loved me more than any man she had ever known, but that I didn't love her.

"You're not a war lover, darling. I know that."

". . . because I never brought up the subject of marriage?"

Daphne reacted to that word with another blush, and again there was anger in her warmth. "All your talk about selfless love," she said, "what was that except a kind of vague yearning for . . . for justification? I mean justification for the use you've been making of me. Selfless love! And even your not wanting to kill—"

"Now wait a minite," I said.

"I don't deny that part of it may have been genuine. What you have to do *is* revolting. But your compromise, darling. 'I'll go in a bomber but I won't kill,' can't you see that there's a lot wrong with that idea? And that what's wrong is that you can't go all the way, you certainly can't give all humanity a complete love when you can't even give it to one human being?"

There was too much to think about, and I guess I was too young to think about all of it clearly. I was a kid. It isn't fair, for the older people to make young kids fight their wars for them. I went back to the subject of Marrow, as if *he* were simpler to think about than myself.

"He sat down on the edge of the bed with his elbows on his knees and his head in his hands. I think he was rather drunk. I watched him closely. He began trying to get me to mother him. I tell you, Bo, one whole class of heroes is nothing but babies! It was surprising how far he let down the bars. 'I'm not as good as they say I am.' And, 'Why was I passed over?' He kept saying he was a failure, always had been. Sent down from his college. Made a poor show of his work for—what was it, a grain merchant? A flying bum, he called himself. Failure, failure, failure. Said he'd always wanted a lot of money, the mad money was a pretense, he was a skinflint. Said he was easily discouraged. Once, he said, when he was about twelve, he got a job at a small apartment house that was built in Holand, really a kind of tenement block, he was supposed to sweep down the stairs and empty the garbage for five dollars a week, but there was a dog, a Doberman pinscher, he was afraid of the dog, and he took to skipping days, and the owner came to the house one evening and sacked him, in front of his parents, and his father bellowed at him, but when his mother tucked him in that night, she said he didn't need to bring money into the family because he brought luck into the house."

Marrow's luck!

" 'The fellows never wanted me. We had a Y in Holand, it was a rickety gym and a library and a room with a piano, and one night, I was maybe thirteen, fourteen, there was this whole bunch wanted to beat me up, or something like that, after a basketball game, I wasn't even on the team, the game got them excited, and they stood out in the yard and chanted my name, and Mr. Buckhout, he was the Secretary, he kept me in his office till it blew over.'

"He said he was puny and pigeon-chested, he bought some springs from Sears, Roebuck to build his shoulders and arms. He said he never got good marks in school. 'Something made everybody hate me.' "

Daphne said Marrow admitted that all his aggressiveness was "bluster and bluff." " 'Why do you suppose Haverstraw is my favorite guy on the crew? Because he's an officer and a weakling. It's easy for a guy to feel like a big shot when he associates with children.' "

And that reminded him: Once, he said, he'd been playing with his friend Chuckie, and a blast of dynamite had gone off on some construction job, on the edge of town, and he thought it was thunder in a clear sky, and he was terrified that it was some sort of *message* or *warning,* and he ran home to his mother. And next day Chuckie called him a coward. "Ever since then," he said, "I've been scared of being scared."

Daphne was positive that it was right after telling this anecdote that he volunteered to her that all his stories of his great swordsmanship were imaginary. "The only thrill I get, it's flying."

I tried to pin Daphne down. "What is he, then? What is it about him that makes you call him what you do?"

"I'm not an expert. This is just a woman's theory."

"I fly with this guy, don't forget that."

Daphne thought a few seconds and then said, "One who loves fighting better than the things he's fighting for."

I tried to think what Marrow might be fighting for. No ideas, no hopes or dreams, certainly. I pictured a white frame house, vintage about nineteen twenty-five, in Holand, Nebraska. Some evergreens that had been put in as "landscaping" have grown far too high for their purpose, and the living room and dining room are dark in the daytime. There is a collie sleeping on the porch. A man in black trousers and a white shirt, with suspenders hanging down and his detachable collar detached, and an unlit half-smoked cigar in his mouth, walks slowly back and forth behind an underpowered motor lawn mower which is spewing out clouds of thick blue exhaust. A woman, nearly white-haired, with a look under her eyes as if a pair of grasping hands had ahold of her cheeks and jaws and were pulling the slack flesh to the sides and downward, comes out onto the porch; the screen door slams, and the collie, who is very old, painfully rises. . . .

"He's a superb flier," I said, "and if he loves war so much, why *was* he passed over?"

Daphne was frowning. "A war lover—my Dugger—your pilot: he's a hero, as I see him, in every respect except that he gets a tiny bit too much satisfaction, 'bang,' Marrow called it, out of some deep-down instinct for . . . perhaps hunting." Daphne was having a hard time with this. "I'm trying to tell you. . . . It's silly for me to try to analyze it, Bo; I'm a woman. It's just something I feel. . . . It has to do with death. That's close to it. I guess when you say the things a man's fighting for, you mean: life. And Marrow doesn't want that, he wants death. Not just for himself, but for everyone."

I remembered Marrow's flashing eyes, that day the three of us lunched in Motford Sage, and the sound of the ladle jangling in the soup tureen when he pounded his fist on the table and said, "I want to kill death." Even death. Death was a bastard, a sergeant. I had a picture of the man in the black pants with the suspenders hanging down: he was skulking in the obscure corners of the dark house, laying an ambush for the boy, ready to roar, ready to jump the boy. Death the Father Almighty.

"So the heroes," I said, "are Marrow, Brindt, Jug Farr? Is that it?"

"No, no, no," Daphne said, "there can be the other kind, who fights fiercely, Bo, when he has to, much as he hates it, because he loves what he's fighting for more than himself—life, I guess. Dunkirk. You only have to say a word like that. London when they blitzed us."

"That stuff you told me about Marrow, here . . ." I shook my head.

"He can't make love, because love has to do with birth, life. When he gets in bed, he makes hate—attacks, rapes, milks his gland; and thinks that makes him a man. . . . You're stronger than he is, Bo—how could you not have known that? He said the medal's yours. It's still on the floor. You can have it if you want it."

I got up and went across the room and there, under the dressing table, was the Distinguished Flying Cross. I picked it up and held it in the palm of my hand: my medal.

"But the tough thing," I said, "is when you have this character on your side, in your own airplane. What are you supposed to do about that?"

"That's very hard," Daphne said. "These people can make you think you love them. I guess the first thing is to know who they are and what they want. . . . But be *careful,* darling."

I was so full of rushing thoughts and feelings that I hardly knew what I was saying or what I was hearing. I was utterly bewildered; nevertheless, I felt stronger than I had for weeks; yet I felt somehow desperate, too. I heard myself saying to Daphne, "Do you think we could make a life together?"

"I don't know," she said. "I don't know, now. I've never loved anyone as much as I did you, yet . . ."

"Did?"

"Darling, you're so American. You get what is and what you want all mixed up together in your head."

Chapter 7

AMERICAN
CULTURE
AND
COUNTERCULTURE

Reading 38

The Right Image

James Horan

One characteristic of modern American politics is the way in which candidates are packaged and merchandised to the public in a manner similar to that used to sell soap. The political aspirant hires a public relations firm which takes charge of his campaign, directing the advertising, deciding on when and where the candidate shall speak, and often even determining what he can say publicly. If the candidate is too conservative or too liberal, these image makers guide him toward the center, so that his views will be acceptable to a maximum number of people. In this selection the young Congressman bears a striking similarity to John F. Kennedy.

"You mean shall we bring up the old man's deal?"

"Of course. Did he mention it?"

"He said his father had called him right after you had left. So it's no secret. Well, let's go in—"

"You still don't want any part of him, Josh?"

"We'll have a drink and brush him off as gently as we can. He does sound like a nice kid."

"Kid? He's as old as you are."

"Years don't mean anything in our business, Finn," Josh said as we entered the bar. "Who knows better than you? It's all experience."

The Press Club Bar was the opposite of the Golden Key: movement, exuberance, laughter, and light enough to see what the devil you were drinking. We stood at the entrance for a moment, surveying the crowded room, with Josh waving to friends and exchanging insults; then he said, "There he is," and we made our way to a table at the far side of the room.

The man who was standing by his chair was in his late thirties, slender, of medium height, with wavy brown hair, warm brown eyes, and an infectious smile, which as long as I knew Kelly Shannon, always got me off center.

He held out his hand, which Josh took.

"Mr. Michaels?"

"Suppose we make it Josh."

"Fine. Then it's Kelly." He looked at me. "Mr. McCool, I hear you're the brains of this outfit."

"You never said a truer word, Congressman," I said as we shook hands.

"I've been coasting," Kelly said, nodding to his glass. "What will you gentlemen have?"

We gave our orders, then settled back.

"I'm really embarrassed about last night," Kelly said. "Twice over since I found out who you were."

"By the way, how did you know it was us—Ian?" Josh asked.

"Who else?" Kelly said with a grin.

I made a noise in my throat, and Josh blandly explained I was only expressing my great friendship for Ian.

"Seriously, I'm glad Tuck Larsen wasn't having a drink there last night," Josh added. "It would have made quite a column today."

"It was a fool thing to do," Kelly admitted. "But he was making cracks from the moment he came in."

"Just what did he say?" Josh asked.

"Apparently he had been stationed in Washington after the war," Kelly said, "and he was talking about the McCarthy-Army hearings. Then he brought up my father. Once I turned around and told him to forget it, he could read it in the history books, but he kept it up, getting more nasty; then he took off after my father. It wasn't what he said so much as the way he said it."

"What exactly did he say?" Josh asked.

Kelly looked up at him. "He made my father sound like a ruthless old son of a bitch who would frame his mother for stealing his socks, and dammit, he was never that—" He nodded to me. "I'm sure Finn will agree."

"Agreed," I said. "I wouldn't want him on my tail, but he was no Joe McCarthy."

"But he did quite a job on a few people down here," Josh said.

"Most of them needed it," Kelly said.

"They sure did," I said. "I know. I was there."

Josh juggled a few peanuts in the palm of his hand, then threw them in his mouth.

"Well, next time meet them in a dark alley," he said with a grin. "It's too damn expensive to slug them in a club."

"That's a promise," Kelly said laughing. "No more matches in the Golden Key."

"Finn and I have discussed your father's proposition. You're aware of all details, of course."

"The senator discussed it fully with us."

" 'Us'?"

"Luke, my younger brother, and Lacey, my sister. You may recall she was married to Professor Lowell—"

"I remember," Josh said. "There was an accident about four years ago
—"

"He was killed near Gallup in a plane crash," Kelly said.

"I remember that," Josh said. "Wasn't it right after he had discovered
that Zuñi pueblo?"

Kelly looked surprised. "I thought only the specialists remembered that.
Are you interested in archaeology, Josh?"

Josh said laughing, "I'm like Custer—I happen to know a few Indians."

"I guess my father's proposition must sound fantastic to you fellows,"
Kelly said.

"That it does," Josh said.

"Well, it's nothing new," Kelly said. "It's been my father's dream as long
as I can remember."

"But is it your dream, Kelly?" I put in. "That's important."

Both Josh and Kelly turned to me, Josh somewhat surprised, Kelly
somewhat thoughtful.

"I'd be a liar if I denied it," Kelly said.

"First governor of New York—then President?" Josh said.

"Far out or not, that's the plan."

"To be perfectly candid, no one knows you outside Westchester County,"
Josh said, "and maybe not everyone there."

"To be candid, Josh," Kelly said with a smile, "your job would be to
correct that."

"But why would you want to be governor—or President? You're a rich
man. A congressman. You have a wonderful family, a beautiful home. Why
try for jobs that admittedly are the toughest in American politics?"

"Albany is in the mainstream, the heart of the most important state in
America—and the crucible for the Presidency. He shrugged. "I know I have
all the natural obstacles a man could have: political obscurity, youth, wealth,
but my father—and my family—insist I have a chance." He looked at me, and
smiled. "I think so too."

"Against the professionals, the machines?" Josh asked.

"Yes. If both of you took me on," Kelly said, "it could be a hell of a fight."

"Interesting, maybe, but with not much of a chance—and I don't go with
losers, Kelly," Josh said bluntly.

"Let's get this straight, Josh," was the cool answer: "no Shannon likes
to lose."

"In this case it's not what you or anyone else likes. It just happens the
odds are against you," Josh said.

"You really think the odds are that much against me?" Kelly asked.

"Definitely."

"Is that the reason you're going to turn my father down?"

"Who said we were going to turn him down?"

"You did—not in so many words. But no hard feelings. You would have to be a fool to walk into this one."

"We've walked into worse," I said.

"Not like this, Finn," Josh said impatiently.

"You're right, Josh," Kelly said. "We were only discussing it last night. Lacey said she would bet us all a steak dinner you fellows would turn it down."

"Women should never have been allowed in politics," I said. "It was bad enough when they let them into saloons."

"I keep telling Finn he would have been great in Cleveland's day," Josh said.

"My father always blows his top when Lacey puts in her oar," Kelly said. "But secretly he respects her opinions. She makes a lot of sense most times."

"I think this might be one of those times," Josh said quietly.

Reading 39

Executive Suite

Cameron Hawley

Most Americans spend their productive lives in factories or offices. What satisfaction they receive from their daily routine on the job is incidental to production; personal satisfaction is not the goal of industry. Some men find business an exciting game in much the same way as others are gratified by success in politics, in athletics, or in other areas. But the problem of American business continues to be that self-satisfaction is reserved for the few. The men in the executive suite cannot understand that their policies often rob others of any job satisfaction in their daily work. The discussion in this excerpt takes place when Avery Bullard, the head of the corporation, dies suddenly, and the other executives seek to understand the secret of his success.

"No, I don't think we can call that Mr. Bullard's idea alone," Don Walling said. "It's something that's in the air today—the groping of a lot of men at the top of industry who know they've lost something, but aren't quite sure what it is—nor exactly how they happened to lose it. Mr. Bullard was one of those men. He'd been so busy building a great production machine that he'd lost sight of why he was building it—if he ever really knew. Perhaps he didn't.''

Julia Tredway Prince's voice, so close to Mary Walling's ears that even a whisper seemed like an explosion in the silence, asked, "Do *you* know, Mr. Walling?"

Mary Walling held her breath through the moment of silence. Could he answer that question? A smile flickered on his face . . . that same tantalizingly familiar smile she hadn't been able to identify before. Now suddenly, she remembered when she had seen it before . . . that night when he had finally designed their house . . . when, after all of his groping and fumbling had frightened her almost to the point of losing faith in him, he had suddenly made everything come right and clear.

"Yes, I think I do," he said. "You see, to Mr. Bullard, business was a game—a very serious game, but still a game—the way war is a game to a soldier. He was never much concerned about money for its own sake. I remember his saying once that dollars were just a way of keeping score. I don't think he was too much concerned about personal power, either—just power for power's sake. I know that's the easy way to explain the drive that any great man has—the lust for power—but I don't think that was true of Avery Bullard. The thing that kept him going was his terrific pride in himself—the driving urge to do things no other man on earth could do. He saved the company when everyone else had given up. He built a big corporation in an industry where everyone said that only small companies could succeed. He was only happy when he was doing the impossible—and he did that only to satisfy his own pride. He never asked for applause and appreciation—or even for understanding. He was a lonely man but I don't think his loneliness ever bothered him very much. He was the man at the top of the tower—figuratively as well as literally. That's what he wanted. That's what it took to satisfy his pride. That was his strength—but of course that was his weakness, too."

Mary Walling listened in amazement. Where were those words coming from . . . those words that he could never have said before but were now falling so easily from his lips? Was that actually Don who was talking . . . the same man who had never beeen able to answer those dark-of-night questions before?

She watched him as he rose from his chair and in the act of standing he seemed a giant breaking shackles that had held him to the earth . . . shaking loose the ties that had bound him to the blind worship of Avery Bullard. He stood alone now . . . free.

"There was one thing that Avery Bullard never understood," Don Walling went on. "He never realized that other men had to be proud, too—that the force behind a great company had to be more than the pride of one man

—that it had to be the pride of thousands of men. A company is like an army —it fights on its pride. You can't win wars with paychecks. In all the history of the world there's never been a great army of mercenaries. You can't pay a man enough to make him lay down his life. He wants more than money. Maybe Avery Bullard knew that once—maybe he'd just forgotten it—but that's where he made his mistake. He was a little lost these last few years. He'd won his fight to build a great company. The building was over—at least for the time being. There had to be something else to satisfy his pride—bigger sales—more profit—something. That's when we started doing things like making the six-teen-hundred series."

He turned and confronted Dudley. "Are your boys proud when they sell the sixteen-hundred series—when they know that the finish is going to crack and the veneer split off and the legs come loose?"

"But that's price merchandise," Dudley said in fumbling defense. "There's a need for it. We're not cheating anyone. At that price the customers know that they can't get—"

"How do you suppose the men in the factory feel when they make it?" Don Walling demanded. His eyes shifted from Dudley to Shaw. "What do you imagine they think of a management that's willing to stoop to selling that kind of junk in order to add a penny a year to the dividend? Do you know that there are men at Pike Street who have refused to work on the sixteen-hundred line —that there are men who have taken a cut of four cents an hour to get transferred to something else?"

"No, I wasn't aware of that," Shaw said—and the weakness of his voice signaled the first thin crack in his armor. "I don't suppose it would hurt too much if we dropped that line. After all, it's a small part of our business."

A voice in Mary Walling's mind wanted to shout out at her husband, urging him to drive in for the kill that would clinch his victory. Couldn't he see that Shaw was defeated . . . that Caswell was nodding his approval . . . that Walt Dudley was waiting only to be commanded?

But Don Walling turned, looking out of the window, and his voice seemed faraway as if it were coming from the top of the distant white shaft of the Tredway Tower. "Yes, we'll drop that line. We'll never again ask a man to do anything that will poison his pride in himself. We'll have a new line of low-priced furniture someday—a different kind of furniture—as different from anything we're making now as a modern automobile is different from an old Mills wagon. When we get it, then we'll really start to grow."

His voice came back into the room. "We talk about Tredway being a big company now. It isn't. We're kidding ourselves. Yes, we're one of the biggest furniture manufacturers but what does it mean? Nothing! Furniture is close to a two-billion-dollar industry but it's all split up among thirty-six hundred manufacturers. We have about three per cent of the total—that's all, just three per cent. Look at other industries—the percentage that the top manufacturer has. What if General Motors had sat back and stopped growing when it had three percent of the automobile industry? We haven't even started to grow! Suppose we get fifteen per cent of the total—and why not, it's been done in a dozen industries? Fifteen per cent and the Tredway Corporation will be five times as big as it is today. All right, I know it hasn't been done before in the furniture business, but does that mean we can't do it? No—because that's exactly what we *are* going to do!"

His voice had built to a crescendo, to the moment that demanded the shout of an answering chorus—and then in the instant before the sound could have broken through the shock of silence, Mary Walling saw a tension-breaking smile on her husband's face. In the split second that it took her eyes to sweep the room, she saw that the smile was mirrored in all the faces that looked up at him . . . even in the face of Loren Shaw.

She had sensed, a few minutes before, that Shaw was defeated, but she had expected a last struggle, a final flare of resistance. It had not come. Instinctively, she understood what had happened. In that last moment, Loren Shaw had suddenly become aware that his brain had been set aflame by a spark from Don Walling's mind—a spark that he himself could never have supplied. Now he was fired to accomplishments that had been far beyond the limits of his imagination. Mary Walling understood the faintly bewildered quality of Shaw's smile, because she, too—long ago—had found it mysteriously strange that Don's mind was so unlike her own.

George Caswell was standing, extending his hand. "We're all behind you, Don. I can promise you that."

"Yes sir, Don, you bet we are!" Walt Dudley boomed.

Shaw shook hands silently but it was a gesture that needed no words to make it a pledge of loyalty.

And now Julia Tredway Prince was standing, too. "I think the occasion calls for a toast. Dwight, would you mind—yes, Nina, what is it?"

Nina was standing in the doorway. "There's a telephone call for Mr. Walling. The gentleman says it's very urgent."

Dwight Prince stepped forward. "There's an extension in the back hall. Come and I'll show you."

Mary saw that Julia was about to speak to her but George Caswell stepped up as an interruption.

"I'm afraid I'll have to run along. The plane's waiting and I—well, I have to be back in New York for a wedding at six. I'll be down on Monday, of course."

"And you'll stay over for the board meeting on Tuesday," Julia said.

"As far as I'm concerned, it's all settled now," George Caswell said. "But you're quite right—we do need the formal action of the board."

Reading 40

F.O.B. Detroit
Wessel Smitter

The assembly line is the most efficient technique devised to build the complex machinery of today's society, and it has become a symbol of the triumph of American industry. Since it was first introduced by Henry Ford to assemble automobiles, however, it has taken a frightful toll in human misery. Gone is the pride of the craftsman in his work. Who can be proud of spending his life putting on left front fenders or mounting rear taillights? The problem of boredom created by compelling men to do repetitive tasks remains a basic cause of absenteeism and shoddy workmanship and has even prompted Swedish automakers to try to do away with assembly lines. In the competition between man and machine the latter continues to be the winner.

One night, coming out of the factory after we'd been in motor assembly a little more than a month, we passed the bone-yard, and there, in with ten acres of other scrapped machinery, we saw the rig. One side was down in the mud; the boom was all screwy, and the big iron claw hung loose and open like an idiot's mouth.

"There's Old Betsy," said Russ. "Let's go in and see what they've done to her."

I didn't see the use, but I went, getting my feet wet and muddy. He went up to the rig and put his hand on the control box.

"Cold iron," he said, serious. "No static, even. But if you was to turn the juice into her she'd soon come to warm life again."

"She'll come to warm life," I said, "when they get the torches to work on her—cut her up and feed her to the open hearths. One of these days she'll be coming over the line in the shape of cylinder blocks and you'll be starting nuts on her."

"You know, Bennie," he said, sliding his hand back and forth along a drive-shaft, "there's something almost funny about the way this steel feels to

From *F.O.B. Detroit* by Wessel Smitter. Published in 1938.

the touch. You get used to having a thing feel the same way, don't you? And when it doesn't—it's almost as though something was wrong. Even during the night she never got really cold. In the morning there was always some heat left in the metal. It must be that way when you feel the hand of someone you've known a long time and—"

"Must be," I said. "Let's get going. If the H.P.s see us fooling around here you'll have a hard time making 'em believe that you're preaching a funeral sermon and not trying to get away with some brass bearings."

"Don't rush me," he said. "What's the difference if we get outa this place a few minutes later than usual? This is probably the last time we'll see the old rig."

"Last time you get sentimental about it, I hope."

"To you," he said, "this machine here is just a pile of old iron—junk. But to me it's more than that, Bennie. To me—it's Old Betsy—still. To you, all machines are alike. Pieces of steel and iron put together—all alike. But they're not, Bennie. Machines do things to us—the men that work with them. Things the engineers never think about. Some machines build us up—help us to make the most of ourselves. Some tear us apart—grind us down. A machine geared to a man—is one thing. A man geared to a machine—is something else. One's human, gives you a chance to be your best self. The other works on you like a gear-cutter—whittling you down, chiseling at you, cutting grooves in you, making you like all the other small gears that work on the line."

He stood there fingering a winged nut on a brakerod, just the bare hint of a smile near the corner of his mouth, that smile that I never knew quite how to take.

"I don't know what you're thinking about," I said, "but I guess it's all right."

"I'm not sentimental," he said, in his quiet way. "At least, I don't think I am. I see things for what they are worth—to me. When I was in the drop forge I had a man's job and did a man's work. It was fun. Remember how I used to stay after the bell rang and try to work out ideas for getting the work done faster, better? I had a chance to use the brains I was born with. Old Betsy, here, gave me a chance to get the most out of myself. When a job was done, I looked it over. Took some of the credit, if it was good. Took some of the blame, if it wasn't. Tried to figure out how to do it better the next time. Old Betsy was geared to my brain—did what I wanted it to do. Gave its strength to my hand, gave its power to my will. I was the boss.

"But in the motor assembly, Bennie, it's different. There the machine is the boss. The machine does the nice work—the hard work—the part that takes skill. The machine's everything and gets credit for the work done. You're nothing until you've learned to be a gear—a small part of the big machine—

until there's nothing left of you but a very small cog without any will. You start and stop when the machine's ready—go slow or fast as the machine tells you. The machine counts—you don't. And why should you? You don't furnish the brains. You don't furnish the skill. All you do is fasten a nut, put on a washer, stamp on a number. The machine does the real job. It's the big boss standing over your head—grinding you down—wasting your strength—whittling away at your brain. Making you a small part of its dead, mechanical self."

"Come on," I said, "it's late. Supper will be waiting for us. We haven't cleaned up yet."

"That's right," he said, picking his way through the mud, "we haven't cleaned up. In the drop forge—we used to clean up every night before leaving. Used to change our clothes and wash the dirt from our faces. Walk out of the gate looking decent. Now we don't—ever. Nobody does. When it's time for the bell we don't think about anything except getting out—getting out. Getting away from the machines. We lay our tools just so—roll our sleeves down—untie the knots in our aprons. We get set for the bell. We get ready to rush out when the bell rings, thinking we'll get rid of the machines for a spell—the machines that eat into us like gear-cutters. But we don't, Bennie. We don't—ever. They stay with us, they get into our blood, leave their dirty imprint on our faces. It's there when we hurry out—there on the river of dead faces streaming out through the gate. And in the morning, when we come back to the machines—it's still there. We go home and use water and soap but we never clean up. The work of the machines that keep whittling and chiseling at us is too deep."

Reading 41

The Drifters

James Michener

In his novel *The Drifters* James Michener looks critically at the values and attitudes of today's youth. Shown in this selection is a new and more frank expression of the old concept of alienation or estrangement from the world. Living under the threat of nuclear destruction, the younger generation feels that all values are relative; nothing is permanent or absolute. One must try to find meaning in a world lacking much contemporary significance; politics, morality, and life in general are no longer important in and of themselves. The great surprise in the excerpt comes not from the younger generation but from the older one. George Fairbanks, the narrator of the story, and Henry Holt, a technical representative for a large overseas company, come to realize that their values are quite similar to those of the young Americans they meet. The difference is that Fairbanks and Holt have "copped out" in a socially acceptable manner, while the youth have expressed their disillusionment in a socially unacceptable fashion. Alienation is, of course, a major factor in American society for it crosscuts all divisions: sex, race, nationality, and age. Many people are dissatisfied with the present government and society and want to change it but do not know how. Perhaps, then, we are all "drifters."

Often as I walked back to my hotel at night I reflected on the discussions I had heard in Inger's and I was amazed at how vocal the young people were in stating their opinions and how little they read to support them. This was a generation without books. Of course, everyone has handled volumes by Herbert Marcuse and Frantz Fanon, but I found no one who had actually read the more easily understood works like *Essay on Liberation* or *Toward the African Revolution* or *The Wretched of the Earth*. It was also true that most of the travelers had read newspaper reports of Marshall McLuhan's theories, and hardly a day passed but someone would proclaim, 'After all, the medium is the massage,' but I met no one who had read the book of which this taut summary was the title or who knew what it meant.

There was always a dog-eared copy of the *I-Ching* somewhere in the hotel, and many had dipped into it, but no one had read it, not even Claire from Sacramento. The strong books of the age were unknown to this group, and I often wondered how they had got as far along in college as they had. On the other had, their verbal knowledge was considerable and they could expatiate on almost any topic. Six pronouncements I noted one night were typical of the conclusions reached every night.

'We have entered what Walter Lippmann terms the New Dark Age.'

'Before 1976 an armed showdown between races will be inevitable in American cities.'

'The military-industrial complex rules our nation and dictates a continuance of the Vietnam war.'

'A permanent unemployment cadre of seven million must be anticipated.'

'By the year 2000 we will have seven billion people on earth.'

'Universities are prisoners of the Establishment.'

But in spite of these statements, I found that most Americans overseas were hard-line conservatives; of the many in Marrakech, the majority had supported the Republican party in 1968 and would do so again in 1972. I took the trouble to check the six young people I had seen unconscious on the floor of the Casino Royale; Claire took me back one morning, and I found that four were solid Republicans, one was a neo-Nazi, and Moorman, the honor student from Michigan who sang ballads with Gretchen, said, 'I don't know what I am.'

I found more than a few supporters of George Wallace, and Constitution-alists, and crypto-fascists, and backers of other ill-defined movements. The basic ideas of the John Birch Society were often voiced, but I met no one who admitted membership.

Most older people who visited Marrakech were surprised to find that among the young Americans, there were practically no oldstyle American liberals. This was true for obvious reasons. To get as far as Marrakech required real money, so that those who made it had to come from well-to-do families of a conservative bent, and throughout the world children tend to follow the political attitudes of their fathers. A boy of nineteen might rebel against Harvard University, country-club weekends and the dress of his father, and run away to Marrakech to prove it, but his fundamental political and social attitudes would continue to be those his father had taught him at age eleven. In my work I constantly met conservative adult Americans who, when they saw the young people with long hair and beards, expected them to be revolutio-naries; they were pleasantly gratified to find that the young people were as reactionary as they were.

Harvey Holt exemplified this response. When he first met the gang at Pamplona he was positive they must be revolutionaries, but after several long discussions involving politics, he told me 'You know, apart from Vietnam and this nonsense about brotherhood between the races, these kids are pretty solid.' Later he said, 'You could be misled if you listened to their songs. You'd think they were going out to burn down New York. But when you talk to them about economics and voting, you find they're just as conservative as you or me . . but they do it in their own way.' I asked him how he thought I voted, and he said, 'Oh, you sympathize a lot with the young people, but I'm sure that in a pinch you can be trusted.'

'To vote Republican?'

'How else can a sensible man vote?' he asked.

I was constantly appalled by the poverty of language exhibited by many of the young people, and these from our better colleges. Claire, as I have said, sometimes talked for a whole hour saying little but 'you know' and 'like wow,' but this had a certain cute illiteracy. More intolerable was the girl from Ohio who said at least once every paragraph, 'You better believe it.' Whenever one of the boys from the south agreed with one of my opinions, he said, 'You ain't just whistlin' "Dixie," bub.' A college girl from Missouri introduced every statement with: 'I just want you to know,' while a young man from Brooklyn related everything to André Gide—he seemed quite incapable of any other comparison.

Two aspects of the intellectual life of these young Americans surprised me. The first was politics. Not one person I knew ever mentioned the name Richard Nixon; they rejected Lyndon Johnson and ridiculed Hubert Humphrey, charging these men with having betrayed youth, but Nixon they dismissed. They would have voted for him, had they bothered to vote, and would vote for him in 1972, if they happened to be registered, but he played no role in their lives. A whole segment of American history was simply expunged by these people; they had opted out with a vengeance.

I say that they would vote Republican in 1972, if they voted, and by this I mean that of all the young Americans I met over the age of twenty-one, not one had ever bothered to vote, and it seemed unlikely to me that any would do so much before the age of thirty-two or thirty-three. To hear them talk, you would think they were battering down the barricades of the Establishment, and some few I suppose would have been willing to try, but they were not willing to vote; in fact, I met none who were even registered.

In spite of this seeming indifference, there were those few I reflected upon that morning when I stood in the Casino Royale amid the stenches and the fallen forms, the few who were painfully carving out an understanding of their world, and their place in it. Because they came from families with income and advantage, they tended to be Republican, and when they settled down, they were going to be good Republicans. Some, like Gretchen, had worked for Senator Eugene McCarthy, but not because he was a Democrat; they would quickly return to creative Republicanism and the nation would profit from the forging process they had gone through.

But when I have said this about politics, I have still not touched upon the mighty chasm that separated them from me: they honestly believed that their generation lived under the threat of the hydrogen bomb and that consequently their lives would be different from what mine had been. They were convinced that no man my age could comprehend what the bomb meant to them, and even when I pointed out that a man of sixty-one like me had been forced to spend nearly half his adult life under the shadow of nuclear bombs and had adjusted to it, they cried, 'Ah, there it is! You'd enjoyed about half your life before the bomb fell. We haven't'. It seemed there could be no bridge of understanding on this point, and after several futile attempts to build one, I concluded that on this topic we could not talk together meaningfully.

Reading 42

The Minister

Charles Mercer

After World War II the position of the Negro in American life steadily improved. Gains in toleration made during the war years were expanded, and overt discrimination declined, especially in the North. A series of court decisions eased legal discrimination in the South. But the real drive for full equality grew out of the struggle against bus discrimination in Birmingham, Alabama in 1955. In this effort the Reverend Martin Luther King, Jr., was thrust into the national limelight. King's campaign for civil rights through the use of nonviolent protest demonstrations received support from many sectors of the nation. In the following years, recreational facilities were desegregated, job discrimination was lessened, and the poll tax was eliminated, giving the Negro greater political power in the South. Massive "sit-in" demonstrations at segregated lunch counters were launched by Southern Negroes in 1960 and were successful because of national pressure, especially against chain stores like Woolworth's which feared the effects of mass picketing upon their business in the North. To a great extent, these civil rights demonstrations were supported by students who wished to speed up the movement for racial equality. This selection describes student "freedom riders" attempting to integrate interstate bus travel.

Name: Katherine Judson. Age: twenty-one. Home: New York City. Occupation: junior, Wellesley College, Wellesley, Massachusetts. Affiliation: Student Nonviolent Coordinating Committee.

In the heat and turmoil of the Nashville bus terminal the young, bespectacled black took down the information carefully, then looked Kathy up and down. "Honey, you sure you're twenty-one?"

"I will be in a few days."

He grinned. "So you want to spend your birthday in jail. You doing this to duck your year's finals?"

"I finished them yesterday," Kathy said. "I had to fly to get here on time."

"Plenty of time," the black said. "This bus don't keep much of a schedule. The drivers keep funkin' out. So you're a SNICK." Thus the Student Nonviolent Coordinating Committee was called. "We got five SNICK's, eight CORE's, three SCLC's, seven independents, and not a single N double ACP."

He looked around at the next bench. "Suzie Polk over there's a SNICK from Howard. Hey, Suzie!" he yelled above the din at a stout young Negro woman. "Here's an ofay to keep you company."

Suzie Polk treated Kathy coolly. What was SNICK doing at Wellesley? Kathy sometimes had wondered herself. A gang of Nashville white youths, jeering and yelling obscenities at the group planning an integrated bus ride to Montgomery, Alabama, made conversation almost impossible anyway. When a couple of youths began throwing tomatoes, shirt-sleeved sheriff's deputies stepped in front of the gang and said, "Cut it out, boys, now just take it easy." Kathy wanted to tell Suzie that *this* was why she had come here, that they were sisters, that all citizens must have equal rights. But of course, those sentiments, which had seemed convincing on the Wellesley campus, would have sounded banal in the Nashville bus terminal.

"There's Dave Murchison." Suzie pointed to a tall, husky-looking young white man who had just come in carrying an airline flight bag and was being greeted warmly by a couple of the black leaders. "He's one ofay Dr. King trusts. Last year during the Greensboro sit-ins he spent a week in jail."

Kathy found it hard to believe. She thought him sort of handsome in an Ivy League biscuit-cutter way: cropped hair, lean face, deadpan demeanor. He stared at her over the heads of the blacks, then made his way to her.

"I'm Dave Murchison. Who are you?"

"Kathy Judson, New York."

He sat down beside her. "I'm at Union Seminary."

Suddenly he interested her. "My father's a minister in New York."

He looked at her more closely. "Martin Judson?" Yes. "Martin Judson of Old Fourth," he said slowly. "So we have a daughter of the Protestant Establishment with us."

She narrowed her eyelids at him. "What Establishment are you talking about, preacher boy?"

He grinned suddenly. "The New York Protestant Establishment begins at the Cathedral and goes south to Trinity at Wall, then curves through the prettier parts of Long Island and up into Westchester. They wear the sword of liberalism but take care never to join any expedition south of the Mason-Dixon Line."

Father a member of the Protestant Establishment? It was ridiculous. Because he had pulled Old Fourth up by its bootstraps and built it into a strong church, he apparently had become a target for the little preacher boys. Good heavens, Father was a radical! When she had phoned him from Wellesley and asked for money to join the freedom ride, he had not demurred for an instant. "I'll send a check right away, Kathy. Glad you want to act on your convictions. Just do me one favor. If you land in jail and SNICK doesn't have the bail money promptly, send me a wire."

At last they climbed on the bus, and Kathy sat down beside Suzie. David Murchison took the seat across the aisle from Kathy. As the bus rolled through the suburbs of Nashville, he talked endlessly, practically telling her the story of his life.

He had been graduated from the University of Michigan, where he had worked at trying to be a writer. "Only thing wrong with that is I don't have any real talent for it." Then why Union Theological? His answer to her question was vague.

"Well, maybe just to irritate my old man. He's dead and doesn't know it. Dead and buried in Scarsdale. I hadn't seen him in three years when I tried to raise some money from him to go to Union. Gosh, it made him mad. He hates Christianity—everything, me included. Says I'm a goddamn Communist."

His father and mother had divorced when he was fifteen, and now she was married to a kooky art dealer and living in Paris. It was his mother who financed him at Union. "She'd like to spoil me. Compensation, I suppose, for walking out on the old bastard in Scarsdale and going off with the art dealer." Did he hate her, too? "No. I sort of like her and feel sorry for her."

There were six white and seventeen black passengers on the bus which sped south through a parched-looking land of yellow clay. The country was as Kathy had expected from her reading about the South. But the atmosphere in the bus was wholly unexpected. In Wellesley and Boston she had heard much about the warm fraternity of fighters for civil rights, but on this bus there was a restraint amounting to coolness between blacks and whites. Dave, a veteran of the new civil war, was the only white whom the blacks trusted fully.

Early in the afternoon the bus stopped where there was a roadside stand, a dilapidated house above a clay bank, a mangy dog asleep in the dust. An old man began padlocking an outhouse as Kathy walked to the stand where a thin woman with a weathered face stared at her grimly. There was nothing to eat, nothing to drink, the woman cried shrilly.

Dave shared his sandwiches and thermos of iced tea with Kathy, who had not thought to bring food or drink. After they climbed onto the bus, he sat down beside her and at once fell asleep. She marveled at him. When she remembered having read that instant sleep was a capacity possessed by most persons who fought oppressive society, she even began to admire him. In midafternoon the black leader called to him, and he awakened as instantaneously as he had slept.

Following a short conference with Dave, the leader addressed the riders. Montgomery was their destination, but first they must pass through Birmingham. He advised them to segregate themselves by color, remain passive, and not try to leave the bus when it paused at the Birmingham terminal. "But Dave has other ideas. He's going to tell you his, and you're free to act as you please. After all, this is a *freedom* ride."

Dave's voice rose easily, and Kathy realized he must be a persuasive public speaker. "My thought is that the Battle of Montgomery is no more important than the Battle of Birmingham. In fact, the more Southern battlefields the better. I think the police may stop us at the Birmingham city limits and arrest any who refuse to segregate their seats. Personally, this ofay plans to get arrested. They say the Birmingham city jail has nice clean sheets and ice cold drinks." There were jeering cheers. "Is there a black man on this bus willing to go to jail with me?" After a lengthy silence a young CORE man said he would be honored. "Anybody else want to see how the better half lives in a Southern jail?

Kathy wondered if he was gazing at her. Remembering suddenly a line from one of her childhood prayers—"Let's get on with it, Lord"—she stood up.

Dave smiled at her and called, "Bless thee, Katherine, in the names of Peter, Titus and Paul. Kathy Judson of New York is looking for a cellmate. Any takers?"

Suzie looked around at her and exclaimed, "Well, I'll be! Come sit with me, Kathy."

"You're a pretty dispirited-looking bunch," Dave said. "Let's put some oil in this tired machine. Let's *lubricate* democracy and make freedom hum. Everybody remembers that rascal John Brown. . . . "

As he led them in the well-known song, Kathy thought: *My gosh, an old-time Gospel singing preacher, turned inside out and twisted all around, with different aims and a language part new, part old, but all tuned to strange ears.*

Half an hour later, as they entered Birmingham, the wailing of a police siren made her neck chill. The driver pulled to the side and stopped the bus. Kathy, thinking of what she had heard about Southern police brutality, was scared. Yet she had asked for whatever might happen to her, so there was no reason to William Blake it and think with the poet: "and the bitter groan of a martyr's woe/Is an arrow from the Almighty's bow."

To her surprise, the policeman who stepped onto the bus was young, good-looking. In a courteous tone he said they had entered the city limits of Birmingham. Then he recited the local ordinance on segregation of bus riders and asked them to conform with the law. When Kathy, Dave and their black seat partners failed to move, the policeman said he would have to take them into custody. Unprotesting, they left the bus with him. Kathy and Suzie rode to police headquarters in the rear seat of one squad car while Dave and his companion rode in another.

At headquarters they pleaded guilty and were booked. After searching through a sheaf of papers, a lieutenant said Dave and his seat companion had criminal records; if they could not post bail of one thousand dollars each, they would be remanded to jail. Dave laughed, and they were led away. Suzie's bail was set at five hundred dollars, and she left with a matron.

"Now look here," the lieutenant said to Kathy. Why should a nice girl like her mess around in things that didn't affect her? It was the most paternal lecture she ever had received. Repent—and go home. She thought of a couple of eloquent remarks but could not bring herself to make them. Instead, she insisted she was guilty, and lacking five hundred dollars' bail, she followed the matron to a reasonably clean cell in the women's block.

A drunken woman yammered down the block, and two cockroaches paraded on the ceiling. After a while Suzie called out her name, and Kathy answered. Having anticipated arrest, Kathy had brought along a paperback edition of *Walden,* which she had started twice in years past but never finished. Now, beginning it again while curled up on her cot, she found herself understanding for the first time why Thoreau went to the pond.

Around six o'clock the matron brought her corned-beef hash, bread, and canned peaches. When she came for the dishes, she lingered for a long time —not to converse, but to lecture. What did Kathy think she was accomplishing? On and on the matron ranted. Didn't she at least want to notify her parents so they could bail her out? No, she had given the lieutenant money for a telegram notifying SNICK headquarters of Suzie's and her arrests, but she was beginning to wonder if the telegram had been sent.

Later in the evening five women who had been on the bus were brought into the block. They said there had been roughing at the bus terminal, and they had been put under something called protective custody. Kathy slept poorly, and the next day she began to understand why the verb "languish" applied to jail. After finishing *Walden*, she started it again and found that the pond had grown stagnant to her.

On the second morning, following a breakfast of bread, powdered eggs, and coffee, she and the six black women riders were taken to the room where they had been arraigned. Two black men riders were brought from their cells and joined them. Kathy inquired about Dave, but the men did not know what had become of him. When the nine were led out and placed by threes in three police cars, she assumed they were being taken to court.

But the cars sped north out of Birmingham along the highway which the freedom riders had followed into the city two days previously. At last Kathy asked, "Where are we going?" Neither of the two policemen in the front seat answered her. It was bewildering and a little frightening, like being caught up in a Kafka creation in which the subject could not relate to the object. She had been arrested and jailed under due process of law, but now the authorities were violating law as flagrantly as the freedom riders. On the police cars raced for what seemed hours.

At last the car began to slow down on a lonely stretch of road fringed by clay banks and pine barrens. When they stopped, one of the policemen spoke for the first time: "Get out!" The woman beside Kathy began to shake and weep. Her terror was infectious, raising unreasonable images of the law gone berserk, of massacre by police guns on the hot and piny clay. Kathy's legs shook as she climbed out.

The policeman stared out at her contemptuously, ignoring the blacks. "This is the state line," one said. "Start walking, and never come back to Alabama."

As they walked north in the heat, cars passed them in both directions. Drivers stared at them curiously, but none stopped. Eventually, Kathy thought, they would reach a town where they could board a bus back to Nashville. It was a sad, a ridiculous ending to her brave protest, her great adventure. Before long the heat began to dissipate her anger into a sullen weariness.

The blaring of a horn behind them warned of some new danger. She looked around at an old outsized limousine such as served airport passengers. Seated beside the black driver was David Murchison, who managed to look at the same time surprised, pleased, sad and angry. Thus possibly General Nathan Bedford Forrest had looked when surrounded in these parts before issuing his famous order: "We'll charge both ways!" But when Dave climbed out of the swaybacked limousine, his order was: "Hop in! Back to Birmingham!"

Not Bedford Forest, but Tom Sawyer, Kathy thought. Into jail, out of jail, back to jail again—and like Huck Finn, she wondered to what purpose. "Now wait a minute," she said.

"You've had enough?"

"Not necessarily. I'd just like some explanation of what's being accomplished."

"We've got 'em on the run."

"I'd say they had us on the walk. How did you get out of jail?"

"My outfit raised bail. Reinforcements are pouring in. Our intelligence network is really cracking. We knew the minute you people were run out of town. Both President Kennedy and the Attorney General are trying to get the governor of Alabama on the phone. We're gathering strength at the Birmingham bus terminal. Before long they'll weaken, and we'll bus it on to Montgomery. Climb in!"

After they climbed into the swaybacked limousine and headed back to Birmingham, Kathy asked him, "Have you ever considered an Army career?"

"No dice. I'm a pacifist."

Some pacifist! Like Uncle Tubby, with his medals, or Father, with his Korean adventures. Onward, Christian soldiers, marching on to jail.

More than a score of freedom riders were gathered at the Birmingham bus terminal when they arrived there. Kathy expected momentarily that they would be arrested, but General Bedford Forrest Murchison proved himself the wiser tactician. They were too numerous now; such a large number of arrests would flood the jail and draw more national attention to Birmingham than the city authorities cared to receive.

Now the police gave them a protective screen against the toughs who wanted to assault them. Now, too, Kathy began to realize that patience was the most important weapon of the resistance fighter. As the hours crept by, she struggled against boredom, fatigue, and—worst of all—a feeling of personal uncleanliness. She would have given almost anything for a shower, a change of clothing, a few quiet moments away from the din—anything, of course, except giving up the effort and going home.

It was a long night on benches which seemed to grow harder as time passed. Their effort to integrate the terminal lunchroom failed when the employees closed it and left. Dave and a white professor from Princeton attempted a sortie out for coffee and food, but they were attacked by a gang of youths and retreated to the terminal somewhat battered. At an early hour of morning, however, a strong force of allies brought them coffee and dry bologna sandwiches.

Wheels were turning in other places, Dave maintained cheerfully. Eventually the governor of Alabama would have to pick up the phone and answer the President of the United States. Eventually something must indeed have happened someplace else, for, about ten o'clock in the morning, they climbed onto a bus and set out for Montgomery.

Ah, Montgomery, first capital of the Old Confederacy, rising from the Alabama River, white columns gleaming through catalpa, sweet gum and magnolia, haunt of Jefferson Davis and the professional auctioneers wearing beaver hats and black tailcoats as they cried, "Niggers is cheap, niggers is cheap . . . " swollen now to one hundred and thirty-four thousand black and white skins, industries capitalized by the North, yet still unreconstructed Confederate. Thus Kathy tried to alleviate her weariness. Thus, too, a black man ahead of her said, "We'll bring those bastards to their knees."

It happened with terrifying suddenness after the bus pulled into the Montgomery terminal. The mob gathered there was much larger, its outraged cries more menacing than the crowds had been in Nashville and Birmingham. Dave led the way off the bus. Kathy, not far behind, saw him suddenly engulfed by several youths. He disappeared, as if the earth had swallowed him. Those behind him began trying to struggle back on, but those still aboard were screaming that the mob was trying to set fire to the bus. Kathy found herself flung into the roaring crowd as by a kind of centrifugal force. She glimpsed a man swing a baseball bat at her and tried to dodge, but someone else shoved her into its arc. There was a numbing pain in her right side, and she went down, struggling for consciousness. . . .

The events that followed always remained vague to her. Somehow she struggled free of the fierce riot and finally was seized by two policemen. When arraigned the pain in her chest was so severe that she begged for the attention of a doctor. What bail was set she could not remember, neither could she recall whether she gave Father's name and address. She kept asking about Dave, but no one seemed to understand her. And then she found herself in a cell with two Negro women.

Perhaps it was that day, perhaps the next, that a doctor came to her cell. Almost at once he had her carried out on a stretcher and transported by ambulance to a women's ward of a hospital. After a time she was rolled off for X rays, and eventually, at some hour of daylight or darkness, a physician came to her bedside. He was a kindly, competent man named Grey, who talked with her as if she were a close friend. She had four broken ribs and a torn liver, besides cuts and contusions about the head and both arms. Her ribs would heal; so would her liver without surgery if she remained immobile, Dr. Grey believed. She gave him Father's name, and he promised to find out what had happened to Dave.

The next afternoon she awakened from a doze to see Dave standing beside her bed. Both his eyes were blackened, his lip cut, his jaw swollen.

He said something corny: "But you ought to see those other guys." He assumed a John L. Sullivan stance and swung his fists. "Take that, Jeff Davis! Take that, Pierre Beauregard! And you that, Braxton Bragg! Not a scratch on 'em." Incredibly, his eyes filled with tears. Even more incredibly, he leaned over and kissed her gently on the forehead. "Kathy, I'm so sorry about that beautiful face of yours. But the doctor says you're going to be all right." Blinking back his tears, he pulled up a chair and sat down gingerly, wincing. "The greatest indignity came when somebody gave me a tremendous boot in the ass."

"Why aren't you in jail?" she asked.

"Released on bail again. Things are really popping. . . ." Montgomery was under martial law. Martin Luther King, Jr., had arrived from Chicago, and when he tried to address a black mass meeting at a church, there had been an even worse riot than at the bus terminal. Reinforcements for the freedom riders were pouring in from the North, as were federal marshals.

Reading 43

The Boy Who Painted Christ Black
John Henrik Clarke

During the 1960s the nation underwent the civil rights revolution (or the Negro revolution). In reality, however, this name is misleading as few black Americans were revolutionaries; they simply sought the rights that most whites already enjoyed. This quest for the guarantees of the Constitution only appeared revolutionary to those whites who believed that the racial double standard was sanctified by the Almighty—and what God had ordained mere men could not rend asunder. Such an attitude is reflected in this reading in the shock with which the white school supervisor viewed the painting of Christ; he was incapable of understanding that it was perfectly natural for a black child to visualize Christ as black.

He was the smartest boy in the Muskogee County School—for colored children. Everybody even remotely connected with the school knew this. The teacher always pronounced his name with profound gusto as she pointed him out as the ideal student. Once I heard her say: "If he were white he might, some day, become President." Only Aaron Crawford wasn't white; quite the contrary. His skin was so solid black that it glowed, reflecting an inner virtue that was strange, and beyond my comprehension.

In many ways he looked like something that was awkwardly put together. Both his nose and his lips seemed a trifle too large for his face. To say he was ugly would be unjust and to say he was handsome would be gross exaggeration. Truthfully, I could never make up my mind about him. Sometimes he looked like something out of a book of ancient history . . . looked as if he was left over from that magnificent era before the machine age came and marred the earth's natural beauty.

His great variety of talent often startled the teachers. This caused his classmates to look upon him with a mixed feeling of awe and envy.

Before Thanksgiving, he always drew turkeys and pumpkins on the blackboard. On George Washington's birthday, he drew large American flags surrounded by little hatchets. It was these small masterpieces that made him the most talked-about colored boy in Columbus, Georgia. The Negro principal of the Muskogee County School said he would some day be a great painter, like Henry O. Tanner.

For the teacher's birthday, which fell on a day about a week before commencement, Aaron Crawford painted the picture that caused an uproar, and a turning point, at the Muskogee County School. The moment he entered the room that morning, all eyes fell on him. Besides his torn book holder, he was carrying a large-framed concern wrapped in old newspapers. As he went to his seat, the teacher's eyes followed his every motion, a curious wonderment mirrored in them conflicting with the half-smile that wreathed her face.

Aaron put his books down, then smiling broadly, advanced toward the teacher's desk. His alert eyes were so bright with joy that they were almost frightening. The children were leaning forward in their seats, staring greedily at him; a restless anticipation was rampant within every breast.

Already the teacher sensed that Aaron had a present for her. Still smiling, he placed it on her desk and began to help her unwrap it. As the last piece of paper fell from the large frame, the teacher jerked her hand away from it suddenly, her eyes flickering unbelievingly. Amidst the rigid tension, her heavy breathing was distinct and frightening. Temporarily, there was no other sound in the room.

Aaron stared questioningly at her and she moved her hand back to the present cautiously, as if it were a living thing with vicious characteristics. I am sure it was the one thing she least expected.

With a quick, involuntary movement I rose up from my desk. A series of submerged murmurs spread through the room, rising to a distinct monotone. The teacher turned toward the children, staring reproachfully. They did not move their eyes from the present that Aaron had brought her. . . . It was a large picture of Christ—painted black!

Aaron Crawford went back to his seat, a feeling of triumph reflecting in his every movement.

The teacher faced us. Her curious half-smile had blurred into a mild bewilderment. She searched the bright faces before her and started to smile again, occasionally stealing quick glances at the large picture propped on her desk, as though doing so were forbidden amusement.

"Aaron," she spoke at last, a slight tinge of uncertainty in her tone, "this is a most welcome present. Thanks. I will treasure it." She paused, then went on speaking, a trifle more coherent than before. "Looks like you are going to be quite an artist. . . . Suppose you come forward and tell the class how you came to paint this remarkable picture."

When he rose to speak, to explain about the picture, a hush fell tightly over the room, and the children gave him all of their attention . . . something they rarely did for the teacher. He did not speak at first; he just stood there in front of the room, toying absently with his hands, observing his audience carefully, like a great concert artist.

"It was like this," he said, placing full emphasis on every word. "You see, my uncle who lives in New York teaches classes in Negro History at the Y.M.C.A. When he visited us last year he was telling me about the many great black folks who have made history. He said black folks were once the most powerful people on earth. When I asked him about Christ, he said no one ever proved whether he was black or white. Somehow a feeling came over me that he was a black man, 'cause he was so kind and forgiving, kinder than I have ever seen white people be. So, when I painted his picture I couldn't help but paint it as I thought it was"

After this, the little artist sat down, smiling broadly, as if he had gained entrance to a great storehouse of knowledge that ordinary people could neither acquire nor comprehend.

The teacher, knowing nothing else to do under prevailing circumstances, invited the children to rise from their seats and come forward so they could get a complete view of Aaron's unique piece of art.

When I came close to the picture, I noticed it was painted with the kind of paint you get in the five and ten cent stores. Its shape was blurred slightly, as if someone had jarred the frame before the paint had time to dry. The eyes of Christ were deep-set and sad, very much like those of Aaron's father, who was a deacon in the local Baptist Church. This picture of Christ looked much different from the one I saw hanging on the wall when I was in Sunday School. It looked more like a helpless Negro, pleading silently for mercy.

For the next few days, there was much talk about Aaron's picture.

The school term ended the following week and Aaron's picture, along with the best handwork done by the students that year, was on display in the assembly room. Naturally, Aaron's picture graced the place of honor.

There was no book work to be done on commencement day and joy was rampant among the children. The girls in their brightly colored dresses gave the school the delightful air of Spring awakening.

In the middle of the day all the children were gathered in the small assembly. On this day we were always favored with a visit from a man whom all the teachers spoke of with mixed esteem and fear. Professor Danual, they called him, and they always pronounced his name with reverence. He was supervisor of all the city schools, including those small and poorly equipped ones set aside for colored children.

The great man arrived almost at the end of our commencement exercises. On seeing him enter the hall, the children rose, bowed courteously, and sat down again, their eyes examining him as if he were a circus freak.

He was a tall white man with solid gray hair that made his lean face seem paler than it actually was. His eyes were the clearest blue I have ever seen. They were the only life-like things about him.

As he made his way to the front of the room the Negro principal, George Du Vaul, was walking ahead of him, cautiously preventing anything from getting in his way. As he passed me, I heard the teachers, frightened, sucking in their breath, felt the tension tightening.

A large chair was in the center of the rostrum. It had been daintily polished and the janitor had laboriously recushioned its bottom. The supervisor went straight to it without being guided, knowing that this pretty splendor was reserved for him.

Presently the Negro principal introduced the distinguished guest and he favored us with a short speech. It wasn't a very important speech. Almost at the end of it, I remember him saying something about he wouldn't be surprised if one of us boys grew up to be a great colored man, like Booker T. Washington.

After he sat down, the school chorus sang two spirituals and the girls in the fourth grade did an Indian folk dance. This brought the commencement program to an end.

After this the supervisor came down from the rostrum, his eyes tinged with curiosity, and began to view the array of handwork on display in front of the chapel.

Suddenly his face underwent a strange rejuvenation. His clear blue eyes flickered in astonishment. He was looking at Aaron Crawford's picture of Christ. Mechanically he moved his stooped form closer to the picture and stood gazing fixedly at it, curious and undecided, as though it were a dangerous animal that would rise any moment and spread destruction.

We waited tensely for his next movement. The silence was almost suffocating. At last he twisted himself around and began to search the grim faces before him. The fiery glitter of his eyes abated slightly as they rested on the Negro principal, protestingly.

"Who painted this sacrilegious nonsense?" he demanded sharply.

"I painted it, sir." These were Aaron's words, spoken hesitantly. He wetted his lips timidly and looked up at the supervisor, his eyes voicing a sad plea for understanding.

He spoke again, this time more coherently. "Th' principal said a colored person have jes as much right paintin' Jesus black as a white person have paintin' him white. And he says . . ." At this point he halted abruptly, as if to search for his next words. A strong tinge of bewilderment dimmed the glow of his solid black face. He stammered out a few more words, then stopped again.

The supervisor strode a few steps toward him. At last color had swelled some of the lifelessness out of his lean face.

"Well, go on!" he said, enragedly, " . . . I'm still listening."

Aaron moved his lips pathetically but no words passed them. His eyes wandered around the room, resting finally, with an air of hope, on the face of the Negro principal. After a moment, he jerked his face in another direction, regretfully, as if something he had said had betrayed an understanding between him and the principal.

Presently the principal stepped forward to defend the school's prize student.

"I encouraged the boy in painting that picture," he said firmly. "And it was with my permission that he brought the picture into this school. I don't think the boy is so far wrong in painting Christ black. The artists of all other races have painted whatsoever God they worship to resemble themselves. I see no reason why we should be immune from that privilege. After all, Christ was born in that part of the world that had always been predominantly populated by colored people. There is a strong possibility that he could have been a Negro."

But for the monotonous lull of heavy breathing, I would have sworn that his words had frozen everyone in the hall. I had never heard the little principal speak so boldly to anyone, black or white.

The supervisor swallowed dumfoundedly. His face was aglow in silent rage.

"Have you been teaching these children things like that?" he asked the Negro principal, sternly.

"I have been teaching them that their race has produced great kings and queens as well as slaves and serfs," the principal said. "The time is long overdue when we should let the world know that we erected and enjoyed the benefits of a splendid civilization long before the people of Europe had a written language."

The supervisor coughed. His eyes bulged menacingly as he spoke. "You are not being paid to teach such things in this school, and I am demanding your resignation for overstepping your limit as principal."

George Du Vaul did not speak. A strong quiver swept over his sullen face. He revolved himself slowly and walked out of the room towards his office.

The supervisor's eyes followed him until he was out of focus. Then he murmured under his breath: "There'll be a lot of fuss in this world if you start people thinking that Christ was a nigger."

Some of the teachers followed the principal out of the chapel, leaving the crestfallen children restless and in a quandary about what to do next. Finally we started back to our rooms. The supervisor was behind me. I heard him murmur to himself: "Damn, if niggers ain't getting smarter."

A few days later I heard that the principal had accepted a summer job as art instructor of a small high school somewhere in south Georgia and had gotten permission from Aaron's parents to take him along so he could continue to encourage him in his painting.

I was on my way home when I saw him leaving his office. He was carrying a large briefcase and some books tucked under his arm. He had already said good-by to all the teachers. And strangely, he did not look brokenhearted. As he headed for the large front door, he readjusted his horn-rimmed glasses, but did not look back. An air of triumph gave more dignity to his soldierly stride. He had the appearance of a man who had done a great thing, something greater than any ordinary man would do.

Aaron Crawford was waiting outside for him. They walked down the street together. He put his arms around Aaron's shoulder affectionately. He was talking sincerely to Aaron about something, and Aaron was listening, deeply earnest.

I watched them until they were so far down the street that their forms had begun to blur. Even from this distance I could see they were still walking in brisk, dignified strides, like two people who had won some sort of victory.

Reading 44

Tomorrow's Hidden Season

George Byram

Mexican-Americans have felt shock waves from the agitation of blacks for full equality in the period since World War II. This minority of more than five million is largely concentrated in the Southwest (Texas, New Mexico, Colorado, Arizona, and California), and in many instances their forefathers were living in the area before the Anglos seized it from Mexico. But this did not keep Mexican-Americans from suffering the same kind of discrimination blacks had received in the Deep South: lack of opportunity in jobs and education, segregated housing, and inequality before the law. This selection has a Chinese cook—and few races were as maltreated in America—teach a Mexican-American boy why many whites consider other races inferior. There is the message that all people should be judged as individuals and not by the color of their skin.

Alfredo rode into the barn, unsaddled Enseouida, replaced the *jaquima* with the halter, snapped on a lead shank, led the colt back and forth inside the barn, cooling it out and letting it dry. He did not allow himself to think and cooled himself out along with the horse.

After putting the horse away, he sprinted through the rain to the house and up to his room. He stripped off his soaked clothes, bathed, and dressed. When he got downstairs, he was surprised to see Burridge at the table. Burridge usually went into Denver each evening. It was also strange that Burridge hadn't changed out of his wet clothes.

As Wong set their meal before them, Burridge began his discourse. He started with Franklin Delano Roosevelt, whom he despised, worked around somehow to Benny Goodman, whose music he liked, and finally got on to a man named Hitler, who had risen to the leadership of a country called Germany.

Alfredo knew about Germany from his study of geography and history with John Wong. Germany had started and lost the world war. Conditions since the war had been chaotic. Now Mr. Burridge was saying that this Hitler was taking advantage of those chaotic conditions and of the world's cowardice.

"I like a strong man, all right," said Burridge. "A man who can take charge, but a man has got to learn not to hate. He's got to remain cool, objective, see the entire picture, and act in the best interests of whatever he's in charge of, whether it's a country, a business, or a farm. Matter of fact, a country and a farm are similar. Hitler's going to realize someday he can't get away with doing what's best for him at the expense of others. Same thing for a man running a farm. He's got to do what's good for the farm and everybody on it. Doesn't mean a man can't get rough sometimes, but he's got to hold his temper. He's got to know what he's doing and why he's doing it."

Then Burridge got off onto Hitler again. Wong was watching him closely.

Alfredo didn't know what Burridge was talking about. He thought Burridge looked a little more flushed than usual. The rambling way Burridge talked was different, too. When Burridge rose, he was unsteady. Wong followed him from the dining room. Alfredo heard Burridge say he believed he'd better not risk the muddy roads tonight and Wong's murmured agreement. Wong went upstairs with Burridge and returned in a few minutes.

After supper, Alfredo helped Wong with the dishes.

"You seem thoughtful," said Wong.

Alfredo kept his eyes on the plate he was drying. "I tried to kill Rod a little while ago."

Now Wong knew what Burridge had been rattling on about. "What did Rod do to you?"

Alfredo told him how it had been between him and Rod. As Alfredo

talked, Wong saw the hate in him. This was new to Wong. He had found
Alfredo to be a good boy. He was headstrong, but he responded to kindness.
He could not be pushed, but he could be led. Show him where he was wrong
and why, leave him alone, and he would come around. Wong realized the hate
was part of that silent, unreachable area that lay behind the hooded eyes. But
Wong sensed something besides the hate. Alfredo was not vicious. What he
had almost done frightened him. The racial issue had caught up with him at
last. Wong knew something about it. He had found his own way through the
maze long ago, but his way, because of his nature and upbringing, had been
a gentler way than Alfredo's would be.

"I don't know that I can help you in this," he said. "Let me ask you. How
would you feel right now if you had killed him?"

During the time it took to dry two plates the only sound was the rain
driving against the kitchen windows. "I know it would be on my conscience,
but if word came tonight he was killed in a roadhouse brawl, I wouldn't mind."

"An honest answer if not a Christian one," said Wong. "But it seems to
me you are worried about what you almost did."

"I felt as if I were someone else. I remember waiting to feel my horse hit
him."

"Would you have done the same thing if somebody else had thrown the
rocks at you?"

Alfredo looked at Wong from under the heavy, upsweeping brows. "What
do you mean?"

"Let's say that, for some reason, Paul came to work for Mr. Burridge and
did the same thing Rod did. Would you have ridden him down?"

"Paul wouldn't do that."

"Of course not. But imagine he did."

Alfredo's eyes never left Wong. "I wouldn't ride him down."

"Why not?"

"Paul and I might get mad enough to fight, but we wouldn't want to kill
each other."

"Why is it different with Rod?"

"Every day when he talks about Mexican women, when he rubs mud into
the horses' coats, when he makes extra work for me, he is in some way killing
me. He knows it and I know it."

Wong sighed. "It's true. The only thing I can do is to show you his side
of it. I hardly know where to begin. At the beginning, I suppose. We've studied
history, you and I. Tell me. Who explored and civilized the world?"

Alfredo couldn't see where Wong was leading, but he answered. "Almost
every nation. The Romans conquered Europe. The Spanish and Portuguese
discovered the new world. France and England joined in the colonization. Is
that what you mean?"

"Roughly. What people were responsible for the industrial revolution, great art, great music?"

Alfredo was puzzled. "Wasn't it everyone? Greece. Italy. Germany. France. Great Britain. America."

"What did the Negro race discover? What did Indians invent? What have either the Negro race or the Indian race added to civilized culture?"

Alfredo thought, but had no answer.

"The truth is," said Wong, "that somewhere very far back the white race took the initiative. Most of what the modern world considers accomplishment was achieved by this race."

"Are you white?" asked Alfredo, not liking what Wong was saying.

"There are said to be four broad colors of man. White, yellow, red, and black. I am of the yellow race. You are of the red."

"Aren't Spanish white?"

"But are you Spanish?"

"I'm Mexican, and Mexican is Spanish."

"Mexican is a mixture of Spanish and Indian." Wong and Paul had talked at length about Alfredo. Paul was sure Santiago was Alfredo's father. Santiago was half Spanish, half Indian. Margarita's parents had been half Spanish and half Indian.

"What difference does it make?" asked Alfredo.

"Just this. For several hundred years or longer white men have been trained to believe that the colored races were inferior. The British in India. America importing Negroes as slaves, and more recently, on the frontier, taking from the Indian his ancestral lands. You remember. Last month we were studying the westward movement of America. Remember the treaty in which America guaranteed the Sioux the Black Hills as their home, inviolate forever? And how shortly thereafter gold was discovered in the Black Hills and America violated the treaty? Remember the remark of the anonymous colonel? If there were two streams filled with gold, one in free country, one in Indian country, white men would prefer the gold belonging to the Indians. There has always been what seems to me a destructive passion in the men who have led the great advances across the earth. They were in a hurry to remove opposition. The easiest way was to kill it. Perhaps it had to be so. Perhaps the job that had to be done was so brutal that only brutes could accomplish it. At any rate, what I'm trying to say is that a man like Rod Murphy is only a few generations removed from those Americans who pillaged the Indians. His training throughout his life by his parents and by his environment has forced him to believe he is your superior." John Wong was startled by the look on Alfredo's face.

"*My* superior! He can do nothing. He teaches himself nothing. *I* am *his* superior!"

"I agree with you," said Wong. "But you're refusing to understand why he's the way he is."

"If to be white is to be so stupid you can't see through color to what a man is, then I'm glad I'm not white."

"Now, you're doing what he does," said Wong. "He hates Mexicans because they're Mexican. You hate him because he's white. What about Mr. Burridge? He's white."

"He's different."

"Exactly. All men are different. Take them one at a time. Don't hate one because he belongs to the same group or race as another, and it would be better if you could learn not to hate at all. It diminishes you."

"Tell Rod Murphy that."

"I wish I could."

"Am I to continue to do his work for him, allow him to make extra work for me, allow him to curse me and my people, allow him to hurt me?"

"No," said Wong. "But whatever you find you must do, try to do it without hating."

"I don't know what to do," said Alfredo in a low voice.

"I think that is why you hate," said Wong. "You don't know what to do."

"Tell me."

"Wait," said Wong. "Do nothing."

"Do nothing! What if Mr. Burridge hired someone to help you dry dishes, and every time you handed him a clean dish he dipped it in the slop bucket and handed it back to you? What would you do?"

Inwardly Wong applauded the aptness of the boy's analogy. "I would go to Mr. Burridge and tell him. He would straighten out the person or fire him."

"I can't do that."

"Why not?" asked Wong.

"I just can't."

"Mr. Burridge saw what happened this afternoon, didn't he?"

"Yes. If he hadn't yelled, I would have ridden Rod down. If it had been anyone else who yelled, I would still have ridden him down."

"You're saying that you respect Mr. Burridge very much, is that it?"

"As long as I am right, he will stand up for me. If I should be wrong, he would not stand up for me, but it would not be because I was Mexican, but because I was wrong."

"What did Mr. Burridge say this afternoon?"

"He told Rod that whatever I said about the young stock was the same as him, Mr. Burridge, saying it."

Burridge and his drinking! thought Wong. When he drank as much as he had during the past several days, he got to where everything in life and everybody were part of some game he played. He had a tendency to experiment, interfering with lives in a way Wong believed he had no right. Burridge was bored. There were few things that gave him the youthful jolt of enthusiasm he craved. In many ways, Burridge had never grown up. Wong knew himself to be more Burridge's guardian than his servant and cook. But to put Alfredo in charge of men—which was, in effect, what he had done—was unfair to the boy. Wong understood, even if Alfredo didn't, why he couldn't go to Burridge. I'll give that gentleman a talking to, thought Wong, if I can get him sober long enough.

"You asked me what I would do if this hired person dipped my clean plate in the slop bucket. If I couldn't go to Mr. Burridge, I'd wash it again and dry it myself. And I would wait."

"How long?"

"As long as I had to."

"That's what I've been doing."

"Keep it up."

"I will, if I can. Today will change things."

"Perhaps for the better," said Wong.

They finished the remainder of the dishes in silence. Wong knew he had not got through to Alfredo. After they had gone to Wong's room, Alfredo could not bring his attention to bear on his studies. He tried, but his mind was in turmoil. He excused himself, went to his room, and stood at the window, listening to the rain.

So white men thought they owned the earth. They thought they were the only ones who had skill, ambition, ability, initiative. They thought because they had all these that they could walk roughshod over all the rest of man. What was it to Alfredo Ortega what the white man had done? Did it reduce Alfredo Ortega? Did it mean that Alfredo Ortega could not accomplish, could not cut as broad a swath across the earth as any white man? It did not. For Alfredo Ortega would be greater than any white man he had yet seen. Yes, even greater than Sam Burridge!

Reading 45

The New Centurions

Joseph Wambaugh

Efforts of Negroes to attain equality with whites by nonviolent means received a setback with the Watts riots in Los Angeles in August 1965. Trouble began with the routine arrest of a young black by a white policeman. Antagonism over housing, unemployment, inadequate public transportation and welfare programs, and long-standing resentment against the police combined to trigger a week-long holocaust. Before the burning, looting, and shooting ceased, there were 34 dead (mostly blacks), 1,032 injured, 3,500 arrested, and $40 million in property damage. The following selection is from a novel by a Los Angeles policeman on duty during the riot and probably is a fair representation of the police's attitude.

Before driving three blocks south on Broadway, which was lined on both sides by roving crowds, a two-pound chunk of concrete crashed through the rear window of the car and thudded against the back of the front seat cushion. A cheer went up from forty or more people who were spilling from the corner of Eighty-first and Broadway as the Communications operator screamed: "Officer needs help, Manchester and Broadway! Officer needs assistance, One O Three and Grape! Officer needs assistance Avalon and Imperial!" And then it became difficult to become greatly concerned by the urgent calls that burst over the radio every few seconds, because when you sped toward one call another came out in the opposite direction. It seemed to Serge they were chasing in a mad S-shape configuration through Watts and back toward Manchester never accomplishing anything but making their car a target for rioters who pelted it three times with rocks and once with a bottle. It was incredible, and when Serge looked at the unbelieving stare of Jenkins he realized what he must look like. Nothing was said during the first forty-five minutes of chaotic driving through the littered streets which were filled with surging chanting crowds and careening fire engines. Thousands of felonies were being committed with impunity and the three of them stared and only once or twice did Peters slow the car down as a group of looters were busy at work smashing windows. Jenkins aimed the shotgun out the window, and as soon as the groups of Negroes broke from the path of the riot gun, Peters would accelerate and drive to another location.

"What the hell are we doing?" asked Serge finally, at the end of the first hour in which few words were spoken. Each man seemed to be mastering his fear and incredulity at the bedlam in the streets and at the few, very few police cars they actually saw in the area.

"We're staying out of trouble until the National Guard gets here, that's what," said Peters. "This is nothing yet. Wait until tonight. You ain't seen nothing yet."

"Maybe we should do something," said Jenkins. "We're just driving around."

"Well, let's stop at a Hundred and Third," said Peters angrily. "I'll let you two out and you can try and stop five hundred niggers from carrying away the stores. You want to go down there? How about up on Central Avenue? Want to get out of the car up there? You saw it. How about on Broadway? We can clear the intersection at Manchester. There's not much looting there. They're only chunking rocks at every black and white that drives by. I'll let you boys clear the intersection there with your shotgun. But just watch out they don't stick that gun up your ass and fire all five rounds."

"Want to take a rest and let me drive?" asked Serge quietly.

"Sure, you can drive if you want to. Just wait till it gets dark. You'll get action soon enough."

When Serge took the wheel he checked his watch and saw it was ten minutes until 6:00 P.M. The sun was still high enough to intensify the heat that hung over the city from the fires which seemed to be surrounding them on the south and east but which Peters had avoided. Roving bands of Negroes, men, women and children, screamed and jeered and looted as they drove past. It was utterly useless, Serge thought, to attempt to answer calls on the radio which were being repeated by babbling female Communications operators, some of whom were choked with sobs and impossible to understand.

It was apparent that most of the activity was in Watts proper, and Serge headed for One Hundred and Third Street feeling an overwhelming desire to create some order. He had never felt he was a leader but if he could only gather a few pliable men like Jenkins who seemed willing to obey, and Peters who would submit to more apparent courage, Serge felt he *could* do something. Someone had to do something. They passed another careening police car every five minutes or so, manned by three helmeted officers who all seemed as disorganized and bewildered as themselves. If they were not pulled together soon, it could not be stopped at all, Serge thought. He sped south on Central Avenue and east to Watts substation where he found what he craved more than he had ever craved for a woman—a semblance of order.

"Let's join that group," said Serge, pointing to a squad of ten men who were milling around the entrance of the hotel two doors from the station. Serge saw there was a sergeant talking to them and his stomach uncoiled a little. Now he could abandon the wild scheme he was formulating which called for a grouping of men which he was somehow going to accomplish through sheer bravado because goddammit, someone had to do something. But they had a sergeant, and he could follow. He was glad.

"Need some help?" asked Jenkins as they joined the group.

The sergeant turned and Serge saw a two-inch gash on his left cheekbone caked with dust and coagulation but there was no fear in his eyes. His sleeves were rolled up to the elbow, showing massive forearms and on closer examination Serge saw fury in the green eyes of the sergeant. He looked like he could do something.

"See what's left of those stores on the south side?" said the sergeant, whose voice was raspy, Serge thought, from screaming orders in the face of this black hurricane which must be repelled.

"See those fucking stores that aren't burning?" the sergeant repeated. "Well they're full of looters. I just drove past and lost every window in my fucking car before I reached Compton Avenue. I think there's about sixty looters or more in those three fucking stores on the south and I think there's at least a hundred in the back because they drove a truck right through the fucking rear walls and they're carrying the places away."

"What the hell can we do about it?" asked Peters, as Serge watched the building on the north side three blocks east burning to the ground while the firemen waited near the station apparently unable to go in because of sniper fire.

"I'm not ordering nobody to do nothing," said the sergeant, and Serge saw he was much older than he first appeared, but he was not afraid and he was a sergeant. "If you want to come with me, let's go in those stores and clean them out. Nobody's challenged these mother-fuckers here today. I tell you nobody's stood up to them. They been having it their own way."

"It might be ten to one in there," said Peters, and Serge felt his stomach writhing again, and deliberately starting to coil.

"Well I'm goin in," said the sergeant. "You guys can suit yourselves."

They all followed dumbly, even Peters, and the sergeant started out at a walk, but soon they found themselves trotting and they would have run blindly if the sergeant had, but he was smart enough to keep the pace at a reasonably ordered trot to conserve energy. They advanced on the stores and a dozen looters struggled with the removal of heavy appliances through the shattered front windows and didn't even notice them coming.

The sergeant shattered his baton on the first swing at a looter, and the others watched for an instant as he dove through the store window, kicking a sweat-soaked shirtless teen-ager who was straining at the foot of a king-sized bed which he and another boy were attempting to carry away headboard and all. Then the ten policemen were among them swinging batons and shouting. As Serge was pushed to the glass-littered floor of the store by a huge mulatto in a bloody undershirt he saw perhaps ten men run in the rear door of the store hurling bottles as they ran, and Serge, as he lay in the litter of broken glass which was lacerating his hands, wondered about the volume of alcoholic beverage bottles which seemed to supply the mighty arsenal of missiles that seemed to be at the fingertips of every Negro in Watts. In that insane moment he thought that Mexicans do not drink so much and there wouldn't be this many bottles lying around Hollenbeck. Then a shot rang out and the mulatto who was by now on his feet began running and Jenkins shouldered the riot gun and fired four rounds toward the rear of the store. When Serge looked up, deafened from the explosions twelve inches from his ear, he saw the black reinforcements, all ten lying on the floor, but then one stood up and then another and another, and within a few seconds nine of them were streaking across the devastated parking lot. The looters in the street were shouting and dropping their booty and running.

"I must have shot high," said Jenkins and Serge saw the pellet pattern seven feet up on the rear wall. They heard screaming and saw a white-haired toothless Negro clutching his ankle which was bleeding freely. He tried to rise, fell, and crawled to a mutilated queen-sized gilded bed. He crawled under it and curled his feet under him.

"They're gone," said the sergeant in wonder. "One minute they were crawling over us like ants and now they're gone!"

"I didn't mean to shoot," said Jenkins. "One of them fired first. I saw the flash and I heard it. I just started shooting back."

"Don't worry about it," said the sergeant. "Goddamn! They're gone. Why the hell didn't we start shooting two nights ago? Goddamn! It really works!"

Chapter 8

Cold War, Korea, and Vietnam

Reading 46

On a Soldier Fallen in the Philippines

William Vaughn Moody

The following poem was written in 1901 at the time when the United States was suppressing the Filipino insurrection, but it is still appropriate in the 1970s. Many Americans opposed imperialism at the turn of the century and questioned whether it was proper for a democracy to hold colonies and forcibly suppress dissent. Some people have continued to question whether it was necessary for this nation to fight two world wars and to engage in the cold war. This poem can be interpreted as asking if the American boys who died in Asia, especially in Vietnam, gave their lives in vain.

STREETS of the roaring town,
Hush for him, hush, be still!
He comes, who was stricken down
Doing the word of our will
Hush! Let him have his state.
Give him his soldier's crown.
The grists of trade can wait
Their grinding at the mill.
But he cannot wait for his honor, now the trumpet has been blown.
Wreathe pride now for his granite brow, lay love on his breast of stone.

Toll! Let the great bells toll
Till the clashing air is dim.
Did we wrong this parted soul?
We will make it up to him.
Toll! Let him never guess
What work we set him to.
Laurel, laurel, yes;
He did what we bade him do.
Praise, and never a whispered hint but the fight he fought was good;
Never a word that the blood on his sword was his country's own heart's
    blood.

A flag for the soldier's bier

"On a Soldier Fallen in the Philippines" by William Vaughn Moody, as first published in *Atlantic Monthly,* February 1901.

Who dies that his land may live;
Oh, banners, banners here,
That he doubt not nor misgive!
That he heed not from the tomb
The evil days draw near
When the nation, robed in gloom,
With its faithless past shall strive.
Let him never dream that his bullet's scream went wide of its island mark.
Home to the heart of his darling land where she stumbled and sinned in
    the dark.

Reading 47

The Bridges at Toko-ri

James Michener

The cold war became a shooting war in June 1950, when Communist forces
from North Korea invaded South Korea across the 38th parallel. This had
been the line assigned to separate Soviet and American forces temporarily
when the country had been liberated from the Japanese in World War II.
During the cold war, however, it had become a permanent line and the
Soviets had developed a puppet state in the North. The United States
declared North Korea the aggressor, and President Truman sent American
forces to aid South Korea. American military forces were initially successful,
but when Communist China entered the conflict the war became a stale-
mate. This first "limited war" confused many Americans who thought in
terms of complete victory and questioned the expenditure of American blood
and money in such a war. In this reading a young attorney in the air reserve
is called to action and, as he faces death, asks that very question.

Brubaker shouted, "Better dodge and duck."

    "Why, is there a war goin' on?"

    "Look!" He pointed toward the trees and as he did so a volley of machine
gun fire spattered the helicopter. Gamidge fell to the ground but rolled over
several times and indicated that he was all right, but above his head the
helicopter burst into flames.

Forney jumped into the ditch and turned back to watch the fire in silence. No other copter would come onto this field. With flames of noon in their eyes the two men in the ditch looked at each other, unable to speak. Then slowly Mike pulled his right foot up.

"Harry," he asked. "Is this what I think it is?"

"Yep."

Scornfully he said, "You sure picked a wonderful place to fight a war." Then he shrugged his shoulders and growled, "We might as well get Nestor in here. Three of us can stand those apes off for days."

He hefted his carbine nonchalantly and started across the rice field to convoy Gamidge but when the sallow-faced Kentuckian stood up, communist bullets chopped him in the chest and he fell. Mike, still wearing his green hat, blasted the line of trees in pathetic fury, for he must have known his carbine could not carry so far. Then he ran forward to where Nestor lay but soon he crawled back to the stinking ditch and tried not to look at Harry.

"Is he dead?"

"Yep."

In silence the two men tried to build protection for their faces, but when they reached into the ditch for stones, an evil smell arose, so that Forney stared back at the ditch and muttered, "I could have picked a better . . ." Then he said bitterly, "They were goin' to give Nestor a medal."

"Why'd you bring the copter in here, Mike?"

"I take care of my men, sir."

"How is it aboard the scow?" Brubaker phrased the question so as to imply that Forney would be returning there when this day was over.

"It's fair, but carrier duty spoils you."

"I liked the *Savo*," Brubaker said, and when referring to himself he used the completed tense, surrendering hope.

Forney caught this and said, "You know what kills me right now? Thinking of Kimiko going to bed with that ape from the *Essex*."

"That would be tough," Brubaker agreed.

The two men looked up at the F4U's and Forney asked, "How much longer will they be able to stay?"

"Not long," Harry replied.

"Well, we got nothin' to worry about. The jets'll be back."

Harry said, "This morning I had a chance to watch jets in action. They're terrific."

"Look at those apes," Mike said, pointing to where communists were starting to move in. From time to time accurate rifle fire pinked the top of the mound and Brubaker thought ruefully of people back in Denver who visualized communists as peasants with pitchforks who overran positions in mass attacks.

"Those guys know what they're doing," he said.

"But they don't known what they're gonna meet!" Mike laughed. Then he suddenly looked at Harry and said, "Why didn't you tell me you didn't have a carbine." And before Brubaker could stop him, he dashed across the rice field, grabbed Nestor Gamidge's carbine and stripped the dead man of ammunition. Two F4U's, seeing what Mike was doing, roared low and held the communists off while the Irishman dodged and ducked his way back to the ditch.

"Boy, now they'll know something hit 'em!" he cried as he jammed the weapon into Harry's hands.

Realization that Mike intended to battle it out here made Harry shiver and he asked, "You think there's any chance they'd allow us to surrender?"

"Those apes?" Mike asked.

The two Americans piled the last rocks before their faces and Harry asked, "Why do you hate them so much?"

"Simple. One Sunday morning in the cathedral I heard the cardinal explain it all," Mike said. A bullet zinged into the mud behind them and Mike grabbed Brubaker's arm. "You understand, sir, I came out here to save you. I don't want to die. There was a fightin' chance or I wouldn't have come. But now we're here, let's go down really swingin'."

He watched one of the communists creep forward for a better shot. "Don't fire too soon at these apes," he whispered. He kept his hand on Harry's arm for at least two minutes. Then, just as the enemy soldier got into position Mike blasted him right in the face. When Mike looked back he saw that Brubaker was busy with his hip knife, slashing away at his poopy suit.

"What are you doin'?" the Irishman exploded.

"Letting some air in."

"Have you gone nuts, sir?"

"Ever since I climbed into my first poopy suit I've been weighed down. I've been sweating and unable to breathe. Like a zombie. Today I want to feel like a human being." He stripped away large chunks of his burdensome gear and stood reasonably free. "I feel better already," he said.

Mike was sure the lieutenant had gone off his rocker but there wasn't anything he could do about it so he laughed and said, "I'm the same way. I couldn't fight these apes without my green hat."

"Why do you wear that?" Harry asked.

"I want people to know I'm around."

"That's what you told the captain. But what's the real dope?"

Mike stopped, looked frankly at Brubaker and said, "When I was a kid we lived. . . ." He stopped abruptly and asked, "Tell me the truth, sir, wasn't that captain a pathetic ape?"

"The way he used windmill all the time."

"In about three minutes now," Mike said, pointing to the trees.

The communists moved slowly and with deliberate plan. Four of them came in from the south, three from the mountain quarter. "I'm gonna keep my eye on those four out there," Mike said.

Some minutes passed and there was a flurry of fire from the three soldiers in the mountain quarter but Forney yelled, "Forget them!" and he was right for the other four lunged forward and tried to overrun the ditch. Calmly Mike and Harry waited until the communists were close upon them. Then they started to fire rapidly. The communists fired back but Mike yelled, "They're crumblin'," and he chopped them down.

"That'll take care of the boys," he shouted. "Now bring on the men." But as he turned to congratulate Brubaker an unseen communist who had sneaked in from the sea quarter hurled two grenades into the ditch. One of them Mike managed to throw back but as he lifted the second it exploded and tore him apart. His body, motivated by the driving forces that had occupied his mind, stumbled forward toward the unseen enemy and pitched into the snow.

Now the sky was empty and the helicopter stood burned out in the rice field and in the ditch there was no one beside him. Harry Brubaker, a twenty-nine-year-old lawyer from Denver, Colorado, was alone in a spot he had never intended to defend in a war he had not understood. In his home town at that moment the University of Colorado was playing Denver in their traditional basketball game. The stands were crowded with more than 8,000 people and not one of them gave a damn about Korea. In San Francisco a group of men were finishing dinner and because the Korean war was a vulnerable topic, they laid plans to lambaste it from one end of the country to the other, but none of them really cared about the war or sought to comprehend it. And in New York thousands of Americans were crowding into the night clubs where the food was good and the wine expensive, but hardly anywhere in the city except in a few homes whose men were overseas was there even an echo of Korea.

But Harry Brubaker was in Korea, armed with two carbines. He was no longer afraid nor was he resentful. This was the war he had been handed by his nation and in the noonday sun he had only one thought: he was desperately in love with his wife and kids and he wanted to see them one more time.

The memory of his family was too much to bear and for an instant he pressed his right hand across his eyes and thought, "The girls will be in the garden now. . . ."

He did not complete the picture for the hidden communist who had tossed the grenades had remained close and now with one carefully planned shot sped a bullet directly through the right hand that covered the American's face. In that millionth of a second, while ten slim Banshees roared in from the sea to resume command of the sky, Harry Brubaker understood in some fragmentary

way the purpose of his being in Korea. But the brief knowledge served no
purpose, for the next instant he plunged face down into the ditch.

Reading 48

On Instructions of My Government

Pierre Salinger

As cold war tension between the United States and the Soviet Union lessened, China was considered as the new threat. This fear arose from the
efforts of that Communist nation to encourage revolution in the third world.
In this novel the American Ambassador and the head of the Chinese legation
have contested for control of the mythical republic of Santa Clara in Latin
America. An armed uprising is considered a defeat for the efforts of both,
since each had tried to gain control of the nation by peaceful means. Although representing two conflicting philosophies of government, the two
men become tennis-playing friends and in this selection discuss their differences.

But his orders gave Han no opportunity to justify himself at the palace—to
leave his first diplomatic post with even a semblance of personal dignity. Even
his personal safety was in doubt. The government radio, rallying Santa Clarans
to the defense of the republic, laid the blame for Jiminez' offensive on Chinese
arms and duplicity, and announced the expulsion of Han as the agent of the
warmongers of Peking.

Han's staff began burning the legation's secret documents in the courtyard
long before dawn. He was on the balcony, watching, when he heard the bass
counterpoint of the guns from the Arroyo Seco through the thin crackle of the
bonfire.

The Chinese legation was not the only foreign mission in Ciudad Alarcon
which had been the scene of night-long activity. When the word had spread
that the Americans were evacuating Santa Clara, it was a clear signal to the
entire diplomatic community that there would be no intervention by Washington and, without it, no guarantee of safety for the personnel of other embassies
and consulates. The diplomatic exodus from Santa Clara would start the

following morning in planes under charter to the Organization of American States. And President Luchengo had left orders, before joining his forces at the arroyo, that Han and his staff were to be aboard the first plane to Guatemala City.

Despite the curfew and the danger to himself, Han left the legation late in the evening for a last look at the city as he had known it. The silence of the streets was broken only by the infrequent rumble of an army truck and the thunder from the arroyo. The guns were heard at persistent intervals now in the slow, rhythmic cadence of a death march.

It had not been his conscious intention to call on Ambassador Hood. There was nothing to be said except goodby and that had a finality Han was unwilling to accept. But the dark, descending streets all led to the plaza—to the palace, where he was the enemy, and to the American embassy, where he had a friend.

The sergeant of the Marine guard was insolent and threatening, his rifle at the ready position. But he finally went to the telephone in the sentry box to relay the message to Hood, and now Han saw the ambassador walking toward him through the bright lights encircling the compound and into the deep shadows of the plaza. His face was grim.

"You shouldn't have come here tonight, Mr. Han."

"I'm sorry. I should have known it would be awkward for you." He glanced toward the embassy. The Marine sergeant had left his position at the gate and was standing on the verge of the plaza, observing them intently.

"It's not that at all," said Hood sharply. "It's dangerous on the streets after curfew, and, I would think, particularly dangerous for you."

"I know," said Han, "I've heard the radio. But I came to say good-by. I leave in the morning."

"That soon?"

"Yes, the orders from my government came today."

"Then I'm glad you came, Mr. Han."

They sat down together on the bench under the hulking figure of *El Libertador*—its green patina glowing in the moonlight, breaching even the shadows with the presence of violence.

"You'll be returning to China, of course."

"To a new assignment—yes."

"Whatever it is," Hood replied, "I hope you will have more luck than either of us has had here."

Han glanced at him in surprise. "You can wish me luck."

"Of course." A faint smile lit his face. "For all of your little sermons to me, you are a bit of a heretic, you know. You came here not entirely to promote the faith, but to reform it."

Han put up only token resistance. "No, I may question the means, but not the end."

"The end," said Hood, "can only be the sum of the means. To question one is to question both." They heard the rattle of rifles from a patrol firing at shadows on the outskirts of the city. "You didn't want it to come to that, Mr. Han."

"No," said the Chinese. "Guns solve nothing." He was silent for a long moment. "You accuse me of apostasy, Mr. Hood. But what of yourself?"

"Unlike you, my friend, I have no rigid gospel to question. Yours has dogma, a continuum of vengeful apostles to enforce it, and certain retribution for those who dare to doubt. My faith has no inviolable scripture and its commandments come down from a papacy with a four-year tenure. It takes little courage to defy it, Mr. Han. I can wish you luck because your heresy is far more dangerous than mine."

Han disagreed. "There can be no credit for either of us. There was peace when we came and now there is war. I think we are poor missionaries."

"Perhaps. But we've at least been on the side of the angels." He put a hand on Han's shoulder. "And we won't say good-by—not yet. We still have an old score to settle."

"The third set?"

"Yes."

"But why?" Han spread his hands in a gesture of futility. "If, as you say, there is little moral choice between my faith and yours, does either of us deserve to win it?"

"One of us—or at least the credos we represent—*must* win it, Mr. Han. One of them is going to prevail, and I would prefer that it be mine."

"But, again, I must ask why. You concede that my faith has doctrine and discipline, and that yours has none—that mine is graven in stone and yours is written in sand."

"But that's just the point," Hood replied. "Mine is capable of reformation precisely because it is not doctrinaire. It can accept new realities and new revelations, and I'm afraid that yours cannot."

"I can't agree," said Han. "In China there is constant re-examination and change."

"Yes, but always toward a more rigid orthodoxy—toward a crueler repression of dissent."

"Please, Mr. Hood. You have had your own inquisitions. You are having them now."

"Agreed. But the dissent continues—and always away from orthodoxy and towards a remission of error. No, Mr. Han, the American faith—however blind or inconsistent—is still the best and, perhaps, the only hope."

"Then our third set becomes academic," said the Chinese. "You are suggesting that you can still influence events and that I cannot."

"I have had no more influence than you," said Hood. "But it's important that we go on trying. If we do—and we must—the time could still come when our third set would prove nothing more cataclysmic than which of us is the better tennis player."

"I would like that," said Han. A faint smile lit his face. I am an atheist, Mr. Hood—and you?"

"An agnostic, I think."

"And yet we have spoken tonight almost entirely in religious allegories. Why?"

Hood thought for a long moment. "Perhaps because the language of diplomacy, or politics, contains no equivalents for such words as right or wrong—moral or immoral." The ambassador stood. "It's very late, and I'm going to insist on dropping you off at your legation.

"It is late. Thank you."

Hood's car was waiting and it was only a two-minute ride to Han's quarters. Neither of them spoke until the driver swung the door open for the Chinese.

"Good night, Mr. Han."

"I hope you're right—that it is good night, and not good-by." His eyes were huge and intense behind the thick lenses of his glasses.

Hood held out his hand. "Have faith."

Reading 49

Company Man

Joe Maggio

The Central Intelligence Agency (CIA) was established in 1947 as the first permanent, all-embracing intelligence bureau in the nation's history. It is responsible solely to the President through the National Security Council and has the task of collecting and evaluating intelligence data abroad. As an undercover agency its operation is secret but it is reputed to have a budget of $1 billion dollars a year and a staff of some 30,000. To its defenders the CIA has played an important and necessary role in the cold war; saving

Guatemala from going Communist in 1954 is cited as one example of the success of the agency. To its critics the CIA is a bungling "cops and robbers" unit that has endangered the nation's security and is not worth its tremendous cost; the hapless failure at the Bay of Pigs in 1961 is cited as an example of its failures. The following tells something of its operation and discusses the experience of one man who has just joined the agency.

The Central Intelligence Agency is more thorough in its choice of employees than any government agency including the State Department, which CIA case officers often use as a cover for many of their worldwide clandestine activities. Many work for the CIA in an informal capacity for years before being asked to come aboard as a CT or Contract Trainee—known officially as the contract A employee. The contract B employee is usually a third-country national, used by an A operative as an "in place" source of intelligence in the target country.

If the man CIA wanted wasn't especially bright testwise, it would provide him with answers to the government tests all formal employees are required to take.

Testing for Martin began when he received a telegram from "E. D. Echols" (word had it there was no such person), CIA's chief recruiter in Washington, which said to start the Federal Testing Program at the University of Miami in Coral Gables. The following morning a call came from the same office concerning Martin's salary request. The caller had a pretty voice and identified herself as Mary Walters, Echols' secretary.

"Mr. Martin, the director of Personnel allows me to offer you a GS-5."

Martin quickly figured how high he thought Personnel would go. SOD came after him, didn't it? And what about his little talk with Mr. Williams?

"Okay," Martin said.

"A 5 then."

"No, I meant, forget it."

"Oh, I see." Then silence. "Mr. Martin, many are coming aboard at a 5, those with your background and qualifications. . . ."

"I don't give a shit about the others, Miss Walters." He was about to hang up but waited until he heard a response, then smiled.

"Wait, I'll ask and call you back."

While Martin waited he began the Federal Testing Program. The level of the testing surprised him because he knew by its nature that he was being prepared for CT's job, not just a job on a contract basis. Maybe he had been too hasty in his demand for a 10 salary. CT status was pretty good; two years abroad counted as three for retirement. Most CT's—once called junior officer trainees (JOT)—were Eastern university dandies bent on a full twenty-year career with the CIA.

The contractee, on the other hand, was the soldier of fortune, tired of low military pay, stale routines and procedures, and interested only in bank receipts. Many were ex-military officers and noncoms who, after added training in CIA methods of tradecraft, would be sent back to their previous military duties sans uniform, at twice their former salary.

Mary Walters called Martin back at the end of the week, and said he had a choice: CT status or the GS-10. He didn't hesitate; he took the 10. Fuck the CT's.

The only common denominator in the recruitment of CT's and contractees was that each had his background extensively checked by the CIA. It was usually much easier for the CIA security "headhunters" to check contractees, especially if they were still in the military—all they had to do was update their 201 files. For the many military reservists CIA recruited each year, the process was longer—some six months. Hometown friends, faculty advisers, professors of CT's would be checked out by security. Without the State Department's or Department of Defense's (DOD) knowledge, under cover as DOD or State officials, CIA security checkers scoured their past; and only if records of credit companies, banks, military service, schools, jobs checked out was the preliminary call given. In the case of men who had been on loan to CIA, an inside contract in SOD's office helped avoid much of the red tape.

After the preliminary investigation into his background was finished, Martin was told to report to headquarters in Alexandria, Virginia, for a personal interview. It turned out to be more of a bull session than an interview. He remembered the interviewer, William Ward, from Latin America. Ward was just marking time until retirement, helping SOD select new case officers now that the big push was on to get more blood in the field. He was a tall, intense man with a fondness for briar pipes, and a seldom-matched dedication to the American intelligence system. As an OSS agent in World War II, he helped train the detachment-101 teams that jumped into Burma. During one operation he led, he saved the life of a young Vietnamese guerilla who fought the Japs as hard as he had. Ho Chi Minh never forgot Ward.

The personal investigation was a joke, too. The investigator, a Rotary type, was unable to convince Martin's friends that he was from the Department of Defense. When he came to "interview" them, they all called him "super spook" and asked how he liked the CIA.

Ward told Martin what to expect when the CIA's head psychologist, Dr. Falk, put him through the headshrinking routine at the CIA headquarters at 1000 Glebe Road.

"Don't sweat him," Ward said. "Just play the game. You love your mother?"

"Always have," Martin said.

"You're in. That's what Falk wants to hear. He's in Room 412."

Central Intelligence liked to amaze itself with thoughts that all its employees had hearts of pure American gold, and were ready to defend motherhood, big business, and the American way.

One thousand Glebe Road was to most residents of Alexandria, Virginia, merely a government building with office space for research and testing, and the Army's Personnel section which looked after the 201 files of those stationed in the Washington area. It was also known as the Broyhill Building, named after Joseph Broyhill, an Alexandria politician. It stood alone on a small corner lot with parking on three sides.

Glebe, the blue, modern, ten-story building that was the second largest CIA training facility in the United States, was devoid of any markings or announcements, except for the address: 1000, in silver numerals located on the front entrance.

Martin was ordered to see Dr. Falk in Room 412, as Ward had said. The verbal test was a long two hours, but not as long as the two-thousand-question test which followed. He passed keeping in mind Ward's advice, and was then sent to be "Black-Boxed" in Room 1E00 at headquarters.

Regardless of where they operated around the world, all CIA case officers were required by CIA policy to take a lie detector test every six months; it was one of the agency's strictest rules. Those who passed were allowed to continue in their current assignment; failures were taken from the field and, according to how badly they failed or their status in the minds of CIA desk chiefs, put in some safe headquarters job which required no top-secret work. Even though the CIA put major emphasis on judging its employees' truth and loyalty from a yes or no from the lie detector, the Black Box, as Martin and his comrades called it, could be beaten.

The method was called Mental Recall Blackout, but it really wasn't all that fancy. It was much like fraternity files, an over-the-years hand-down of systems that help a student pass the exam. Mental discipline was needed to beat the Box; lowering the rate of body hyperactivity was also a help. So many an employee called on the carpet for the Box put blotters in their shoes, took a few Valium; some smoked grass. Those who took a hard line to pot, usually the contractees or longtime employees who had no interest in that method, took about four aspirin, some "downs" if available.

Martin used grass. When he was seated and "wired" and waiting for the questions to come at him in quick and tricky fashion from the "Box man" he let his mind wander. He could have recalled the love of Kari, the smell of the ocean, and their lovemaking in the lower bunk of the sloop as the vessel sailed trimmed to course; or the hot mug of tea laced with honey she would hand him as he came off watch during a long passage. But he knew to keep up with the answers and not cause the Box to jerk when the "Box man" threw the letup pitch.

So he used the comedy of a situation that occurred when he was sixteen. He had been invited to a party by some of the more worldly members of his high school crowd. Rumor said a man was coming who would "service" the boys, and a woman for the girls. It was a new adventure for Martin, who never thought of sex with a man. The man "serviced" all the boys in a dark room. He worked one bed, his lady friend the other. When the evening was over and the man and lady came into the living room, Martin found himself face-to-face with a close relative, an uncle who was always passed off as a model of creativity and good taste by his parents.

Martin used that incident mostly when he was boxed. He used others, but that night still flashed back to him in horror, revelation, and finally laughter lasting many years. It took his mind off the questions and he never lost to the Box.

Two days later, Martin called SOD headquarters to ask how he had done and was told to report the next day for formal processing as a contractee, GS-10.

After formal processing—filling out forms for loans available at the Federal Credit Union, and for next of kin—Martin met the members of his training group: "Chief " Dawson Sands, a former Ranger sergeant major who wore a pair of Arab Paratroops wings given to him by King Hussein for helping train the Arab Legion Airborne; and two reserve officers, one a Kentucky high school basketball coach, the other a public health inspector with a background of Air Force training. Later that day they found out none of them was going to be sent—for the moment at least—to the field. Instead they were told to report to headquarters the following morning.

Martin met Loring Caldwell at the entrance of headquarters as he entered the building at 8 A.M. Very little was known about the tall, well-tailored man in his forties; word had it he was once a top-flight forger and counterfeiter and had done a stretch in Sing Sing for murder. Every time Martin met him he looked as though he just stepped out of a men's fashion advertisement—every thread, hair and crease just right.

They walked across the vestibule with the white marble American emblem—the eagle grasping conflicting weapons of life—the only place in headquarters that it was stated: Here is the CIA. They handed ID cards to the U.S. security guard, an erect old soldier who wore his ribbons and campaign decorations on his uniform, and then pinned them on their jackets.

Each card was different for staffer or trainee. CIA trainees wore the three-by-five temporary ID tags on a pin, while staff members had their ID's hanging around their necks on long silver chains. New recruits and those dealing with low classified items just had identifying pictures and some special numbers; others, mainly staffers dealing with top-secret projects or highly classified operations, had little red blocks on the front of their cards. The more red blocks, the more top-secret or classified items they had access to; it was a status thing to agency employees.

SOD had a corner office on the third floor. In the long, main hall were paintings of Harry Truman, who gave a start to what has mushroomed into CIA. There were pictures of other CIA leaders including the founder, "Wild Bill" Donovan, and other CIA memorabilia captured from China and Moscow were in showcases.

Glebe Road training lasted six weeks, during which time SOD's Ground Branch received their cover background. Cover was the name of the game, Martin learned. CIA cover organizations were in many ways a secret intelligence operation unto themselves, even with respect to CIA's own government.

During CIA indoctrination the officers gave a forceful lecture about "living your cover"; they provided case histories of the many people who were important CIA case officers in foreign governments and even in the United States, but whose friends always thought they were employed by some other agency.

Pat Nunan was a short, balding man with a large stomach, red blotches on his face and nose, and an uneven mustache. He also was head of cover for SOD. He greeted Martin and the others as they walked into Room 3D108 on the third floor of CIA headquarters. The cover office reminded Martin immediately of a small loan shark's office: one main desk staffed by spinsters, lots of small cubicles, and Nunan—who certainly could have been cast as the loan operator himself.

"Gentlemen." He smiled gaily, fingering his mustache as the three were seated at a long table. "Let's see. SOD, Ground Branch. There are very few CIA-SOD covers a sharp civilian can't detect if he is sharp enough. Remember that."

They were taught that every embassy, trade mission, and travel group that ventured into friendly or cold-war countries had a CIA case officer under cover as a travel agent, citizen, diplomat or plain traveler. "Blow it, and your job with CIA will be gone. Blow it bad enough and they will be fishing you out of a river somewhere," Nunan warned.

On embassy staffs, CIA case officers were hidden by bureaucratic titles: adviser to the ambassador, special projects assistant to the ambassador; every embassy security staff had CIA men under cover. Many ambassadors have suddenly been put in delicate positions, their careers in the State Department threatened by CIA case-officer activities and policies.

"Ah, former military. Splendid," Nunan thin-lipped to himself as he went over the SOD car file records. Closing the file box, Nunan handed them laminated ID cards and explained how the cover system worked.

"Gentlemen, you're now part of DOA—that is, if anyone is to know, you are Department of the Army civilians. I'll read you this cover, which is on these ID cards. They must be lived to the fullest. Do you understand?"

When no one replied, he went on. "As the ID card says, you're now part of the United States Army's Technical Training Advisory Group. This organization does not exist except for purposes of cover." He smiled. "Nor do I." He smiled again, like a little boy who knows something no one else on the block does.

"These are all 450 SOD covers," he said, caressing a larger metal file box. "Business, AID, State Department, Army, Navy, and a host of others you don't currently have a 'need to know.' "

"Must be a hassle to keep them in order," one of the men said.

"Computers. The entire intelligence community uses computers now; they keep track of all covers. Each desk has this many covers or more, and each is organized somewhat similar to ours at SOD. Over ninety percent of CIA activities are hidden under cover. A few people—some old-time Washington newspaper reporters—know the system. But CIA policy states that if any case officer, trainee, staff or clerical worker meets or discusses anything with a member of the press—anything, no matter how trivial—it must be reported within twenty-four hours to the branch chief. The text and topic of conversation will be studied by security force, and the reporter's name will be put on a special list that will keep him under scrutiny, watched by security."

Reading 50

The Only War We've Got

Derek Maitland

The American war in Vietnam was the most controversial in the nation's history. At first CIA advisors assisted the French in their efforts to suppress the Communist Vietminh. After the French left in 1954, United States military personnel directed the South Vietnamese war effort against the Vietcong and their North Vietnamese supporters. After 1963 commitments were stepped up so that the conflict became virtually an American war. To Yankees who became cynical about the war and who would much rather be back in the States the stock answer was, "It's the only war we've got." The following conversations reveal what the war was all about to some of the participants. To the Vietnamese it brought American money; to some naval officers it brought the opportunity to win the medals so indispensable to their careers; to a construction worker it brought a chance to make big money; and to some blacks it was a chance to learn how to fight Whitey.

'You no go home!!' screeched the young bar-girl picking herself off the floor once again and diving back on to the construction worker's lap. 'Me velly poor. No momma. No poppa. No money to buy lice. Hab bludder in army. . .'

'Ah shaddup,' the construction worker roared, bouncing her back on to the floor again.

'Another drink for every man at the bar!' cried the Navy captain, and there were several men in the room who came close to being seriously hurt in the rush. Wilkinson quickly slipped a notepad on to his knee and took out a ballpoint pen.

'Have you been bombing North Vietnam, Captain?' he asked the Navy type.

'That's just what I been doing for the past twelve months, buddy,' the captain roared. 'Bomb the shit out of them—that's what I say. What about you, Bill?'

'Er, the captain's a little drunk,' Bill said nervously.

'Had much trouble with those Russian surface-to-air-missiles?' Wilkinson asked the captain.

'Why those SAMs couldn't hit a bull in the ass with a bass fiddle!' the Navy captain roared. 'We fake our way around them, don't you worry.'

'Er, what the captain means,' Bill hastily explained, 'is that the surface-to-air-missiles around Hanoi pose a serious problem to our air operations, and that the pilots have a healthy respect for them.'

'Heck, don't you go listening to Bill. He's here to keep our big mouths shut.'

'I suppose you've flown missions over the South, too,' said Wilkinson. 'What kind of ordnance do you use, and what types of targets do you hit?'

'Well, buddy, I'll tell you. We mostly like kicking the shit out of Vietnamese villages, and my favourite ordnance is napalm. Man, that stuff just sucks the air out of their fucking lungs and just burns them little slant-eyed mothers up.'

'Er, what the captain means is that air strikes in South Vietnam are often flown against Viet Cong structures, but the operations are always supervised by a Forward Air Controller, or F.A.C. aircraft that watches from the air. Ordnance used is the conventional seven-hundred-fity-pound bombs and twenty-millimetre cannon.'

'Have you flown any missions apart from those over North and South Vietnam?'

'You bet your sweet ass, I have. Why, we get orders every day to sortie over . . . over . . . er,' the captain caught a glimpse of Bill's stricken face and coughed. 'Yeah, er, well I tell you—those bastards over there throw up everything at you. Why they even throw the kitchen sink if they've got one. The greatest concentration of anti-aircraft fire of any war in history—that's what they say—and it's true as I'm sitting here. Why, even the kids have slingshots.'

'Er, what the captain means,' said Bill, 'is that he has occasionally been required to fly missions in the extreme western part of the Demilitarized Zone, and he has a healthy respect for the flak there.'

'You're goddam right,' said the captain.

'Of all the targets you've hit, which one was the most satisfying?'

'Shit, the best time I had was when we were assigned to hit that fucking suspected Viet Cong vegetable garden. Man, I dropped napalm right in the middle of the goddam cabbages, and my wing men splashed it with six of those seven-hundred-fifty-pound cannisters that spread the goddam blaze all the way to the beets and carrots.'

'What the captain means is that the great variety of tactical targets right throughout Vietnam calls for a perfect flexible response.'

'Captain,' said Wilkinson, 'can you reduce your impression of the war down to a simple phrase?'

'Sure I can,' said the captain, 'It's a fucked-up war.'

'What the captain means,' Bill explained, 'is that it's a fucked-up war.'

'Yeah, and now I'm going home!' roared the captain. 'Good-bye Vietnam!'

'We're all going home!' cried the construction worker.

'You can't go home!' shrieked the bartender.

'You no go home!' screeched the bar-girl, leaping up from the floor to transfer her ardour to the Navy captain, whom she literally smothered with kisses.

'I can't go home!!' bellowed the young Navy coxswain, hurling the broken bar-stool away from him and moving in on the juke box.

'Why not?' the construction worker roared.

'I only just got out here, an' I aint even seen active duty yet. They got a brand new river patrol boat waitin' for me down in the Mekong Delta, with twin engines an' fifty-cal machine guns an' armour platin' an' mortars an' Christ knows what else. I ain't got any medals yet. I aint killed any Cong yet. *I aint done nothing'* . . . What am I gonna tell the Legion? What about my folks?'

'What about me?' roared the construction worker. 'How am I gonna make a living anywhere else? I'm a goddam truck-driver back in the States. Where am I gonna get eighteen hundred dollars a month for doing nothing'? Where am I gonna get an airconditioned French villa an' servants an' a Dodge car an' a piece of ass whenever I want it? Not back in the goddam States, or anywhere else—that's for sure.'

'What about me?' bellowed the Navy captain. 'I've gotta go home to sit on my ass in San Diego harbour. Where am I gonna get a Phantom jet again? Where am I gonna get the chance to drop bombs again?'

'What about me?' cried Wilkinson, as a sudden nasty thought struck him. 'Where else can I - get twelve-year-old Vietnamese girls who look as if they're seven, and are not a day over thirty?'

'What about me?' cried Heavenly Orchid, smothering him with passionate kisses. 'I velly poor. No momma. No poppa. No money to buy . . . !'

'What about me?' shrieked the bartender who owned half the bar 'if Amellicans go, I lose bar, I lose business, family starve, I lose face . . . *I lose everyt'ing!!!*'

'It's the only war we've got!' the captain bellowed. 'Think about it!' But a sudden uproar in another bar next door broke through the train of drunken thought, for the men in that bar had also got around to the Big News and the Paris peace talks, and in the middle of the floor a young Negro infantryman sank down on his knees with a look of sublime happiness and raised his arms above his head and cried: Lordy, Lordy, Ah's a-comin' home!'

'Yeeeeeah man,' the mahogany faces around him chorused.

'Ah's a-comin' home, Lordy, cos ah aint gonna fight no war no more,' the infantryman cried.

'Yeah, man. Hit it. Hit it,' the others yelled, a-skatin' an' a twisting together in the packed bar.

'This aint my war, Lordy. This aint my war. Ah'm too young to dah. Ah'm too young an' black an' beeeoootiful . . . an' . . . an' ah'm goin' back to Harlem an' . . .'

'Yeah. Yeah. Yeah.'

'. . . an' an'm gonna tell Whitey "You fight your own wars from now on. Ah don't want anything to do with your wars no more. Cos ah'm black an' ah don' fight for Whitey . . ." '

'Get it, man. Get it . . .'

'Ah'm gonna go back to Harlem an' ah'm gonna get me a beeeoootiful black chick an' ah'm jist gonna have a ball.'

'Yeah, man,' a big fat staff sergeant sang from the corner of the bar. 'We's all goin' home an' we's gonna fight for ourselves for a change . . .'

'Yeah. Yeah. Hit it, Sarge.'

'We's gonna fight our own war back there in Harlem an' in Detroit an' in Watts an' in 'Bama an' Georgia an' . . . an' . . . all over the goddam place.'

'Yeah, Sarge. Yeah.'

'We's gonna fight them white cats. We's gonna fight a war of our own . . . a war of national liberation. And man,' the fat sergeant chuckled, 'Whitey's gonna get one hell of a big fat shock when he sees what we's been learning' over here.'

'*But I don' wanna fight no more!*' the young infantryman cried.

'But you gonna have to, boy,' said the fat sergeant. 'You think you finished here, boy? You aint even started yet. There's a bigger war gonna happen back there, boy. A *real* war.'

'*But ah don' wanna fight any more wars!*'

"You gonna have to fight, boy, just like the rest of us. Cos you're black and they's white. You're just gonna have to fight.'

Reading 51

The Only War We've Got

Derek Maitland

The basic reason for the unpopularity of the war in Vietnam was the confusion over its objectives. As the war dragged on and on, it was repeatedly asked what was the United States doing in a domestic quarrel half way around the world where our basic interests were not threatened. The usual justification for the American war effort was that if we didn't fight Communism in Vietnam, the other nations in Southeast Asia would soon fall behind the Bamboo Curtain with the result that the safety of the United States would soon be endangered. This "domino" theory is ably expounded in the following.

'A toast, Colonel!' he cried. 'To . . . to . . . the great American soldier we once knew who didn't have to fight his way through crowds of stinking, bearded hippies with their idiotic placards to get to his troopship. Who didn't have to feel like a criminal every time he took a shot at the enemy in the front-line. Who didn't have to fight his way through another goddam stinking crowd of hippies and posters when he got home from the war.'

'Bravo, Shenrul!' cried Monk, and the two men threw back their bourbon with gusto.

'Scuse me, Shenrul,' Monk mumbled as he wiped the bourbon off his chin and mopped up the front of his blouse. The General eyed him coldly for a second and then screwed the cap back on the bourbon bottle and pushed it to one side. Monk made an effort to pull himself together.

'War and politics don't go together, Colonel,' The General continued. 'Politics and politicians change from day to day, and so do their policies. And what about the soldier? Does he just pick up his rifle and go home when a goddam civilian who knows nothing about running a war says the war must stop?' Colonel Monk grinned stupidly at him. The General grunted with exasperation and leaned forward.

'Look at it this way, Monk. Why are we fighting in Vietnam?'

Monk made a massive mental effort to concentrate, one eye on The General and the other gazing wistfully at the bourbon bottle.

'To save South Vietnam from the Communists,' he said.

'What else?'

'To . . . er . . . guarantee her right to freedom and . . . and . . . her freedom to chose her own future.'

'And what will happen if we pull out?'

'South Vietnam will become Communist, I guess.'

The General sighed 'You're damn right it will. But what else would happen, Colonel?'

'Well, the Domino Theory would happen. Thailand and Laos and Cambodia would fall under the Communists. Then Malaysia and Indonesia and the Pacific Islands . . . and Australia and New Zealand . . .'

'And the whole balance of power in this half of the world would shift in favour of the Communists. Right?'

'Yessir, and before long we would be fighting the Reds in San Francisco Bay.'

'. . . and right up along the West Coast . . .'

'. . . and along the Potomac and the great Hudson . . .'

'. . . and on the steps of the White House itself . . .'

'. . . and in Whispering Falls, Wichita . . .'

'Whispering Falls, Wichita?'

'That's my home town, General,' said Monk, proudly.

'Oh, yeah, The General grunted. 'So you see, Colonel, don't you? The future of South Vietnam is in our hands. The future of South East Asia and the Pacific is also in our hands. And the future of the great United States itself depends upon us. And what happens if the United States—God forbid—becomes Communist? The rest of the world will fall under the Communists. *So we have the future of the whole world in our hands here!!*'

'You're goddam right,' cried Monk, taking advantage of the emotional pitch of the moment to grab for the bourbon bottle and pour another slug.

'So there it is, Monk. Black and white. Clear-cut as only good military logic can be. None of this confused, defeatist civilian crap. You wouldn't want to go back home knowing that if you had stayed here you could have saved the whole world, would you, Colonel?'

'Oh. No sir,' said Monk. 'I'd never sleep easy again.'